INCEST

UNDERSTANDING AND TREATMENT

Domeena C. Renshaw, M.B., Ch.B., M.D.
Professor, Department of Psychiatry,
Loyola University of Chicago
Stritch School of Medicine, Chicago

Foreword by Ralph Slovenko, LL.B., Ph.D.,
Professor of Law and Psychiatry,
Wayne State University
School of Law, Detroit

Boston   Little, Brown and Company

CONTENTS

FOREWORD

INCEST is a fascinating subject—it has been that way from time immemorial—and this is a fascinating book about it.

In mythology, the incest offender is severely punished, even in the absence of intent. Oedipus was destroyed by the gods although he unknowingly violated the taboo. King Arthur's downfall followed his sexual involvement with Margeuse, who, unknown to him, was his half-sister. Raskolnikov in Dostoevski's *Crime and Punishment* killed the old woman who symbolized incest.

All states in the United States make incestuous fornication or incestuous intermarriage a crime. The strength of the prohibition is in proportion to the relationship, the penalties ranging from one to fifty years in prison. In the United States, however, the concept of incest as a crime is generally defined more broadly than in other countries. Many states in the United States have enlarged the prohibited degrees of relationships beyond the father-daughter, mother-son, and brother-sister relationships to include grandparent-grandchild, uncle-niece, and first cousins. The legal prohibition of incest in other countries has tended to contract as the family unit diminished socially, but the law in most states in the United States has remained unchanged though the contracted nuclear family is more prevalent.

The incest law in many states in the United States does not cover nonconsanguineous sexual relations as between adoptive or stepparents and their children. Thus, these statutes seem to be based on the hypothesis of harmful biological effects without regard to psychological impact. Many of the statutes were enacted before a 50 percent divorce rate made the stepparent situation common. In any case, the stepparent may be subject to prosecution for contributing to the delinquency of a minor or child molestation. In this book Dr. Renshaw recommends the criminalization of incest only in the area where a minor or participant is exploited by another of a close relationship (including a stepparent).

Dr. Renshaw appropriately begins with a discussion of the law in the various states showing that the application of the law in many cases results in severe restrictions on evaluation and treatment. Questions arise: What laws are desirable? How ought incest be defined? What are the consequences of incest? What kind of treatment programs are appropriate? Largely because of the stigma and secrecy surrounding incest, accurate statistics and empirical data on the subject are hard to come by. Some survey statistics suggest that as many as five percent of individuals and one in ten families may be involved in some form of incest. The numbers are widely believed to be increasing. As Dr. Renshaw points out, the stresses of mobility, marital discord, family disintegration, faulty sex education, job instability, and various other social causes of emotional distress are all contributing to the rise in incest. She suggests, though, that in some cases incest may be quite normal to the culture.

Much can be done to improve treatment techniques in detected cases. Many physicians and other professionals, however, close their eyes (consciously or unconsciously) to incestuous behavior. Dr. Renshaw strives to lift the veil. She points out incidents of withdrawal, avoidance, ignoring the subject, feeling anxious and overwhelmed, disbelief, cover-up, panic, silence; and she offers instruction on how the doctor can handle it differently.

In the course of the book Dr. Renshaw poses and responds to many intriguing questions: Who commits incest? Is there a special incest personality? What are the restraints concerning incest? When do they form? How do they develop? What was the early parent-child relationship like? Was it affectionate? How do relationships differ in families where incest does or does not occur? Are women who experienced brother-sister coital consensual incest more likely to initiate mother-son incest? Are men who experienced brother-sister incest more likely to try father-daughter incest? Are parents who themselves enjoyed incest contacts as children more likely to encourage sexual contacts between their own children? How long must stepparent and child live together to obtain the emotional state of real relatedness? This book says important things about incest, and it says them with clarity, sensitivity, and inventiveness.

RALPH SLOVENKO

PREFACE

INCEST is a word unknown to some and misunderstood by many. While incest is listed as a criminal offense, many health care professionals have no clear idea of what constitutes incest or that some incestuous acts are reportable by law. Academic writings on the subject abound, yet may confuse rather than clarify because of lack of adequate definitions. An article on incest may alter its perspective from a legal to a moral or psychosocial frame of reference without explanatory transition, seemingly without an author's awareness of a switch, leaving assumptions of forced coitus and crime. Sometimes force and violence to a person are involved, but not as often as the presumption exists or is unconsciously planted. From dissatisfaction with the vagueness, generalities, hushed professional discomfort, and often inept clinical management of incest cases came my idea to research this "uneasy" subject.

Only during the writing of this book in 1980 did I recall that I first heard of a case of incest (without knowing the word) at the age of six in the tiny village of my birth, Douglas, South Africa. My mother was whispering to her mother that a sixteen-year-old girl we knew was pregnant by her alcoholic father and that her hyperobese mother planned to rear the baby as her own. My grandmother said that was a clever idea since no one would know because that lady always looked pregnant! Both laughed heartily. I asked what was so funny and was promptly told to go out and play. My memory of that gossip was recently verified.

As a teenager I read of incest in legends, mythology, and novels. It was comfortably distant and unimportant. Later a fellow medical student quite casually and comfortably told me that she never went home alone for vacations or weekends since her mother's remarriage.

Her stepfather would pretend he was drunk and make sexual overtures. She considered her mother foolish and frigid and her stepfather not much better. She quite sensibly was not about to get entangled in their conflicts, so always took a girlfriend along. I was impressed with her poise.

Then in 1964 as a mission doctor in Natal I saw my first crisis case of incest. A 20-year-old single woman, unconscious, dehydrated, and six months pregnant, was brought in with burns from self-immolation over 80 percent of her body. When intravenous fluids restored lucidity, I asked the reason for the suicide attempt. "The baby." "Who is the father?" "My uncle." "How old is he?" "Sixty. He supports the family." She slipped into a coma and died.

Her mother and six of her nine sisters all talked at once as I stepped into the corridor. The mother spoke only Hindi but sent for her son in the car outside. He said the dead girl was sixth of the 11 children, quiet, and hardworking. They claimed ignorance of her pregnancy or any likely cause for suicide. There was a long silence when I told them she said she was pregnant by her maternal uncle, who owned the house and general store in which they all worked. With dignity the old lady firmly told her son to tell me that her brother was old and crippled but a good man who would never do such a thing. Her seven children shook their heads in unison. In the face of this united denial and a call for me to go to the emergency room, I could only tell them to watch that no sister be alone with the uncle at any time, in order to avoid another tragedy. I knew that their financial dependence on the uncle must be the reason for their denial. A colleague later told me that in this province incest was not uncommon and was usually successfully secreted in the family. He suspected incest in some cases of illegal abortions. He knew of many families who simply accepted and raised the child.

Some years later as a practicing full-time academic psychiatrist at Loyola Medical School in Chicago, I occasionally evaluated a child and family sent by the courts before a court hearing for alleged incest. I also heard from patients in individual psychotherapy expressions of incestuous fears or fantasies or of youthful sibling sexual activity. In the meantime a close personal friend who had married her first cousin (contrary to her own physician's advice) in 1954 raised five bright, healthy children.

In 1972 I began to treat married couples with sexual problems in a special clinic designed to train young professionals to deal with sexual problems in their future clinical practice. By this time literature on incest, mainly telling of the pathological consequences, was accumulating. What surprised me in the 1970s, therefore, was that while some persons were upset at the time the incest experience occurred, most had coped well. Moreover, quite a few of these same adults we were seeing in the Loyola Hospital Sex Clinic had none of the reported or predicted dire sequelae of incest. My curiosity was raised.

I then began to gather more explicit data, to scour the medical journals, to collect books and press clippings. I recognized how anxiety-provoking the topic of incest was to colleagues, trainees, friends, and relatives. At times during this eight-year search for clarification of incest, I have felt as if I were cutting a path in a dense forest with a small paring knife. I had avoided thinking carefully about incest for most of my life. I had in many ways been an observer of many different facets of incest for years, yet I was vague and confused. It became a personal challenge only when, as a medical educator, I was forced to face my own ignorance. Incest became more complex the more I read, listened, and attempted to teach about it.

By now I was sure that professionals in health, law, and religion and in the community at large deserved an integrated basic text on this topic.

This book represents my path to an improved understanding of incest. I have tried to share this and my own ways of treating those in search of help. My goal is to reach interested family physicians, pediatricians, obstetricians, psychiatrists, medical students, social workers, psychologists, counselors, nurses, ministers, lawyers, and any others who wish to understand incest more clearly. Then they can assist families in their own communities to cope with incest more successfully when it causes problems, and perhaps by public education they can prevent inappropriate sexualization of affection within the family.

I am aware that there is much to be learned and hope young researchers will be inspired to do substantial well-designed fieldwork. It will be difficult to do and to obtain funding, but it is a worthwhile endeavor.

Special acknowledgment is due to my husband, Robert, whose dialogue and encouragement helped me to complete this work. And to Nancy Romano, my secretary—her patience, loyalty, and endurance were remarkable.

D.C.R.

INCEST

Understanding
and Treatment

1

INTRODUCTION

TABOOS against incest or customs requiring incest have been known in human society since the beginning of recorded history. Sigmund Freud considered that conscious or unconscious incestuous feelings and their control shaped the development of the personality. Greek mythology, through Sophocles, told of the tragedy of Oedipus Rex, who unknowingly killed his father the king, married his mother the queen, and then blinded himself when he discovered the facts. This story is the origin of the Freudian term *Oedipus complex* or a child's desire for sex with a parent of the opposite sex. A parent's desire for sex with a child was not given emphasis in Freud's psychoanalytic writings. Incest has been considered by some writers to be the most extreme form of deviant behavior or the universal crime, and is regarded legally as a felony and morally as a serious sin. Yet, there are cultures in which the practice of incest is carefully regulated by rituals and in which specific acts of incest, including marriage between close family members such as brother and sister, cousins, and other relatives, are the norm.

How do most people learn about the laws of their land? Usually by being told the laws or by unknowingly breaking them (as in the Oedipus story) and then taking the consequences. Parents, elders, ministers, and school teachers are the customary authorities who transmit cultural expectations and the many "thou shalt nots." Failing such instruction, human behavior shows a primitive drive toward need satisfaction and is guided only by environmental restrictions such as discovery, accusation, or punishment of what is considered unacceptable or wrong. Some persons may not know or care that incest constitutes a wrongful act in their society. Participants may enjoy the sexual exchange in privacy. Incest varies widely in the age and actual affectionate or sexual activity of participants, as well as in the degree of coercion, force, and physical or psychological harm involved. The reporting of incest to church or civil authorities may be late or capricious or may occur only when there is physical abuse or a pregnancy. Medical or psychiatric help may be sought in such a crisis, or under legal pressure.

Quite normally, physical and affectional needs search for expression within the family. So may sexual needs, unless clearly directed outside the family circle. For centuries, Judeo-Christian religion has openly taught that all nonprocreative sex is sinful: fornication, adultery, and incest. Ecclesiastical, civil, and penal laws on incest have changed through time and do not always correlate with what is accepted or prohibited. From ancient times to the present day, laws, special exceptions, or suggested reforms regarding sexual offenses have evolved in the religious and secular life of every culture.

In modern times, with the evolution of the medical specialties of psychiatry and pediatrics, incest cases are handled by pediatricians and psychiatrists as well as by family physicians and obstetricians. It is interesting to note that the *Diagnostic and Statistical Manuals of Mental Disorders I, II* and *III* [30, 31, 32] do not include any separate category for incest. Another vague, nonspecific diagnostic label is usually chosen, such as adjustment reaction of childhood, parent-child problem, pedophilia, or atypical psychosexual disorder. This represents professional avoidance of the issue.

Human development, including sexual development, occurs—for better or for worse—within the intimacy of family life, which includes relaxation of dress codes; some natural, customary, accidental, or casual exposure to nudity; sometimes crowded quarters or common beds; and general learning through exploration of self and family as well as other peers. Seeing and touching family members, at any age from infancy into late life, may result in normal sexual arousal. These normal sexual feelings are initially undifferentiated and may be evoked by a child or an adult, by an animal, or even by an inanimate object (e.g., sliding down a pole or banister). A breast-feeding mother may quite normally experience sexual arousal because of nipple stimulation by her sucking baby (or even by a breast pump). These are physiological arousal feelings, which persons may or may not interpret as erotic. A breast-feeding mother may worry because these feelings are evoked by her infant rather than by her husband, but countless thousands of breast-feeding mothers are not incestuous.

Such normal day-to-day sexual feelings must be felt, understood, and controlled as part of lifelong psychosexual maturation. Learning about sexuality is unfortunately still unstructured and accidental. Too often, sex education is by experience, despite parental attempts to suppress sexual knowledge, drives, and expression. Pleasurable interpersonal physical responses, closeness, attention, and excitement invite repetition. In the case of sexual behavior, the pleasure and excitement may coexist with uncomfortable emotions such as fear, guilt, or confusion. Sex play with a partner forbidden by parents may generate anxiety or heightened sexual desire. On the other hand, the forbidden love object may be abandoned to avoid parental disapproval. The outcome of sexual sanctions depends on many complex factors in each coupling.

If a trusted and loved family member tells a child that proposed or actual sexual activity between them is good and beautiful but "it's our secret," the secrecy and collusion may generate closeness, excitement, anxiety, perplexity, or all of these feelings. When there are other good family relationships, a confused participant may innocently check with another family member. The inquirer may be genuinely surprised if there are unexpected results: disbelief, blame, rejection, anger, attack upon the inquirer or the other participant or both. Open acceptance of incest is rare in contemporary Western culture but is known to occur in urban families originating in incest-accepting communities. In some families, a daughter may show distress at being the only child not receiving father's sexual favors [16].

Incest usually arouses strong aversive feelings in incest-rejecting cultures. Sometimes these negative emotions preclude an objective assessment of the persons involved, the incest context, or the situation to be evaluated by professionals or others. Few people (including physicians and health professionals) can comfortably discuss incest in the necessary depth and sexually explicit detail without becoming uneasy and confused and experiencing conflicting emotions. Because a clear working definition of incest is not available as yet, studies and reports do little to enhance the clinician's understanding. Condemnation rather than clarification may provide relief for an author but gives little assistance to those in search of ways to evaluate and treat incest in clinical practice.

In the 1948 Kinsey study of human behavior in the male, the incidence of incest was dismissed as insignificant: "[Incest] occurs more frequently in the thinking of clinicians and social workers than it does in actual performance" [84]. The 1953 Kinsey report on human behavior in the female found that 4 percent of the 12,000 women questioned reported sexual contact with a male relative before puberty [85]. There are not details of whether sex play or full intercourse was involved. Some recent textbooks on human behavior and sociology state that incest is rare [49, 82]. Of 1356 sex offenders [56], 147 were convicted of incest, but that tells little of incidence in the community at large. Family physicians and other health workers know that incest periodically comes to their attention.

Some authors report estimates of a 500 percent increase in confirmed cases of incest each year [81]. Recent television documentaries have stated that 20 million women have been the victims of incest.

The pendulum of estimates is thus making a wide swing from negligible to epidemic occurrence.

True incidence cannot, of course, be reported until acceptable working definitions evolve. The weakness of the emerging literature on incest is the absence of such a satisfactory or practical working definition of incest, which is complex behavior. A one-word definition will not suffice. Adult-child incest may differ from adult-adult incest as much as consensual incest differs from rape incest. Child-child exploratory sex play between siblings may be noncoital and quite normal. Subgroupings of incestuous behavior, such as heterosexual versus homosexual, will be needed. A specific chapter of this book is devoted to developing definitions adequate for evaluation and for the professional communication necessary to assist those incest partners and families in need of help.

Studies of convicted incest offenders (most frequently fathers or stepfathers who have committed father-daughter incest) must be interpreted with caution, since for every case brought to trial there are hundreds that do not reach legal attention. Reasons for the latter may vary from more effective secrecy to being able to afford confidential private psychiatric care to avoid the courts when a crisis occurs. Retrospective case studies list many incest-promoting factors: cultural pressures for incest; a failure to desexualize family affection; family isolation; ignorance of incest prohibitions; family disintegration; affinity kinships; alcoholism; drugs; unemployment; physical contiguity (same bed); and psychiatric problems such as pedophilia, retardation, and manic-depressive or psychotic illness. Sometimes poverty is mentioned as a factor, but this may relate more to resultant family disintegration than to poverty per se. Incest occurs in well-educated, white-collar families as well as in uneducated, blue-collar, and primitive families.

Careful large studies recording ethnic, religious, social-class, geographic (including urban versus rural settings), and educational factors as well as types of incest are sorely lacking. Researchers as well as volunteer participants in incest studies (anonymous or identified) must be protected from legal snarls related to current criminal laws. Only then may we begin to provide needed information about incest in the population at large. One hundred cases would represent only a small pilot study, which would have to be replicated many times over before even the most cautious conclusions could be drawn.

Data on incest gathered from mental health clinics and psychiatric situations as well as from prisons and court reports are obviously skewed, since they represent only those persons who reach the attention of public agencies. White-collar families who are confidentially treated by private doctors are not included. Nor are those incest participants who have not used nor perhaps ever needed health care. How large is this group? No one knows yet.

It is alleged that a great deal of unreported information on incest was gathered at the time of the first Kinsey report (1948). Since this was not made public at the time, and still awaits publication, nothing can be said about it. The Kinsey studies [84, 85] are highly respected because together they include thorough personal interviews of some 20,000 men and women. Reports of incest from this large group would prove valuable and perhaps provide an indication of the general incidence of incest in the white population between 1940 and 1953. Further studies must follow.

Sometimes a history of incest may emerge quite incidentally in the course of a thorough life history taken for medical reasons or written as part of an autobiography. When special searches have been launched by inviting incest participants to tell about their experiences, the researchers have advertised for those "pro-incest" or for those "damaged by incest." This approach acknowledges researcher preconceptions in search of confirmation. Such studies are based on a small, selected sample and often use questionable or unreliable methods. When published, however, they have become best-sellers because of their readable journalistic style, highly erotic content, and sensational marketing.

Incest seems today to be a media theme whose time has come. The *Chicago Tribune* (2 August 1979) pictured brother and sister David Goddu (aged 22) and Victoria Pittorino (aged 24) who were adoptees, reared apart, who knowingly met and married in Salem, Massachusetts, in May 1979. Since their marriage had violated incest laws in Massachusetts, Victoria's distressed adoptive mother allegedly brought charges [163]. Both siblings received a suspended sentence. Incest again made the *Chicago Tribune* (18 August 1979) when a 42-year-old woman, Jean Lillie, married her 19-year-old soldier son, Christopher. Both were given suspended sentences for the misdemeanor of an unlawful marriage.

Press coverage recently has ranged from advocating the joy of incest to severe indictments of incest as child abuse, which include dogmatic statements that incest always leaves irrevocable psychic damage [28, 118]. These extreme positions often generate more heat than light.

All persons, lay and professional alike, when confronting incest (real, fantasized, or in print), struggle with three emotional, physical, intellectual, and moral responses: (1) avoidance, (2) attraction, and (3) attack.

Incestuous desires (attraction) are natural, physiological sexual feelings. A variety of unconscious or deliberate mechanisms must be developed to control (avoid) and deny (attack and repress) these natural sexual feelings, which are real. Values are later accorded to all behaviors and reactions. In an intact family that espouses a sexually conservative belief system, many preconscious and conscious ways of controlling all sexual expressions are recurrently taught and learned. These controls assist as defenses against incestuous arousal (as well as sexual feelings for nonfamily) that may lead to unacceptable behaviors. In Anglo-Saxon families, physical affection other than in the marital bed is mostly restricted to infants. Prolonged caressing and hugging is only for babies and for private interactions between the parents. Perhaps this assists incest avoidance by physical distancing. Perhaps separate beds and bedrooms help too.

Normal learned defenses against incest are modesty, privacy, desexualized affectionate exchange, the labeling of premarital sex as sinful, sexual appropriateness, and encouragement of romance outside the family (with strong injunctions to avoid premarital pregnancy). These essentially are also general sexual prohibitions. How and why do these barriers work in most cases? How are effective messages given that it is appropriate to express affection, loyalty, and love to family members, but *not* sexuality?

Incest occurs in the setting of everyday life. Often (but not always) it may be in the framework of a loving and caring relationship between adult and child. There may be debate about a child's legal age of consent or about the presence of subtle coercion owing to parental power and child dependency, but child-adult incest need not include physical abuse—indeed much affection and tenderness may be exchanged. Although discovery of incest may create a sudden crisis in the family, school, or neighborhood, it is important to emphasize that incest is not necessarily violent, nor is adult-child incest always child abuse. The resultant panic on discovery may be far more traumatic to the child incest partner than the sexual contact from which he or she is to be protected.

Care may be more readily offered to the whole family by objective professionals who are informed and comfortable, rather than morally outraged and condemnatory. Family members may care a great deal about each other although they practice incest, and caring is a strength in a family. Understanding incest does not mean condoning it. Also, optimum treatment might far more readily occur in a setting where incest is decriminalized, but this may be a generation away. Professional intervention at present, unfortunately, has a tendency to break up the family immediately and place the parent in jail and the child in an institution or foster home for years. To "save" the child, the family is destroyed. The rupture disintegrates all important relationships and prevents valuable family therapy in the time of crisis. Tragically, later restoration of the family unit may even be totally precluded. The law and health professionals may be viewed by the family as antagonists and considered more destructive to the family than the actual incestuous sexual expression. For the child, institutional care or a series of foster placements may mean emotional neglect and more sexual or physical abuse. Laws on mandatory reporting of child abuse recognize this reality and include abuses other than parent-child abuses under the same reporting act. All of these possible untherapeutic outcomes of treatment need to be clearly kept in mind when each case is professionally evaluated for management. The death penalty for incest occurred in the past; the death of the family is too often today's penalty for reported incest.

Before incest is discovered, "keeping the secret" may be a cause of anxiety to both incest partners, yet it may also be a strong emotional bond between them. A combination of affection and sexual pleasure binds persons closely to each other. Secondary gain from the incest may also occur when one partner exploits the other to obtain privileges, favors, or material rewards. At times an envious sibling sees the money or rewards, begins to watch, and then reports the incest to someone. A thorough history should always include information about this materialistic aspect of the incest relationship, which may have perpetuated sex for gain rather than affection. One incest partner may control the other by blackmail, threatening to tell unless the incest behavior continues. Such threats may be a reason for the recurrence of sibling incest.

Internal sexual controls or sociocultural incest barriers are learned behaviors that are needed for incest avoidance. When desexualized affection is not learned in a family, incest occurs. Therefore, incest may be considered a sexual learning disorder and possibly amenable to special sex education in a family therapy setting.

Since adequate treatment strategies are in rudimentary and trial stages, follow-up studies of family outcome are almost nonexistent. Ideally, in the future, different models of incest treatment will be compared to select optimum management techniques for a specific family or individual.

Understanding of family values as well as the cultural context remains an important first step for health professionals, so that response by immediate attack (arrest) or by avoidance (neglect, transfer or closure of cases) may be reduced. Acceptance of the dignity and worthiness of the participants (not necessarily of their incest act) is important as we search for further understanding. Successful therapeutic intervention with each family or individual depends on motivation to change. Outside controls may be provided by a legal mandate: treatment or jail. Often sent unwillingly to therapy, such a family may nonetheless learn to express affection without sex, to refuse sexual overtures within the family, and to discern who is an appropriate or a legally prohibited partner. This is especially true for children of divorce reared in newly constituted families, which is so common a phenomenon in western culture today.

It is not easy to treat cases of incest. They test every fiber of the character of the physician or counselor, especially in a program collecting numerous incest cases. "Burn-out" or emotional depletion is known to occur in professionals unless a team approach evolves to provide dialogue, consultation, and mutual support. Professionals dealing with incest receive gratitude rarely and animosity often. They are outsiders to the family. Their challenge is to stay objective, but this is difficult. An incest case may be confusing, because the emotions of the helping professional may shift from attack to avoidance to attraction during the course of a single hour. These mixed emotions may be anxiety-provoking and upsetting but need first to be recognized, then understood, and then accepted within the self.

Consultation with a colleague can and often does provide objectivity for the health professional. For many incest partners, psychotherapy is not available when needed. At other times therapy is neither requested nor perceived as of any value, yet may be mandated by the courts and much resented. Patients may come once and then disappear, move, or relate again in crisis only.

The defensive mechanisms of some individuals prevail at the time of incest or later, so that they obtain perspective regarding the incest without any professional help. These persons may escape from the family (as children or adults) and may sort out their own conflicting feelings of attraction and avoidance. They may love, fear, pity, or hate the incest partner, but they work out their own sense of responsibility for participation or they work out a sense of satisfaction at escaping the incestuous involvement. Perspective and resolution can occur with forgiveness of self, sometimes of the incest partner, and of the silent (nonprotective) family member such as the other parent or sibling who may have known but was afraid to intervene. Life and marital adjustment later may be satisfactory.

For some persons, there may be psychic trauma or residual incest wounds of varying depth and degree. Incest fantasy may cause severe distress and require individual rather than family therapy. With or without psychotherapy, emotional reactions to incest can heal. Finally, understanding and self-acceptance may be achieved. There may even be a strong sense of self-satisfaction at having emerged and adapted well in spite of, or even because of, the incest experience.

To keep an open mind and to avoid prejudgments in working with incest are challenges for the mature, empathic evaluator and therapist. Benefit and growth may be achieved by retaining an awareness of the three shifting responses of attraction, avoidance, and attack within the self and in others who deal with incest.

There are, therefore, numerous perspectives on incest. The anthropologist, the sociologist, the lawyer, the social worker, the doctor, the psychiatrist, and the pastor all see a separate segment of this highly complex and still poorly understood aspect of human sexual behavior. The participants and their families have still other views. These differing perspectives will be explored in later chapters.

2

DEFINITIONS OF INCEST

AT present, there is confusion, misunderstanding, and an absence of meaningful communication in ordinary conversation and in scientific studies regarding incest, which is complex sexual behavior. Specifically, what constitutes incest? Is it only sexual intercourse between two people of family kinship or blood ties? Is mouth-to-mouth kissing or breast-caressing also incestuous? Could sexual arousal resulting from visual contact or seductive looks or signals be incestuous? Is a distressing or arousing dream or fantasy about contact with a blood relative incestuous? Wide differences between psychological and moral or legal definitions, as well as many levels of understanding incest, emerge.

Since helping persons must understand, communicate professionally with, make plans for the management of, and treat those who come seeking help to obtain relief of distress, any attempt to clarify incest must, therefore, consider these differing dimensions of incest: commonly used definitions, legal definitions, religious and moral definitions, biological definitions, and psychosocial definitions.

COMMONLY USED DEFINITIONS

Webster's dictionary [169] offers these definitions of incest:

> 1. Sexual intercourse or inbreeding between closely related individuals especially when they are related or regarded as related (as by reason of affinity or membership in a tribal kinship, group or clan) within degrees wherein marriage is prohibited by law or custom: compare endogamy, exogamy, inbreeding.

2. The statutory crime of cohabitation, marriage, or sexual intercourse without marriage of parties related to each other within the degree of consanguinity or of affinity within which marriage is prohibited by law. (*Consanguinity* is being related by blood or descended from a common ancestor. *Affinity* is being related by marriage.)

LEGAL DEFINITIONS

Legal definitions of incest differ between countries and within countries. In the Middle Ages, the Catholic Church exercised both secular and religious authority. With separation of church and state, statutory law in England in the sixteenth century evolved as secular expression of the dominant community morality. The death penalty for incest by hanging or beheading was customary in Europe up to the end of the eighteenth century. In England in 1583, Queen Elizabeth had repealed the incest death penalty, but Cromwell restored it from 1642 to 1660. Incest was an ecclesiastical offense from 1660 until the Punishment of Incest Act was introduced in England and its colonies in 1908, with legal penalties varying from seven years to life imprisonment. Today most jurisdictions in the Western world except France list incest as a crime.

In the United States, no uniformity exists among the states regarding the kinship degrees of forbidden relationships or the age of legal consent for sexual participation. A majority of states restrict the crime of incest to first- and second-degree blood relatives. Some states include affinity relatives. In Illinois, the law is as follows:

> *Incest* is a statutory offense, usually a felony, which consists of either marriage or a sexual act (intercourse or deviate sexual conduct) between persons who are too closely related.

> *Aggravated incest* is an act of sexual intercourse or deviate sexual conduct between father and daughter only, "daughter" being a blood daughter regardless of age or legitimacy or a stepdaughter under the age of 18. Knowledge of the relationship is an element and only the father is guilty of the felony of aggravated incest.

> *Incest* is an act of sexual intercourse or deviate sexual conduct between mother and son, or brother and sister of the whole or half blood. Knowledge of the relationship is an element. Both participants are guilty of the felony offense.

Since aggravated incest is considered by law to be only that between father and daughter (not between mother and son), it has been contended that the law discriminates against men by not penalizing the woman (*People* v. *York*, 329 N.E.2 845, Ill. App. 5th, May 26, 1975). In Hawaii, a Polynesian man 10 years younger than his sister was jailed whereas the sister was not penalized for consensual consanguineous adult-adult incest.

One man raised the question of his own illegitimacy, attempting to support a plea of not guilty of consanguineous incest by so doing, but his plea was not upheld at trial (*State v. Russel*, December 22, 1971, Calif.). He claimed that since his parents were apart at the time of his conception he was not a direct relative as accused.

For the crime of incest heterosexual intercourse must take place, yet many incest offenders are behind bars, convicted for noncoital contact and in affinity rather than consanguineous relationships [56, 103, 110, 158].

The popular movie *Midnight Cowboy* starts with the fleeting implication that the main character's sexually permissive grandmother, who raised him, has personally coached him in the erotic arts. She tells him that he is the finest stud, thereby encouraging his odyssey to New York for fame and fortune as a male prostitute. In the Australian criminal code, grandfather-grandchild incest is considered criminal, whereas grandmothers are not mentioned. This raised the question of discrimination against men in a case of consensual adult-adult coital involvement between an unprosecuted grandmother and her grandson [151].

The state of Illinois does not permit marriages between first or second cousins. Yet such marriages are permitted by some religions and by other states and several countries abroad. Thus paradoxically there may be religious dispensation for first or second cousins to marry, but Illinois priests, ministers, or rabbis may not perform the marriage ceremony, which would not be valid by current civil law. Therefore, religious dispensation may be obtained in Chicago, but the couple must find another state for a valid church wedding. A midwestern couple, first cousins aged 70 and 72, discovered that Wisconsin and Indiana allowed them to marry only because both were older than 65 years.

On a practical legal level, most prosecuted incest cases today are concerned less with permission to marry than with adult-child sexual conduct. The minor in incest cases usually goes through juvenile court, under protection of the local or state child service agency. Usually, for the child this has meant removal from the home and placement in a psychiatric hospital and then in foster homes, because in many states incest is categorized as criminal child abuse.

The Abused and Neglected Child Reporting Act in Illinois mandates that professionals report (anonymously) sex offenses involving children under 18 years. For physicians, ambiguity may arise because there is also a confidentiality contract of absolutely privileged communication between doctor and patient (as is also legally the case between priest and penitent and lawyer and client). This legal privilege of confidentiality is not extended to nurses, social workers, teachers, and other child care workers, who are legally required to report incest.

The Law Reform Commission of Canada [90] submitted in November 1978 (in French and English) a thoughtful and useful 56-page report on sexual offenses, with reform recommendations, of which the segment on incest is given below:

> Section 150 of the Criminal Code defines incest as sexual intercourse between two people who by blood relationship are either parent and child, brother and sister, half-brother and half-sister, or grandparent and grandchild. Incest is an indictable offense, carrying with it a maximum penalty of fourteen years imprisonment. No offense is deemed to have been committed, however, where the parties do not know that they are blood relatives.
>
> Practical court experience has shown that the overwhelming majority of incest trials concern illicit intercourse between fathers and daughters at the age of puberty or during the period of adolescence. By contrast, the judicial record is mostly silent on prosecutions for incest between persons over the age of majority.
>
> In its Working Paper 22, the Commission recommended that incest between consenting adults should no longer qualify as an offense. It was thought that incestuous relations not involving children or adolescents did not deserve to be treated with the full rigor of the criminal law. This recommendation elicited numerous letters and considerable comment on the part of the public. The Commission even received one petition signed by some three hundred people asking: "Please do not take incest out of the Criminal Code!" Despite the evident sincerity of such correspondents, the Commission continues to believe that incest between consenting adults ought no longer to fall within the purview of criminal justice. This position is based on several grounds.
>
> As outlined above, the reform of laws dealing with sexual offenses should be based on three fundamental principles:
>
> 1. The protection of the integrity of the person,
> 2. The protection of children and special groups, and
> 3. The safeguarding of public decency.
>
> It is not the function of the law to intervene in the private lives of citizens and to attempt to cover all sexual behavior. Certain forms of sexual behavior are regarded by many as sinful, morally wrong, or objectionable for reasons of conscience, or of religious or cultural tradition. Certainly incest is universally regarded as repugnant behavior. But the criminal law does not, and indeed should not, cover all such actions. As was said in the 1957 Report to the British Parliament of the Committee on Homosexual Offenses and Prostitution (the Wolfenden Report): "Unless a deliberate attempt is to be made by society, acting through the agency of the law, to equate the sphere of the crime with that of sin, there must remain a realm of private morality and immorality which is, in brief and crude terms, not the law's business."
>
> Accordingly, in the absence of any exploitation of au-

thority or dependency, it is felt that incestuous behavior ought not be treated and punished as a criminal act.

Nor can it be argued, within this framework, that the genetic risk of inbreeding justifies the intervention of the criminal law. The substance of this argument is that sexual relations between those who are related by blood create a serious risk of genetically defective children. In the first place, the available scientific evidence is controversial and does not support the contention that the offspring of blood-related parents are necessarily more likely to be born with genetic defects. But even if this contention could be made out, we would still have to ask whether this is an appropriate problem for the criminal law. It should be remembered that the law does not intervene to prohibit marriage and subsequent procreation by persons who are not related but who may exhibit genetically serious mental or physical disabilities. Nor does the law permit compulsory sterilization of such persons.

As to the argument that the criminal prohibition of incest is necessary for the protection of the family, it must be asked whether the criminal law provides an appropriate solution for the problem. Incest is above all a family disturbance; it is not a cause but a symptom or result of a disturbance within the family, a disturbance generally present *before* the offense took place. The criminal law and the criminal process are notoriously weak in dealing with family problems. This is true even in situations involving general prohibitions, such as cases of family assault, of which assault upon a spouse and child abuse are two examples.

The Commission believes that incest should above all be a matter of social and psychological treatment; secondly, a matter of regulation by family and child welfare law; and only thirdly, a matter for the criminal law. The Commission further believes that the only valid basis for the intervention of the criminal law is the protection of children and adolescents from the abuse of authority and from interference with their right to mature unmolested toward sexual self-determination.

As the law now stands, such protection is not necessarily afforded: the provisions of the Code are limited in scope, and section 150 defines restrictively the degrees of kinship within which sexual relations are prohibited as incestuous. Moreover, the offense as it is presently defined contains no element of either violence or exploitation, the two elements the law seeks to repress in dealing with sexual offenses. Finally, the present law does not extend the same protection from exploitation to male and female persons.

Under the scheme proposed by the Commission, children under fourteen years of age are protected by the absolute prohibition against sexual interference, whether with or without consent. However, in order to reinforce the legal protection of adolescents between the ages of fourteen and eighteen, already proposed, from exploitation of dependency or exercise of authority, it is suggested that such exploitation or exercise of authority be presumed where the young person is between fourteen and eighteen years of age and the adult accused shares with the former a close degree of kinship. This position is consonant with the abolition of the crime of incest between persons of equal status, of majority or minority, but goes no further. It would emphasize that the essence of the offense is the exploitation of a minor grandchild, child, sibling, niece or nephew. The new formulation would thereby retain the protection now accorded to the young by section 150 (incest). Indeed it would widen the family circle beyond the present provision so as to bring the brothers and sisters of a parent under its ban, since these persons are frequently in a position to exploit young people. Such an approach provides an appropriate response to the growing concern for the exploitation of children, a concern which is evidenced, for example, by the . . . Year of the Child in 1979.

As to consensual relations between brothers and sisters between the ages of fourteen and eighteen, it should be remembered that such relations presently come within the definition of "sexual immorality or any similar vice" within the Juvenile Delinquents Act. Thus such behavior is presently dealt with as a form of juvenile delinquency rather than as a criminal offense, and the Commission believes that the juvenile court is the appropriate forum for such problems. Should the juvenile offender be transferred to the ordinary criminal courts, the presumption of exploitation would not apply because the juvenile offender's age would have been less than eighteen years at the time at which the delinquency was alleged to have occurred.

The Commission is aware that its recommendation may well elicit strong opposition from certain sectors of the public, if only because of the age-old stigma attached to incest. It also acknowledges that in the final analysis it will be up to Parliament to assess public opinion and decide whether decriminalizing incest between adults would be impolitic at present.

This thoughtful directive from numerous Canadian professionals, needed as it is by the Western community at large, went unheeded. It was tabled because of other Canadian political and legislative priorities. An opportunity for courageous leadership from Ottawa was avoided by politicians. As a practicing psychiatrist, I endorse its wisdom and call upon United States and other legislators to study its content for comment or action.

RELIGIOUS AND MORAL DEFINITIONS

A valid academic question may be raised: Is incest a moral absolute, or is it only relative to certain circumstances? Ignorance of relatedness (e.g., as a result of being reared apart) is generally considered an exonerating factor. Danger of death or an emergency may allow dispensation from religious incest laws. Killing is another strong social taboo, but is not a moral absolute, since church, society, and society's legal system recognize times when killing is appropriate (war, self-defense, or for punishment of certain deeds). Many difficult moral questions remain regarding incest.

Impediments to marriage have changed through time and with various belief systems. The word *religion* is thought to be derived either from the Latin *religio* (reverence) or from the French *religare* (to tie back). Control of undesirable human impulses such as aggression and free sex has been an important focus of old and new religions. Sex for procreation (therefore, restricted to marital partners) is a strong Judeo-Christian theme. Parent-child or sibling incest violates the marital contract.

In antiquity, belief systems considered sexual relations between family members as models of godly behavior and therefore not only acceptable but even required. Regal incest occurred among the pharaohs and also among Egyptian citizens in the Seventeenth and Eighteenth Dynasties of the Ptolemies [103]. Ancient Persian religious writings [148] recommended incestuous unions as "pious." For pre-Columbian Peruvian nobility, brother-sister marriages were required by religious laws while pre-Christian Greeks varied from condemnation to praise of incest [103].

The polytheistic Roman Empire is said to have officially banned consanguineous or incestuous marriages to the sixth degree of relationship. Various emperors declared themselves gods, above Roman law and exempt from the harsh Roman punishment of enforced suicide for incest.

When Emperor Constantine took the throne in about 300 A.D. he became a Christian. Incest laws delineated a penalty of death by burning plus confiscation of property. Inheritance laws forbade marriages of cousins up to the sixth degree. For centuries, incest was considered a mortal sin by Christians as it had also been by Jews. Hebrew prohibitions of incestuous acts were spelled out in Lev. 18:6–18, with the death penalty imposed in Lev. 20:10–21. Prohibited relationships included both consanguinity and affinity; Jews abhorred the alleged carnal promiscuity within Canaanite families. Prohibitions in Mosaic law are still directed only at the male since he is considered the only active partner in coitus.

The Fourth Lateran Council 1215 A.D. in Rome liberalized marriage laws for Roman Catholics, clearly forbidding only first-cousin unions. However, at the same time the Inquisition was set up to pursue witches. An accusation of incest (among other allegations) ensured that the named persons would be interrogated, tortured, and burned in the name of Christ. In the following centuries, incest in the community at large was apparently rife [103]. Changing religious attitudes fostered the Reformation and the Protestant movement, together with the Counter-Reformation within the Roman Catholic church. Along with other reforms, incest laws were liberalized so that today dispensation for second-cousin marriages and, in many circumstances, first-cousin marriages is readily granted by most Western religions.

Eastern religions have a diversity of prohibitions of kinship marriages. The ancient Chinese applied a death penalty for some incest, whereas modern China inflicts banishment and beating for sex with a relative closer than the fifth degree. In northern India, Hindu Brahmins do not allow marriage between those of the same surname, regardless of blood relationships. Only third or more distant cousins may marry. In the south of India, Hindus allow certain first-cousin (cross-cousin) marriages but not others. For example, mother's brother's children and father's sister's children may wed, but mother's sister's and father's brother's children may not. The latter (parallel) cousins are taught from infancy to call each other brother and sister to reinforce the marriage prohibition. In colonial times, British law had to be evaded to continue the custom of first-cousin marriage. The coastal region of Andrah Pradesh has the highest incidence of first-cousin marriages in India.

For Muslims, the Koran allows all types of first-cousin marriages. Arranged marriages are customary. Any nonmarital sexual relationship, incestuous or otherwise, is considered a severe family disgrace requiring revenge. Illegitimate (also incestuous) offspring are reluctantly accepted and raised by the family, although the child is considered unmarriageable. In remote villages, stoning of the unfortunate pregnant woman may occur. On the other extreme, the Ismailis, a group of devout Muslim followers of the Aga Kahn, who set himself up in France as a god, accept brother-sister marriages, which are considered criminal except in France.

The views on incest of Confucians, Shintos, and Buddhists are not mentioned here because of a lack of adequate source materials.

The cultural and religious mosaic that is present-day America awaits study of attitudes and values regarding close kinship marriages. Romantic love rather than family pressure for property preservation may propel some cousins to consider marriage. If they live in a state that forbids a first-cousin marriage, they will simply seek a state where it is legal.

Regarding the current public moral stance on sexualized affection within the family there is nothing reliable known yet.

BIOLOGICAL DEFINITIONS

In discussing human genetics, publications and textbooks do not mention the word incest. In this science, only biological facts are of concern. The terms *inbreeding, interbreeding,* or *con-*

sanguineous mating are used to describe both animal and human pairing. There is a paucity of material on human inbreeding. In an erudite text on population genetics [94], there are detailed descriptions and mathematical probabilities for offspring outcome for sib, parent-offspring, and cousins matings, but the system of inbreeding pertains to lab mice rather than to humans. In the nonhuman mammalian world, father-daughter, brother-sister mating is determined solely by propinquity and dominance; there is no other deterrant [63, 73].

Pedigree, or a record of ancestry, is an important aspect of genetic study. Elaborate charts are drawn up regarding heritable characteristics and disorders. Since genetics concerns itself with outcome, there is high interest in gene combinations and their expressivity. The effects of inbreeding may be optimally observed in small, closed population studies. Pedigreed inbreeding agriculturally achieves 10 percent superior individuals, 10 percent "runts" or less desirable individuals, and 80 percent average individuals: therefore, 90 percent satisfactory individuals. The superior 10 percent are then again inbred to achieve yet more desirable characteristics. The final outcome is elimination of undesirable recessive traits from a particular species and the evolution of superior species. In other words, inbreeding is finally effective for the group as a whole but less so for some individuals, particularly those inheriting congenital diseases, since damaging genes are usually incompatible with survival [74, 109].

It has now been clearly established from the genetic study of human pedigrees that mutation, or changes within chromosomal material, is quite sporadic and more important in nonfamilial than in familial conditions. Many persons are carriers of congenital disorders but do not manifest the disease. However, if they mate with a person (blood relative or random) who carries a similar recessive gene, some of their children may be affected. There is a high incidence of Tay-Sachs disease in Ashkenazic Jews, but no history of inbreeding. To explain this, it must be remembered that although each person is genetically unique there are similarities among people. Children resemble parents; brothers and sisters and other relatives usually look more alike than unrelated persons. Genetic similarities may extend beyond the immediate family to others within the same ethnic and geographic group, since most persons do not mate totally at random but usually marry someone who shares their cultural background. Intermarriage and large-scale genetic exchange owing to random matings has increased with migration and travel. Nevertheless, most persons seek someone similar in appearance to self: "likes attract." Genetically, the term *assortative mating* is used as a synonym for selection of a mate who is more similar than would be expected by random. Another departure from random mating is inbreeding, where marriage partners are related to each other by blood.

Inbreeding causes a more marked decrease in the variability of the genes (which account for differences such as color, hair, eyes, etc.) than does assortative mating. The probability of identity by direct descent is known as the *inbreeding co-efficient* and is often represented by the symbol f. For random matings $f = 0$. For complete inbreeding $f = 1$ (rare in humans other than in children of consanguineous parent-child incest). The average known inbreeding co-efficients are $f = .0005$ (France), $f = .003$ (Japan), and $f = .02$ (Andhra Pradesh, coast of India), where there is a high percentage of first-cousin mating. Children of first-cousin matings usually show 5 percent recessive genes compared to 4 percent in children of unrelated parents [95]. First cousins have one-eighth (12.5%) and second cousins one-sixteenth (6.25%) of their genes in common for both desirable and abnormal chromosomes. A child of a consanguineous parent-child mating has 50 percent and that of a consanguineous brother-sister mating 25 percent of the same genes.

Hartl [74] mentions that children of first-cousin marriages were shown in some studies to be average, in others to be less capable than noninbred children, and in still others outstanding. Apparently the pronounced inbreeding effects mentioned in some studies [144] are not always observed. Franklin and Eleanor Roosevelt were first cousins who married and had four healthy children (as have numerous other such couples). If there is a rare hereditary disease carried by both first-cousin (as by both unrelated) parents, then the chance of transmitting the disease to their children will, of course, be higher than related or unrelated parents only one of whom is a carrier. Theoretically, beneficial traits owing to recessive genes could also be increased by inbreeding, as is pursued in thoroughbred animal husbandry.

It is conceivable that destructive hereditary defects would finally be eliminated from the population at large by death of negatively affected offspring as a result of inbreeding. It must be repeated that the biological effect upon the children of incestuous relationships is extraordinarily difficult to assess from available medical literature. With humility it must be admitted that available scientific studies are few and flawed; their reliability is questionable because there is no correction for such factors as maternal age, adequate antenatal care, or attempted abortion [3, 4, 143, 144, 157]. Too often there is loose speculation, with opinions rather than facts repeated from text to text. Geneticist George F. Smith has stated [149]:

> Ideally, we would like to follow the results of these incestuous pregnancies from the time of conception into adult life. Unfortunately many studies on incestuous matings only produced information about the infant during the neonatal period and shortly thereafter; thus critical information is lost about early fetal loss, stillbirths, neonatal deaths, mental retardation and debilitating conditions which had their onset in later life.

Dr. Smith stated that studies in the United States, France, and England [3, 21, 157] had shown detrimental effects of close inbreeding, for which he suggested three possible explanations: chance occurrence, data collection bias, and synergism in action of genes rendered homozygous by inbreeding. He gave a critique of the largest study published to date of 161 births to 141 mothers from Czechoslovakia [144]. In this group 14 percent of the mothers and 6 percent of the fathers were themselves mentally retarded, most of the mothers were teenagers, two were deaf-mutes, two had epilepsy, and two had congenital syphilis—all factors increasing pregnancy risks. Many received minimal prenatal care. Their infants (88 from father-daughter incest, 72 from brother-sister matings) were born into troubled homes with low environmental stimulation, which compounded any genetic disadvantage. An unusual number of the incestuous couples produced multiple progeny: six couples had two children each, two had three each; two had four each, and one woman produced five children by her father. Dr. Smith concluded that these incestuous parents were not a representative sample of the general population and that reported physical and mental subnormality of offspring could relate to parental subnormality rather than inbreeding.

Ideally (in an academic sense) children of incest need to be studied longitudinally. A genetic profile must be obtained and then compared with offspring of mothers of similar age and social status. Affluent mothers in private medical care pregnant from a consanguineous mating should be studied and compared with women in the court and welfare system. Observations and available studies to date confirm that the initial gene pool of each participant, whether in random or inbreeding matings, determines the offspring outcome. Unrelated carriers (healthy in appearance but with a high-risk gene profile) may mate and produce infants with abnormalities. These persons are not prohibited from marrying, nor are they considered criminals. Prediction of a possible abnormality from consanguineous mating is not yet possible; such abnormalities may have been in the past grossly exaggerated in less-than-objective reports. All too often, an incestuous offspring's life may have been terminated unduly. For affinity matings, e.g., matings between adoptive siblings or stepsiblings, the offspring's inbreeding co-efficient is no larger than that of the offspring of random matings.

Genetics places a special emphasis on the common good, the community at large, and, with scientific concern, has been less condemnatory regarding incestuous matings. Geneticists may yet provide professional leadership and direction for essential data gathering. Great areas of ignorance remain regarding children of first-line blood relatives. Although few in number, these children deserve scientific study: both the malformed (who are most likely to reach geneticists and therefore constitute a biased sample) and the healthy ones. Contemporary geneticists may then avoid bias in the study sample, not lose an important potential study population, and, finally, understand the biological consequences of incestuous unions by long-term follow up.

Psychosocial definitions

Psychosocial definitions of incest vary from obvious avoidance (e.g., the total absence of any mention of incest in DSM I, II, and III) to attack (defining incest categorically as child abuse, or viewing incestuous fantasy, fondling, or coitus as severely deviant or damaging). The National Center on Child Abuse and Neglect uses the term *intrafamily sexual abuse* for incest "which is perpetrated on a child by a member of that child's family group and includes not only sexual intercourse but also any act designed to stimulate a child sexually or use a child for the sexual stimulation, either of the perpetrator or of another person." This is a sweeping definition that gives great power to an accuser and a burden of proof on accused partners. Is "any act" a kiss on the lips, a piggyback ride, breast-feeding? These acts may quite normally be designed to give affectionate stimulation to a child but may accidentally trigger a sexual response in the child or relative. A responsible, sensitive parent may recognize the sexual aspect and explain to the child that the boundary between affectionate and sexual feelings is narrow and must be avoided in the future. The sexual aspect is perhaps more startling, upsetting, or threatening (therefore, in need of control) than the degree of relationship. Contemporary cultures exist (Middle East, Polynesia) where groups of mothers openly rub their child's genitals. This is done affectionately, with smiles, cuddling, and special songs. This custom of deliberate adult-child sexual activity is not surreptitious and not considered wrong, sinful, or incestuous according to local belief systems, nor are the children involved reported to have developmental or adjustment problems.

A clearer and more objective distinction between incest and child abuse is, therefore, called for in the United States by reform of unclear child abuse laws. Incest is not necessarily violent nor is it always child abuse. Involved partners may care a great deal about each other. There may be no exploitation, fear, or force. Today a 12-year-old alone, with confidentiality, may receive treatment for venereal disease. Fourteen-year-olds may obtain contraceptives and sign themselves in and out of Illinois psychiatry hospitals. Society thus gives double messages about the age of consent.

In this era, divorce and remarriage both have a very high incidence. An estimated 40 percent of children are from divorced families. Critical legal consideration must also be accorded, therefore, to stepkinships. In such relationships, there has not been an opportunity over a period of years for protective family bonding to develop. Desexualized, concerned caring on the part of a new stepparent or stepsibling will take time and teaching. It is a giant leap of expectation that a healthy 28-year-old stepfather and 13-year-old adolescent stepdaughter should have no sexual feelings for each other. A home usually provides close quarters, relaxed dress code, and reduced privacy. In the situation just mentioned, much extra protection by the mother would be needed in the way of a close relationship with her new husband, a strong family moral code, and sex education so that her daughter may learn that sexual feelings in the newly constituted family are normal but inappropriate except between the parents. Affinity incest is a risk to be anticipated especially by the incoming stepparent in all reconstituted families.

There remains the important question of exactly what constitutes an act of incest. Legally, *incest* means coitus, but new child abuse laws say "any act." In psychosocial writing, the frame of reference may switch within a single paragraph from describing fondling to presumption of intercourse. Coherent professional evaluation and exchange of information as well as dialogue with an involved family or community is thus compromised by confusion and misunderstanding. This might be reduced if the psychosocial definition of incest were made more complete, factual, and descriptive of the actual behavior [140].

I propose the following three-stage classification system to describe all incest cases:

1. Incest Diagnosis
   More than one may apply and be listed:
   a. Consanguineous (blood relative) or affinity (related by marriage) incest
   b. Consensual, coercive, or forceful
   c. Coital or noncoital incest
   d. Heterosexual or homosexual incest
   e. Adult-adult, child-child, adult-child, or group incest
   f. Rape incest
   g. Pedophilic incest
   h. Exhibitionist incest
   i. Multiple deviance incest (e.g., exploitation, prostitution, transvestism, child pornography, sadomasochism)
   j. Fantasy or dream incest
   k. Incest craving or envy
   l. Incest-accepting family, culture or religion
2. Physical Diagnosis
   Are physical signs of incest, e.g., vaginal or anal tears, present or absent?
3. Other Psychiatric Diagnosis
   In addition to incest, is a psychiatric disorder present or absent? Diagnoses in this category might include no psychiatric diagnosis,

alcohol abuse, drug abuse, mental retardation, infanticide, depressive disorder, conversion disorder, parricide, avoidant disorder, dissociative disorder, anxiety disorder, somatization disorder, or adjustment disorder, etc.

It becomes thus immediately apparent that there are numerous diagnostic aspects to be considered. Subdivision into child (under 12 years old), minor (12–15 years old), and adult (16 years old and over) incest [56] is not considered of real value clinically. The age of sexual consent varies in each state, as does the age of legal consent.

Clarity in a psychosocial definition could be of great value in the final understanding and treatment of "the incests" in clinical practice. My justification for a separate category Incest Diagnosis is that the more comprehensive the description the more helpful clinically. Culturally some incest behaviors are not only accepted but expected and may not be at all damaging emotionally or maladaptive to the individual or the community. In some incest cases there may indeed be traumatic reactions physically or psychologically and, therefore, categories 2 and 3 are needed. This format might begin to establish more coherent academic reporting and clinical management, as in these examples:

CASE 2-1. Incest Diagnosis: Affinity incest, adult-child (stepfather-stepson), homosexual, pedophilic, consensual, noncoital (mutual masturbation); Physical Diagnosis: none; Other Psychiatric Diagnosis: none for the adult partner (homosexual pedophilia already stated). Here it is clear that the stepfather, a homosexual pedophilic, seeks young boys; the affinity relationship is quite incidental. From the known pattern of pedophilics, the stepson will be of little sexual interest when he matures to puberty, but the stepfather's pattern of pedophilia will continue with other available young boys, whom he may or may not coerce or molest (the stepson was cooperative). Stepfather will need both legal and psychiatric attention for optimum remediation, although the outlook for changed behavior is guarded. The child needs also to be evaluated as does the mother and the rest of the family.

CASE 2-2. Incest Diagnosis: Consensual incest-accepting family group incest, adult-child, child-child, and adult-adult heterosexual coital incest; Physical Diagnosis: none; Other Psychiatric Diagnosis: none. This situation was revealed quite incidentally in a suburban Chicago school. The family regularly rotated weekends at three extended family homes which was reported when a 15-year-old girl complained to a woman teacher that she was upset at her mother and father's refusal to allow her to date a classmate "because it's my weekend to go to Uncle Orval." The girl was an average student without behavioral problems. She had no emotional distress about the incest, only about being forbidden to date the peer whom she liked.

CASE 2-3. Incest Diagnosis: Adult fantasy incest (in retrospect) of child-adult heterosexual consensual intercourse. Physical Diagnosis: none; Other Psychiatric Diagnosis: post-traumatic stress disorder or obsessive-compulsive anxiety disorder. Current reality will need to be explored to understand why this 30-year-old divorced male now has the stressful symptom of constant preoccupation with fantasies of himself as a 12-year-old having intercourse with his mother. How long has he been distressed with this as a given cause? How long has he been divorced? How is his job? What does he see as the cause of the divorce? Who filed for the divorce? Was his mother a factor in the divorce? How was his sexual function during the marriage? What are his sexual outlets now? Was there ever sex play or intercourse with his mother at age 12 years or any age? What is his present relationship with his mother? Such explicit questions are needed in order to evaluate the current meaning of the presenting symptom. Is this symptom of distress at incest fantasies an avoidance of dealing with his present pain and grief at the loss of his partner? Is it regression to wishing for a totally accepting sexual partner?

These examples illustrate the process of formulating the behavioral component of the Incest Diagnosis, then making a Physical Diagnosis, and then any Other Psychiatric Diagnosis. This procedure is really not unlike a complete evaluation of a patient with a slipped disc who also suffers from schizophrenia. In a case of adult-adult rape incest, there may be body bruises, lacerations, vaginal bleeding, or anal lesions to be repaired. All of the necessary medicolegal lab tests will also need to be done [133].

In a case of recurrent adult-child pedophilic heterosexual incest, the child (if frightened or forced) may have night terrors, anxiety attacks, hysterical seizures, depression, dissociative withdrawal, or other psychiatric symptoms. If there was warm and loving fondling without coercion or terrorism, there may be no psychiatric sequelae from the sex exchange. However, there may be much distress at being discovered and questioned, fear of getting the parent or self into trouble, or fear of losing the parent or being brought to the police, a clinic, a doctor, or to court.

Past incest may be reported by an adult not as a presenting complaint but quite incidentally. However, the incest history may relate to a presenting symptom of a sexual dysfunction such as sexual aversion, vaginismus, or dyspareunia (in the absence of an acute physical cause). The history may reveal a lifelong guilt and self-abhorrence regarding sexual attraction and fantasy of genital play with father or brother in the absence of any such actual activity [117]. In other cases there may have been full coitus for years with a father or brother or both and no sexual symptom; that is, there was a satisfactory life and marital adjustment, and the incest was incidentally reported as part of a complete sexual history of each partner taken in the course of sex therapy sought because of a sex symptom of the spouse [132].

Each individual case of incest, therefore, needs a full and explicit definition of the physical, behavioral, and emotional components. The immediate, intermediate, and long-term outcome will evolve during treatment and careful follow-up.

3

ANTHROPOLOGICAL
PERSPECTIVE ON INCEST

Francis X. Grollig, S.J., Ph.D.
Professor, Department of Anthropology
Loyola University of Chicago

Is incest ubiquitous? For an anthropological perspective on incest a valid question is, Do the natives practice or prohibit incest or both? A cross-cultural research of 54 randomly selected tribes found in the Human Relations Area Files [18] revealed that incest is ubiquitous. In the United States, according to Harris [15], Kinsey and his associates found "in a sample of about 12,000 individuals, nuclear family incest occurs at the rate of five per thousand."

Brigham Young married his wife's sister. Joseph Smith married his wife's sister. So did some 10 percent of the 1,642 Mormons whose bigamous unions are recorded. Is this incest? Legally, yes, but for this religious group, no. It was *sororal polygyny,* or polygamous unions with two or more sisters. Early Mormons endorsed the practice of polygamous unions. While "available records offer no corroboration of the accusation that many polygamous marriages were incestuous, they . . . suggest the source of such reports in the surprisingly common practice of marrying sisters" [17]. But Vivelo [35] adds: "Basley mentions the Mormons of Utah before 1892, among whom marriage of men to daughters and sisters and of women to stepsons was extensively practiced." For them, it was a culturally approved sex pattern.

Polygamy is tolerated in many tribes; some allow fraternal and sororal cousins to marry, but fraternal polyandry is rarely observed. Even more rarely found is regal incest, when the king (e.g., the Inca in Peru) or the queen (e.g., Cleopatra in Egypt) may or must marry a sibling although such a union is forbidden to "lesser mortals."

From a real superabundance of tribal data, incest practices of six tribes are discussed here.

INCEST IN SIX TRIBES

Araucanians

Sororal polygyny was common among the Araucanians. It was reported as such as late as 1946. Among these South American Indians, the maternal cross-cousin was the preferred spouse for the boy. Drinking sprees frequently wound up in incestuous sex relations. Latcham, who worked among the Araucanians, reported [25] that "when drunk, they give themselves up to sexual promiscuity that respects no conditions or relationship . . ."

About the same group half a century later, Faron [9] wrote, "The incest barrier is theoretically immutable and its transgression unthinkable," and Hilger [16] reported, "Incest is considered a disgrace. No instance of it between brother and sister having the same mother was known [and] no case of incest between mother and son had ever been heard of; [but] several between father and daughter were known." However, there was a reported case of incest between half siblings. Young Araucanians who engaged in incest were subject to strong censure, but they were not ostracized. Elsewhere, Faron emphasized that "in all fairness . . . what matters is that today incest is not of the order described in the past."

Culturally, prohibition of incest may change on occasion. An example would be the inheriting of his father's wives by a son. Among the Araucanians this was true, but the son did not inherit his own mother.

Ngonde

The inheriting of the father's wives but not the boy's mother is also found among the African Ngonde. But for the boy to have intercourse with a wife of his father before the father's death was a severe offense necessitating special purification. While the Ngonde do not consider some extrafamilial sexual relations outside of marriage incest, familiarity between father and daughter-in-law is regarded as evil.

There is an extended account of an individual among the Ngonde who had had intercourse with his father's sister, who is called his classificatory mother. The whole affair became public knowledge when the "supernatural" penalty—syphilis—was discovered. Health and happiness allegedly came back to the group when the four required cows were ritually killed and eaten. Some rituals were also performed if a son (even with permission) had intercourse with one of his living father's wives, but the elaborate ritual killing of the sacrificial animals was performed at the time of the father's death [36].

Eskimo

For the South Alaskan Eskimo there were cases of incest, though not frequent, between parents and children, but this was not approved socially. Among one of the tribes, the Koniags, men on occasion do marry their own mothers, but such unions are not approved.

When dealing with a group such as the Eskimo, it is well to remember that they inhabit a great territory, and some of the cultural data applicable to a part of the group may not apply to others of the same group. So it is no surprise to find wife-lending "reputed to some of the groups, but denied of other groups" [5]. And Langsdorff, who was among the Eskimo in 1805, wrote of two tribes [24], "The Koviaks practice polygamy and incest; the Kodiaks cohabit promiscuously, brothers and sisters, parents and children." At that time, when commenting on the incest, he had said they "follow the example of the sea dogs and sea otters" as one Aleut put it.

The Copper Eskimo classify both half siblings and adopted children in the same category with natural children. They surround them with the same marriage regulations and incest taboos. Among the Copper Eskimo there is a custom of exchanging wives (more or less permanently), which leads to an extension of the family. Because the children of the two families are considered brothers and sisters, marriage between them is forbidden [19]. Even children who have neither parent as a common (biological) parent are considered (classificatory) siblings. This means that C, the son of A and B, and F, the daughter of D and E, become classificatory siblings if A and E (and B and D) at any time participate in a spousal exchange.

One example of incest among the Copper Eskimo was reported by Jenness [19]: One girl would sleep with her brother or her cousin, aged 17, even though there was no question of marriage, and eventually married her stepcousin.

Tallensi

In the African Tallensi tribe, sexual relations between brother and sister are designated as sinful [10]. Basically it is a question of lineage: "Sexual relations with a sister or a daughter are so much less reprehensible than incest with a wife" of someone of the same lineage because the sister or daughter belongs to them "equally by birth" [10]. This means that incest with a sister or daughter is less of a fault because these persons belong to the same lineage. But sexual activity with someone else's wife involves competition for one who does not belong to the lineage. This competition destroys the moral unity or solidarity of the group. Accordingly, in a case where a man has had relations with his sister or daughter, his lust is considered foolish and contemptible, but not punishable. Yet the Tallensi forbid a man to have "sexual relations with, or even to sit on the same mat with, his daughter-in-law" [10]. Vengeance then is in the hands of the ancestor spirits who determine when the guilty person shall be stricken. For the Tallensi this conduct destroys the basic father-son relationship and the familial bonds. Therefore it is spiritually punished.

Iban

The oceanic Iban culture dictates a long list of prohibited persons with regard to incest. One tribe, the Sea Dyaks, at the end of the nineteenth century were very particular as to their prohibited degrees of marriage; they opposed in principle the intermarriage of relatives. Roth [31] comments: "This is one reason for the fertility of their women as compared with other tribes who are fast vanishing around them. . . . A man may not marry his mother" or his stepmother, mother-in-law, daughter, stepdaughter, sister, stepsister, half sister, wife's sister, father's sister, or mother's sister!

Faced by all of these cultural prohibitions, one Iban tribesman found that his ideal mate would be his first cousin, and he married her. But "the people refused to visit him unless he asked . . . forgiveness. To obtain this he killed a pig and threw the whole of it into the river" [31] along with a chopper and a plate. This bloody but vicarious expiation, therefore, allowed the couple to be accepted by the tribe. Two other cases are reported in which uncles married their nieces with similar sacrificial animal blood ceremonies.

Ojibwa

Hallowell [14] recounts a long story of an Ojibwa boy who had seduced his aunt and had had intercourse with her only once. Since it was only once, they were not visited with any sanction or sickness; they were not "even forced publicly to confess the incest." But such is not the ordinary Ojibwa way to handle incest. Household relatives violating the tribe's moral standards merit severe reprisals: "Here belong the tales of incestuous rape sometimes by the father or grandfather, but more commonly by the stepfather. Although such incest brands a man, the girl's reputation is more seriously damaged; she usually leaves home and may even be forced to leave the community" [23].

It is somewhat difficult to reconcile this with Landes's 1937 statement [22] indicating that incestuous marriages were common enough "except between siblings," while sexual intercourse was found among individuals of all categories including even classificatory siblings, with no penalties beyond caustic remarks. However, Hallowell details the beating given to an Ojibwa man who seduced his brother's wife.

PENALTIES FOR INCEST

After Oedipus, in Greek mythology, realized that he had unintentionally committed incest with his mother, he blinded himself. In their mythology, the Bontocs considered that the gods abandoned and punished them, when their culture heroes, being brother and sister, committed incest [33]. In the literature at least a dozen tribes mandated the death penalty for incestuous unions. Sometimes this meant death for both persons, sometimes only for one. However, the greater number of tribes have a less than lethal penalty for incest.

Is the incest taboo unique among humans? Endeavors to explain an apparent incest taboo founded in nonhuman primate behavior has led to field studies (as opposed to observations made of animals in captivity). These have detected an apparent avoidance of mother-son copulation among several genera, including the chimpanzees. Various reasons (especially the dominance hierarchy) have been adduced to account for alleged mother-son copulation avoidance. Swartz and Jordan [34] have coined a new word, *protomorality* (in animals) as the label for their explanation.

Aceves [1] notes that just because incest is prohibited in a given culture does not mean that it does not occur. Perhaps it was the very variability of cultural phenomena that drove Levi-Strauss [30] into his structural functionalism, which places the burden of definition for a trait not on the essence of the thing or the person defining it, but on its function in any observed culture. Families must be interdependent for the efficient survival of society. Therefore the incest taboo functions to promote marriage into other families. The fear of biological damage is not an adequate explanation for the prevalent incest taboo [30]. Structural formalism was also used by Emile Durkheim [30] to account for patterns of suicide. Perhaps this is why in some classic societies (e.g., Rome) both incest and enforced suicide as its punishment occurred.

A reprint of Malinowski's "Brother-Sister Avoidance among the Trobriand Islanders" taken from his *The Sexual Life of Savages in Northwestern Melanesia* notes: "I was told that if a man came by chance upon his sister and her sweetheart while they were making love, all three would have to commit *lo'u* (suicide) by jumping from a coco-nut palm." Understanding of human nature as he was, Malinowski commented that more likely than not all would pretend that they had seen nothing and the brother "would discreetly disappear" [20].

In India, among the Santal Parganas, social ostracism is the penalty for incest, and those who fail to participate in the ostracizing activities are themselves given the same penalty. Although an outcaste cannot regain his caste by his own efforts, the parents of offending incest partners may arrange and pay to have them "eaten into caste again" [32].

One thing that seems to emerge in these cross-cultural studies is the apparent inequality of punishment that is given to persons both of whom have been detected in the same incident of incest. The Tiv of Africa, for example, make the boy so caught pay a fine—and the girl becomes his marriage ward! Father-daughter incest was considered "great foolishness" but the father did not even have to pay a fine. Among the Azande the involved persons "were quite happy together, and the criticism of their neighbors left them quite calm" [6].

Like the Tiv and the Azande, the Lozi are also Africans, but their treatment of those guilty of incest is different. Mere presence together alone in a hut is sufficient to bring a brother and sister to court on the incest charge. Even though the judge does not believe that they are guilty, the boy has done wrong (just by being in that circumstance) and has to provide an animal for a sacrifice to blot out the "conventional offense." A Lozi wife may claim a divorce if her husband is seen alone on a path with his mother-in-law.

The Eastern Apache Indians were reported as late as 1941 as equating incest with witchcraft, and the penalty for the crime could be death. Perhaps what is most stunning about this penalty is that it is the parents who must burn or kill the children. "Public exposure and beatings are the mildest punishments meted out to those discovered in incest. Just as often the extreme penalty is demanded" [28].

Besides witchcraft, magic seems to surface in incest contexts. Basically this involves "sympathetic magic" as, for example, sticking pins into the head of a voodoo doll to cause the desired effect (pain) in the head of the person being hexed. Among the oceanic Ifugao, a magic mock combat is staged to undo the relatedness of the couple [3] who have contracted an incestuous union.

Another oceanic community, the Toradja, although not condoning incest, allow it under certain circumstances. The "piacular offering" causes the guilt of the incest to float down the river. When such an offering is being made, at one point in the ritual, the hands of the two persons are put on the dead offerings, a fowl and a pig, and a relative prays: "Here are two people who have committed incest; actually they should be killed themselves, but we now kill a pig and a fowl in their place." Sympathetic magic carries away guilt, and tranquility is restored—even though the incestuous situation remains. The community tolerates what it cannot effectively terminate [8].

Among primitive peoples, *incest* may not necessarily indicate that intercourse has taken place. A clear example of this is identified as ceremonial incest among the Negritos. Just to cause a girl to sit next to her father-in-law is a sufficiently serious offense that requires her ritual purification.

Some societies demand (at least under some circumstances) the death penalty in cases of detected incest. Of the North American Tlingit we read:

> There were many known cases where a man and a woman of the same phratry fell in love and lived together until found out. Songs tell of pathetic and forlorn hopes of these forbidden lovers. The penalty for incest was death, both

persons being killed by their respective clansmen. In spite of this penalty incest was common enough to make the law less rigorously enforced [26].

Olson [27] agreed with this observation about the Tlingit, adding that either marriage or elopement within the moiety was punishable by death.

The legal procedures involved in choosing the alternate penalties is not known, but among the Arapaho, "When an Indian is caught in incest with his own daughter, he is either killed or his name is immediately dropped and people cease to respect him" [7].

Some incest restrictions seen today in some tribal societies may be the results of acculturation. For example, among the Tarahumara, who have had Roman Catholic missionaries with them for centuries, "sexual relations with brother, sister, parent, child, first cousin, aunt, uncle, godmother, godfather, are regarded as incestuous" [4]. Three Tarahumara cases are discussed. In the first, it was considered a joke when one man married his stepmother; in the second, a civil marriage license was refused when a man wanted to marry his first cousin on his mother's side, so they just cohabited without a civil blessing; and, finally, the child born of incest between a brother and his sister was killed by its mother. It seems that murder was socially more tolerable to the tribe than incest. Incidentally, no one would marry the boy, but the girl did get married.

Among the Nayar, a central Kerala group of Asia, the most important factor in the social organization is the lineage, and Gough [12] reports "intra-lineage incest was a crime punishable by death." Among the African Twi there is an extension of the incest taboo to both blood and clan lines. Rattray [29] wrote: "Perhaps no other sin was regarded with greater horror among the Ashanti [Twi]. Both parties to the offence were killed." But among the oceanic Ifugao, Gluckman [11] reported, incest was punished by death:

> If an Ifugao father commits incest with his daughter, his own family cannot take action against him, because "a family cannot proceed against itself." . . . But he might be punished by the girl's mother's family on the ground that he had committed an offence against one of its members.

The Indonesians reckon descent by clan, and incest was punished by death. Among the Indonesian Toradja:

> People in some areas are stricter than in others. Whereas in Lage and Onda'e the two never escaped the death penalty, in Pebato and Poe'oe-mboto they were spared if they gave to the villagers four buffaloes one or two of which were slaughtered at the sacrificial feast . . . at which atonement was made for the incest committed. When this offering had been made, the two guilty persons were separated;

if it appeared that they were seeing each other again, then they were killed [2].

Under conditions like these, it is no surprise that a girl, pregnant from incestuous intercourse, would not identify the child's father: Her easiest plea was that "a spirit had done it" and, the authors added, "They sometimes knew how to dish up quite a story about their experiences" [2] with the spirits!

The Amazonian Jivaro are headhunters. They regard incest and any illicit sexual intercourse with the greatest of horror. Karsten [21] tells us they punish it "by cruel ill-treatment, sometimes even by both parties being put to death." In the wake of such executions horrible blood-feud killings may ensue when relatives get involved. A high percentage of individuals treated at one Amazonian medical post was the result of such blood feuds, according to the Jesuit Jose Guallart, who worked with them for more than a quarter of a century.

Summary

Cross-culturally incest manifests as sororal polygyny among the Araucanians, inheriting of the father's wives among the Ngonde, parent-children incest cases among the Eskimo, brother-sister incest among the Tallensi, uncle-niece incest marriages among the Iban, a case of aunt-nephew and even mother-son incest among the Ojibwa. This is not a complete taxonomy of incest situations among even the tribes named, but does explore something of the diversity of incest practices.

The sororate practice allows or demands that the surviving husband marry the sister of his deceased wife, and the levirate allows or demands that the surviving wife marry the brother of her deceased husband.

But there is another side to the incest coin. One side shows what is tolerated or even preferred in terms of sexual practices; on the other side appear some of the penalties for acts of incest—as each tribe defines it. Some tribes mandate the death penalty; others give a penalty less than death. Finally, some tribes allow for expiation sacrifices (e.g., killing a pig instead of a person). My conclusion is that perhaps the time has come to use with caution any *universal* anthropological statement about incest.

References

1. Aceves, J. B. *Identity, Survival, and Change.* Morristown, New Jersey: General Learning Press, 1974.
2. Adriani, N., and Kruyt, A. C. *De Bare's Sprekende Toradjas van Midden-Celebas (de Oos-Toradjas)* (2nd ed.), Vol. 1. Amsterdam: Noord-Hollandsche Uitgevers Maatschappij, 1951.

3. Barton, R. F. *The Mythology of the Ifugaos.* Philadelphia: American Folklore Society, 1955.
4. Bennett, W. C., and Zingg, R. M. *The Tarahumara: An Indian Tribe of Northern Mexico.* Chicago: University of Chicago Press, 1935.
5. Birket-Smith, K. *The Chugach Eskimo.* Copenhagen: Nationalmuseets Publikationsfond, 1953.
6. Bohannan, L., and Bohannan, P. *A Source Notebook on Tiv Religion.* New Haven, Conn.: Human Relations Area Files, 1969.
7. Dorsey, G. A., and Kroeber, A. L. *Traditions of the Arapaho.* Chicago: Field Columbian Museum, 1903.
8. Downs, R. E. *The Religion of the Bare's-Speaking Toradja of Central Celebes.* The Hague: Uitgeverij Excelsior, 1956.
9. Faron, L. C. *Mapuche Social Structure.* Urbana: University of Illinois Press, 1961.
10. Fortes, M. *The Web of Kinship among the Tallensi.* London: Oxford University Press, 1949.
11. Gluckman, M. *The Ideas of Barotse Jurisprudence* (2nd ed.). Manchester: Manchester University Press, 1972.
12. Gough, E. K. Nayar: Central Kerala. In D. M. Schneider and K. Gough (Eds.), *Matrilineal Kinship.* Berkeley and Los Angeles: University of California Press, 1961.
13. Guallart, J. Los Jivaros. Unpublished data. No date.
14. Hallowell, A. I. *Culture and Experience.* Philadelphia: University of Pennsylvania Press, 1955.
15. Harris, M. *Culture, Man, and Nature.* New York: Crowell, 1971.
16. Hilger, M. I. *Araucanian Child Life and Its Cultural Background.* Washington, D.C.: Government Printing Office, 1957.
17. Hill, M. S., and Allen, J. B. (Eds.) *Mormonism and American Culture.* New York: Harper and Row, 1972.
18. Human Relations Area Files, Inc. Ann Arbor, Mich.: Universal Microfilms International, 1968.
19. Jenness, D. *The Life of the Copper Eskimos.* Ottawa: F. A. Acland, 1922.
20. Jennings, J. D., and Hoebel, A. E. *Readings in Anthropology* (3rd ed.). New York: McGraw-Hill, 1972.
21. Karsten, R. *The Head-Hunters of Western Amazonas: The Life and Culture of Nu Jibaro Indians of Eastern Ecuador and Peru.* Helsingfors: Centraltrykeriet, 1935.
22. Landes, R. The Ojibwas of Canada. In M. Mead (Ed.), *Cooperation and Competition Among Primitive Peoples.* New York: McGraw-Hill, 1937.
23. Landes, R. *The Ojibwa Woman.* New York: Columbia University Press, 1938.
24. Langsdorff, G. H. *Voyages and Travels in Various Parts of the Nu World,* Vol. 2. New York: Da Capo Press, 1968.
25. Latcham, R. E. Ethnology of the Araucanos. *Royal Anthropological Institute of Great Britain and Ireland Journal* Vol. 39, 1909.
26. Oberg, K. Crime and punishment in Nu Tlingit society. *American Anthropologist* 36:145, 1934.
27. Olson, R. L. *Social Structure and Social Life of the Tlingit in Alaska.* Berkeley: University of California Press, 1967.
28. Opler, M. E. *An Apache Life-Way.* Chicago: University of Chicago Press, 1941.
29. Rattray, R. S. *Ashanti Law and Constitution.* Oxford: Clarendon Press, 1929.
30. Richards, C. E. *Man in Perspective.* New York: Random House, 1972.

34

31. Roth, H. L.   The Natives of Borneo. Edited from the papers of the late Brooke Low, Esq., London. *Royal Anthropological Institute of Great Britain and Ireland Journal* 21:110, 1892.
32. Skrefsrud, L. O.   *Traditions and Institutions of the Santals/Horkoren Marc Hapramko Reak' Katha,* transl. with notes and additions by P. O. Budding and S. Konow. Oslo: Oslo Ethnographic Museum, 1942.
33. Stewart, K.   *Pygmies and Dream Giants.* New York: Norton, 1954.
34. Swartz, M. J., and Jordan, D. K.   *Culture: The Anthropological Perspective.* New York: Wiley, 1980.
35. Viveio, F. R.   *Cultural Anthropology Handbook.* New York: McGraw-Hill, 1978.
36. Wilson, M. H.   *Good Company: A Study of Nyakyusa Age-Villages.* London; New York: Oxford University Press, 1951.

4

FAMILY ASPECTS OF INCEST

SINCE incest very literally is a family affair, optimum clinical evaluation and management involves studying each family within which incest occurs. The structure and tasks of the small group or social unit that we call the family are usually taken for granted. A family provides for physical survival by nurturance of all members, especially its young, through homemaking, nutrition, working, earning, and coping with environmental conditions. Beyond physical care, social, religious, and political values plus the laws of the land filter to each individual through the family, which, therefore, is an essential primary learning and teaching unit. Recognition of the powerful role of the family in shaping children is old. Neither Plato in 600 B.C., nor the Oneida community in 1850, nor Karl Marx in 1917 was successful in their deliberate attempts to alter the structure of the family, replacing parents with other primary educators in the toddler phase to produce ideal future citizens. In essence, these communal experiments broke up the traditional family unit to create newly constituted, complex, expanded units with the specific tasks of educating the young to conform and to be loyal to the ideal of the government or the group, rather than to follow individual inclinations or parental desires.

Israeli kibbutzim are also experimental communes, closed groups resembling families. There are conflicting data regarding mating and marriages of children reared there. One study [146] postulates that co-rearing results in romantic aversion and negates intermarriage. Another states that the marriage avoidance of kibbutz-mates is exaggerated [25], since they can and do marry.

What is of importance to clinicians is to search for a better understanding of why incest occurs and possible ways to deal with it. Let us begin the search here through a study of the structure and tasks of the family, factors that lead to incest avoidance, factors that promote incest, and false accusations of incest.

FAMILY STRUCTURE AND TASKS

Definition

The word *family* comes from a Latin root *famulus* meaning "servant." Webster's dictionary [169] gives a series of definitions of family, one of which includes "all servants of the household"—a bygone luxury. Another is "a group of persons of common ancestry," who today may be scattered across the globe and not even know of each other's existence. All family members are related by blood (consanguinity) or by legal marriage (affinity).

Ideally the family has a leader (formal or informal) and meets the needs of its members, who are expected to show intense family loyalty. The family is expected to conform to the society within which it is an essential unit. Cultures differ in their learned personal priorities: church, "king and country," or family. All are authorities demanding allegiance, which may at times be conflicting.

Family structure

Only within the last few decades have scholars begun to analyze and delineate the psychodynamics of the "traditional" and evolving family [2, 36, 41, 75, 93, 96, 181]. Two important basic family divisions or axes are described by Fleck [41, 42]. First is the *generational boundary*—parents (or surrogates) who nurture, lead and teach; offspring who must learn and follow. This same line separates sexually active parents and those to whom sex is forbidden in the family. The second axis is the *sex division* within which gender role learning occurs, e.g., what work is done by each sex and how each sex behaves publically and privately. Fleck regards maintenance of these two structural boundaries as the most important life tasks of every family, pointing out that nonverbal cues and example or role modeling are how it is accomplished. No matter what type of family style, the generational boundaries and sex divisions must be taught to the young by the elders. The action of one member affects all others in a family group.

EXTENDED FAMILY. For centuries, the multigenerational extended family system was an almost worldwide norm. Married children remained in the parents' home. Local custom dictated whether the couple stayed with parents of the husband or of the wife. Grandparents, single or married aunts, uncles, cousins and other relatives were part of the household, with elders retaining family leadership and mandating child-rearing practices and conformity of all consanguineous as well as affinity members. Soon after World War II, the predominance of the extended family lessened markedly. However, in the 1980s small numbers of divorcees are returning with their children to their birth families to establish a new style of extended family.

NUCLEAR FAMILY. In the United States, industrialization, urbanization, and economic independence gradually fostered the evolution in one living unit of the nuclear family: two natural parents, two sexes, and two generations when the children are born. Father was out working and mother stayed at home. This was the idealized and commercialized norm into the 1960s. However, 1978 statistics show that this family style now comprises only 7 percent of families in the United States. The economy, working mothers, plus the very high divorce rate have changed society's family pattern considerably. The residual nuclear family may be a single-parent family. For the demands of urban living, babysitters are now extensively used instead of extended family members to meet the demands of child rearing. In the face of realities such as both parents working or a working single-parent situation, rotating (or regular) babysitters assume an important parent-surrogate (authority) role and form an integral part of the family's structure.

STEPFAMILY. Statistics report that now over 25 million stepparents engage in child rearing, and 40 percent of United States children are labeled children of divorce. Sometimes there are reconstituted stepfamilies with children from two to four previous unions, after divorce or the death of a spouse. Since the remarriage rate seems to keep pace with the divorce rate, stepfamilies today are common affinity kinships [15, 161, 166]. The younger a child is when a parent remarries, the more likely it is that the stepparent perceives the child to be his or her very own. Many stepfathers become adoptive fathers by request, through the courts.

ADOPTIVE FAMILY. It has been estimated that 3 to 5 million married persons in this country are infertile. One million persons in 1980 tried to adopt a child. For the most part, procedures favor infancy adoptions to promote early, long-standing, close, and intense parent-child bonding relationships. For closer identification as a family, physical and ethnic characteristics are usually approximated, again to assist acceptance by the whole family and by the community. Legal adoptions are binding until death and are considered to be affinity family ties. Informal adoptions may occur within an extended family system, upon the death of a parent, the birth of an illegitimate child, or when an elder is solitary or childless.

FOSTER FAMILY. It is estimated that one million foster homes are involved in the care of children from broken homes. Each state functions as the financial surrogate parent, with selected families paid to perform as surrogate kin to one or more children assigned to them. Foster families, like any newly constituted family, are not duplicate nuclear families. They are complex. Some foster for altruistic motives. Others do so for needed income. At best, they may provide a haven from stress and meet many nurturant needs. At worst, they may recapitulate emotional trauma, exploitation, or physical or sexual abuse.

The move into a foster home is often an even greater trauma than the change to a stepfamily, where at least there is a hope and promise of permanence and one parent and often a sibling or more who is known. In a foster home, all are new, adults and children alike, and fearful unknowns include uncertainty about the duration of stay. How long before I move? Where next? Other children come and go. What will happen to me?

INFORMAL FAMILY. Many different family styles and structures have evolved on a small scale in contemporary society. Others may yet emerge. For all intents and purposes, they may be considered affinity kinships within the community, although legal responsibility may be unclear. Communal family clusters, homosexual families, and informal living-together arrangements (LTAs) may all rear children. Common-law marriages of the past usually comprised consanguineous children and were so recognized by the law, although the derogatory term *bastard* designated the natural offspring. Today's LTA families may have one natural parent plus a live-in boy friend or girl friend who is expected to function as a semipermanent surrogate parent, without the legal affinity ties of a marriage. One or both members of the couple may not wish to, or be free to, marry. The duration of such a newly constituted informal family may vary from brief and temporary to many years. Sometimes a remarriage occurs, forming a legal stepfamily and possibly resulting in adoption of the children. Ignorance or confusion about role and relationship will require repeated clarification so that the children may learn kinship bonds and appropriate desexualization of affectionate attachments that may develop with relatives.

Family tasks

Certain universal social values have shaped family goals and tasks for as long as recorded history.

CONTINUITY. Continuity of the family through its progeny is probably a primary and timeless consideration.

NAME, FAME, AND PROPERTY. Name, fame and property are usually tangible and important components of each family's aspirations and endeavors. Retaining the family property and name had much to do with regal incest and religious exemptions from marriage prohibitions. When some wives today retain their birth family surname, children may be given both the father's and the mother's surname for continuity of the family names.

PHYSICAL NEEDS. Physical needs may be mundane, but meeting them is an essential family task. All members need shelter and warmth, food and fluids, air, sleep, elimination, sensory and motor stimulation and activity, order, personal space, privacy, safety, and protection from harm. Adult caretakers in the family—parents, grandparents, other blood kin, adoptive or foster parents, stepkin, or babysitters—all have shared the responsibility of altruistically tending to recurrent dependency demands of young or ailing members. However in some cultures, exploitation of children is accepted: pagan child sacrifice, child brides, child beating, and child labor. In the last century, child abuse laws have emerged in the West to protect the person and rights of each child, handicapped or healthy.

EMOTIONAL NEEDS. The emotional needs and desires blend in each person in the family. They are essential and include the desire and need to touch and be touched, to care and be cared about, to accept and be accepted, to understand and be understood, to listen and be listened to, to encourage and be encouraged, to appreciate and be appreciated, to need and be needed, as well as to share problem solving, to trust or rely, to express frustration or conflict, to relate appropriately to others, to give and receive desexualized affection, to build self-esteem, to develop mastery and autonomy, to be creative nonsexually and sexually, and to search for life's meaning. All of these are complex, ongoing human needs with various degrees of expression at any particular time. When they are met, a sense of security and well-being develops. In incest-rejecting cultures, sexual needs may not be met in the family, except by spouses.

SOCIALIZATION AND EDUCATIONAL TASKS. The family must meet both the physical and the emotional needs of each member while conforming to the rules of the larger society in which the family lives, since status and social approval are important aspects of a family's stability. In ancient times, before modern schooling, the family (through elders) was the exclusive teacher of the younger members.

Each family member gives, receives, and applies teaching related to the following intellectual and social skills:

1. Language(s)
2. Self-care
3. Food gathering and preparation (hunting and planting replaced today by jobs, paychecks, and supermarkets)
4. Clothing (weaving and animal hides replaced by department stores)
5. History, pride, and identity of the family and race (now done by schools)
6. Weather, water, and fire (replaced by television forecasts and utility bills)
7. The pathways to other villages (replaced by road maps and airline schedules)
8. Training for assigned jobs such as carver, weaver, warrior (replaced by diplomas, the draft, job hunting)

9. Social roles and specific ways to regard, formally address, or relate to family members and other notables (replaced by informality and few if any guidelines)
10. Marriage partner prohibitions and preferences, often by arrangement of elders (replaced by freedom of choice and romantic expectations but few if any statements regarding kinship prohibitions)
11. Pleasure, leisure, laughter (often relegated to television commercials and comedians, sometimes taught as family-generated interpersonal fun)
12. Religion and moral values (marked change to little religious education at home in the nuclear family regarding God, prayer, and church attendance)
13. Government, politics, and defense (mostly relegated to television and schools)
14. Money management (mainly relegated to schools)
15. Body functions, health, and sickness (mainly relegated to mass media and schools)
16. Sex education (mainly silence at home, often misinformation from peers)

It is remarkable that all of these complex physical, emotional, and socialization tasks of the family proceed (with more or less success) although they are rarely conscious and even more rarely explicitly discussed.

Pertinent to an understanding of the occurrence of incest is an in-depth exploration of the nuances of how sexual learning and partner prohibitions actually take place in families in which incest does and does not occur.

INCEST PREVENTING FACTORS

Learning by "osmosis"

Effortless unconscious absorption from family surroundings ("osmosis") is how much everyday learning occurs. Is this how individuals learn about incest avoidance?

In an informal verbal survey, 20 men and 20 women were asked: "How and when did you know that your father [mother] was sexually out of bounds?" The most frequent responses were "I just knew," "I don't know *how* but I always knew," "It's difficult to say when, but I think from age 5 or 6. No one said anything, but I knew." Most (27) of the 40 respondents were raised in intact nuclear families; 8 were in stepfamilies from infancy; 3 were raised by grandparents; and 2, by mother only.

When do persons know the meaning of the word *incest*? Few of the

40 nonpatient subjects surveyed had occasion to see or hear the word *incest* before their late teens or later. One said he looked it up in a dictionary at age 12 on seeing it in a novel. However, he was not helped by the dictionary definition. He did not understand what *carnal knowledge* meant. Is the word *incest* as secret as the behavior? In the past few years, the word has emerged from whispers to appear on paperback covers and magazine articles, so osmosis learning may today be assisted by specific reading.

Vital questions to raise are, When (at what age) do persons become aware that sexual gratification with relatives is forbidden? Who tells the child? How do relationships differ in families where incest does or does not occur? Is it really a state of nebulous osmosis or "just knowing" that parent-child, family, and sibling sexual gratification is forbidden? Is the sanction learned in formal religious teachings? Do incest violators also "know it is wrong" yet proceed despite possible consequences?

There is as yet no scientific data base from which to answer these questions. Large samples from all socioeconomic and educational levels are needed, as are cross-cultural studies within the United States and abroad. Much is yet to be learned.

Effective establishment of sexual prohibitions or incest avoidance is thought to occur through complex, dynamic, nonverbal yet explicit parent-child cue giving [96, 119]. Exactly what, how, and when is not spelled out. When anti-incest cues have not been learned, then it is necessary even in an intact nuclear family, but especially in reconstituted families, to discuss incest avoidance openly in the family group—usually in family therapy if it has come to professional attention.

A wholesome marital relationship

A respectful relationship which includes openness and satisfactory sexual expression for both parent partners is the epicenter of all other family relationships. Affection and love may enhance (but are not imperative for) a wholesome relationship. Such a relationship of respect may exist in conditions of poverty, crowding, ill health, or unemployment. From this primary dyad, the offspring emerge and learn how to relate to others each day as they grow. When this parent-parent bond is emotionally and sexually wholesome, it ensures for the couple appropriate expression of both sexual and affectional energies. Therefore, parent-child sexualized affection will be unlikely.

Few modern newlyweds receive any practical premarital education about intimacy—its risks, stresses, and joys. Individual partner expectations may concur or differ widely. Children may arrive whether the parents are ready or not, even in this modern era of easy contraception. A wanted child may enrich the parent bond and become a tangible expression of their dreams, which they may then together work for. However, a child may distance the partners, who may compete for the affection of the child. A variety of coalitions may form, especially if parents differ in child-rearing beliefs, or if they are not finding emotional satisfaction in their own relationship.

If there relationship is wholesome, they may be able to talk about drifting apart after the arrival of a baby. Without blaming each other, they can discuss a perceived priority of a close "us" husband-wife relationship to enhance their parent roles. If there are sexual dissatisfactions—fear of another pregnancy, fatigue—these will also benefit from dialogue so that resolution may be achieved. If sexual communication is kept open in a couple's relationship, they can discuss feelings of arousal towards a child when these normally, although unexpectedly and inappropriately, arise.

Theoretically, a wholesome relationship between parents is the best protection against parent-child incest. Even in a healthy parent relationship, however, psychopathology (e.g., a personality disorder, alcohol or drug abuse, psychosis) may stress and break through this incest barrier.

Maintaining generational boundaries

Fleck [42] has postulated that fulfilling five basic overlapping and interrelated family functions maintains intact generational boundaries so that inappropriate sexual outlets may be avoided:

1. Parental coalition (often or usually disrupted in incest families).
2. Nurturant tasks (often in incest families there is role reversal—a child meeting a parent's needs).
3. Enculturation or teaching of offspring (e.g., that incest is acceptable or that it is wrong).
4. Emancipation of offspring (which may be delayed owing to lack of peer sociosexual contact should prolonged incest have restricted a child's autonomy).
5. Family crisis management by parents (incest may represent a defense against the crisis of open rupture when parents have an unsteady coalition. Discovery of incest may become a crisis and severely damage the family structure by placing father in jail, child in an institution).

Bonds between family members are said to be held firm by erotic and affectional ties [96]. The parents form a permanent union and are permitted and even expected to have sexual relations, but direct sexual relations within the family are prohibited to the children. How they learn this prohibition and yet obtain "erotic gratification" from parental figures who give nurturant care is not clear [96].

Parsons [119] wrote that child-parent closeness should be frustrated gradually to prevent excessively close family ties which might impede investment of interest and energy in the extra-familial world.

The importance of maintaining the parent-child generational boundary is emphasized by Lidz [96]:

> Different types of affectional relationships exist between parents than between a parent and a child. Yet the situation is complicated because of the intense dyadic relationship heightened by erogenous feelings that properly exist between the mother and each pre-oedipal child and by the slow differentiation of the child from his original symbiotic union with the mother. The generation division serves to aid both mother and child in overcoming the bond-development that is essential to enable the child to invest in learning and peer groups and gaining his own identity.

Each individual must, therefore, be frustrated; one cannot achieve completion as an adult within the contemporary family of origin because one cannot or may not find sexual gratification linked with affectionate family relationships. The individual must then move to seek a new sexual union with someone outside the family who fulfills his or her image of a complementary partner [96].

Teaching and learning values

Learning to avoid incest may be achieved as part of general learning about values, ethics, and morals. Each marriage partner, churchgoing or not, brings a set of beliefs, values, and moral goals: for self, for the other, for the marriage, and for their offspring. These goals and values consist of a hierarchy—God, religious authority, government and law, their own parents—and relate to social, sexual, financial, recreational, and ethical behaviors. Learning about a greater-than-self and an afterlife is usually promoted first by elders, parents, and the society and culture in which a child is raised. The concept of soul will not be a spontaneous exploratory finding on the part of a child [80, 155].

Parents represent religion and the law of the land to their children and also represent the child in the courts and in church; therefore, *parents transmit values.* They tell a child what is right or wrong, acceptable or not. One crucial parental task is to assist each child to develop adequate internal controls to "become the law to themselves" without the constant external controlling presence of a parent or a policeman.

Internal controls usually concern respect for persons, property, social and sexual customs, the law, and the church of choice. In all cultures, the concepts of shame (fear of public exposure) and guilt (an internal feeling of wrongdoing) are also taught by parents or elders in a family to the young regarding lying and stealing, and then about vaguely unacceptable "thoughts, words, and deeds," together with what is good, pleasing, and praiseworthy. Moral teaching encompasses human relationships, language, land, food, family ties, social skills, survival and living skills, school, sex, marriage, death, work customs, higher expectations, and behavioral prohibitions.

Teaching specifically about the moral unacceptability of incest would be an important first step towards incest avoidance. Incest education must be emphasized in reconstituted families, where close relatives live nearby, or where marriage prohibitions are strictly mandated by religious or legal protocol. If obtaining or retaining property takes precedence over custom, then legal and religious dispensations will be sought for marriage between close kin.

Teaching and learning about affection, love, touching, and sex

Incest avoidance may perhaps be assisted by improved explicit teaching about the appropriate expression of affection, touching, love, and sex.

Affection is learned altruistic behavior with significant cultural differences in its expression. It is both a verbal and a nonverbal form of communication, and includes positive looking, talking, touching, trusting, concern, caring, sharing, and doing for or with another. There are many definitions of affection: kind feeling, attachment, love, warm regard.

The capacity to relate to other persons is a learned response and forms an important aspect of an individual's identity and personality [35, 36]. It is also an ability that "carries over," that is, allows the individual to relate to multiple others if the very early, primary object relationships or attachments have been pleasant, predictable, rewarding, reassuring, and secure. This aspect of affectionate relating builds trust—which takes time and testing to develop.

Between infant and parent (or other primary caretaker) the building of attachment or the capacity to relate is usually a complex, bilateral give-and-take of sensory cues:

1. Tactile: holding, stroking, touching, feeling, petting, rocking, tickling, being wet, drooling, hurting [18, 72, 116].
2. Visual: seeing the person, the face, the eyes, the smile, tears, a scowl, a frown, or angry gestures.
3. Auditory: hearing talk, singing, laughter, crying, yelling, noises.
4. Olfactory: smelling mother's perfume or baby's bathing soap, which is associated with mother; smelling father's pipe tobacco.
5. Temperature: comfortable warmth of body closeness, acute discomfort at being cold physically or distant personally.
6. Spatial: the comfort or general sense of safety at being skin-to-skin as an infant; being held in a secure balanced position; later having ownership and some privacy, e.g., bed, closet, room.

The messages from infant to parent are also complicated, constant, subtle, and often preconscious, yet they are essential in the development of the infant's sense of self and in the continuous relationship feedback. The value placed by the parent (or parent surrogate) upon the child as a person worthy of respect, attention, concern, and desexualized love will determine the child's self-esteem. In return, the parent's gratification will be heightened by a positive response from the infant, which further evokes smiling responses from the parent [156].

Both child and parent have wishes and needs to be fulfilled by the other; these are vastly unequal because of the totally dependent state of the human infant. Strong, protective parental responses are evoked by a helpless infant, who intensely desires the constant presence and touch of mother. These are powerful and early bonds [17]. As the toddler grows, there will be expeditions to test with delight the mastery of mobility, but there will be many returns to see, hear, or touch mother even briefly for security or for emotional "refueling" [101, 102].

One theory of love [53] holds that motherly love, by its very nature, is unconditional, whereas fatherly love is earned and conditional; the child needs to fulfill certain expectations to receive it. Fromm also describes an ascending hierarchy of love: brotherly love, motherly love, erotic love, self-love, and God love. Brotherly love is seen by Fromm as fundamental altruism. Lacking exclusiveness or symbiosis, it includes responsibility, respect, psychological independence, yet care and concern for the other. It is not restricted to one's own flesh and blood (which he sees as no achievement), but encompasses those who do not serve a personal purpose, yet evoke a compassionate feeling. Motherly love, besides unconditional acceptance of the child, has also a willingness to bear the separation essential to the child's development. Erotic love Fromm sees as restricted by nature exclusively to one person. It does not generalize and is deceptive in its intensity, which may wane later.

From the responses to 20,000 questionnaires, a Toronto sociologist developed a typology of numerous different styles of love: romantic, pragmatic, possessive, playful erotic, altruistic, and combinations of these, all possible at various times in an individual's life [92].

Falling in love is described as "the sudden collapse of the barriers that existed until that moment between two strangers" [53]. Others have described falling in love as "suddenly my eyes opened," or "limerence"—a yearning for reciprocity [160]. Shakespeare, in *A Midsummer Night's Dream* recounts Titania's willingness and readiness upon awakening to fall in love. She becomes enamored of Bottom, despite his ass's head. Fromm considers such an experience of sudden intimacy very short-lived, and warns that should the exclusiveness of "falling in love" lack the qualities of altruistic brotherly love then the couple are separated from the rest of mankind with a brief sense of "erotic fusion" or "egotism à deux." Often fantasy distorts reality. Tannov's study reports a duration of two days to two years at most for limerence experiences. Could an erotic fusion state explain some prolonged incest dyads? Nin [117] describes incest thus: "We only love ourselves in the other." Similarly Shakespeare's Titania casts her dream on the first available object.

Fromm makes the important point that selfishness and self-love, far from being identical, are actually opposites. Self-love is an honest appraisal of self with integrity and recognition. Selfish persons are incapable of truly loving others, since they seek only their own need fulfillment. This may well be true in adult-child incest, where adult sexual needs are met at the price to the child of loss of needed peer relationships. Developmentally, cross-generational affection is different from that of peers, which is also important for growth. Freud [51] postulated that each person's repressed incestuous longings for the opposite-sex parent were essential to personality development, but this is not widely accepted.

It has been said that in the United States the family is now organized almost exclusively around romantic love as its binding force. There are almost no arranged marriages and relatively few kinship, financial, or vocational ties. No overt messages are given to today's children as to whom their future marriage partner will be. They learn about romance and "living happily ever after" from nursery rhymes and television.

Stories and free play are acknowledged to be the "work" of the child—important in developmental learning about being a person [102, 182]. Containment of anxiety through make-believe is achieved in play and fantasy [75]. Play encourages further development of the child's personality. Guided play and stories about children not being able to marry family members is therefore good teaching about acceptable and unacceptable romances and marriages. Sexual fantasies toward parents on the part of a child may in fact be normal rehearsal for later sexual development. Since mother is the first wife and father the first husband known to the child, identification and complementary modeling occur in every healthy parent-child relationship. Explicit dialogue allows growing children to accept such normal child-parent sexual fantasies and repress them without anxiety: "Daddy's my husband. You'll grow up and marry someone else."

Such an incest-avoiding teaching strategy must occur deliberately in all reconstituted families: stepfamilies, foster families, adoptive families, and informal families. It is also desirable before reunions of extended families. Any new relationship may innocently become important, affectionate, and loving. If this occurs between consanguineous strangers, sexual feelings may follow unless desexualization is assisted by honest, open discussion that romantic considerations must be frustrated by the law of the land, which does not allow marriages between stepsiblings, first cousins, and other close relatives.

The capacity to relate affectionately is a response, that is, a personality strength developed throughout life by each individual. Various ways of relating affectionately may be learned in each individual's birth family, from peers, from one's own children or grandchildren. These are:

1. Minimal verbal or physical (touch) expression of affection between persons, yet they know they can count on each other.
2. Personal distance, hard work, and providing money equals caring equals love equals affection.
3. Affection displayed by liberal touching, hugging, and light kissing expresses caring.
4. Caring equals discipline, on the biblical theory of "spare the rod and spoil the child"; minimal praise and much criticism.
5. Affection equals touching equals love equals sex, and therefore touching and tenderness are used only as a prelude to intercourse.
6. Various combinations of these.

There is a wide cultural variation in customs regarding skin-to-skin touch. All mammals, including humans, nurture their young with breast milk; this requires prolonged body contact. Deprivation of this needed mother-infant touch causes marked developmental and mating problems in both monkeys and humans [18, 72, 116, 153]. Semitic and Latin cultures express all emotions more abundantly through touch than do Anglo-Saxons. In the West, boys and men have been taught from childhood that touching is "sissy stuff" and that male-male touching is definitely prohibited except in contact sports. Men also learn that sustained male-female touching is mainly for courtship and a direct prelude to intercourse. On the other hand, girl-girl, parent-girl, and woman-woman affectionate touching is accepted and often expected in families and friendships. If the sexual differences in touch expectations and expressions are not learned, there may be many disappointments and frustrations in a marriage when a woman wants caressing only and a man expects sexual intercourse.

Sex, like touching, is learned behavior, as is its inaccurate synonym, love. At times sex and love may be synonymous, but there may also be a wide gap between "making sex" and the warmth of love even when no genital sex is involved. Love adds caring, sharing, respect, loyalty, and commitment. Human sexuality is an innate physical capacity that responds to subtle social training. It combines the instinctual with social and moral learning.

In primitive cultures, much sex education was provided by elders at puberty initiation rites. These occurred separately for each sex in a small group temporarily isolated from the village. Each family sent the boy or girl at physical puberty to learn about sexual, marital, and cultural "dos and don'ts." Afterward, the village celebrated their passage into adulthood, and families began the process of matchmaking.

The contemporary family does not arrange marriages and for the most part has remained silent at home regarding essential sex education, sometimes even opposing what little sex education a school may attempt to provide. Therefore, *the incests must be regarded as sexual learning defects.* Normal kinship affectional bonds can become normally sexualized responses but must not be directed toward a socially and morally forbidden family member. Sexual urges are normal feelings. Incest is a forbidden act. Hunger is a normal feeling. Stealing food is a forbidden act. If inappropriate (and illegal) sexual exchanges—the incests—are to be successfully controlled, every person must learn these cultural realities.

Is there some special way that an early parent-child relationship that is close and affectionate is desexualized to build incest taboos? Conversely, how do future incest partners eroticize the family affectional bond? Is there a specific avoidance of, or an inability to make, important peer affectional relationships outside the family? Does moral or social restriction about choosing a potential outside peer sexual partner keep incest partners within the small group of the family, selecting an available, compliant, dependent relative? Did early Mormons, in their religious sanctions of incest, develop specific types of sexualized affectional bonds that later allowed acceptance of adult-adult, consanguineous group coital incest? (Leader-father Joseph Smith's marriage included daughters, sisters-in-law, and others.)

Parents are acknowledged to be the most valuable teachers, facilitators, role models, and reinforcers of learned behavior and of values and attitudes about behavior. Hence the endurance of the family as a unit within which parents rear their children. Jacques Barzun, in his 1944 classic *Teacher in America,* has a superb passage [12] on the power of parental teaching:

> What is it and why is it a human comedy? Think of a human pair teaching their child to walk. There is on the child's side strong desire and latent powers: he has legs and means to use them. He walks and smiles; he totters and looks alarmed; he falls and cries. The parents smile throughout, showering advice, warning, encouragement and praise. The whole story, not only of teaching, but of man and civilization, is wrapped up in this first academic performance. It is funny, because clumsiness makes us laugh, and touching because undaunted effort strikes a chord of gallantry, and finally comic because it has all been done before and is forever to do again. All the knowledge, skill, art and science that we use and revere . . . is a mere repetition and extension of the initial feat of learning to walk. But this extension does not take place by itself. Most of it has to be taught slowly and painfully. . . . Children are not born human, they are made so.

Let us extrapolate Barzun's very positive story of learning to walk to a child's faltering steps towards sexual discovery. Is there smiling and encouragement when the child discovers the genitals? Yes, if the child's genital touch relates to proper toilet behavior. No, however, if there is a lingering genital touch or discovered masturbation. Instead of no sex education, negative sex education follows by parental warning, negation, frowning, and sometimes severe punishment. The more dependent the child, the more loved or feared the parent, or the more the negatives are repeated, the stronger and longer lasting will then be the learning that all sex is damaging and evil.

Is this perhaps the true "secret weapon" against incest, namely, the suppression (deliberate or conscious) and repression (less conscious) of all sexual feelings or expression as bad, wrong, unacceptable? Perhaps incest prohibition is learned in the context of the global condemnation and prohibition of natural and normal sex. It is, if so, an inordinately high personal price to pay for incest avoidance, since early aversion toward normal sexual expression may endure for years and may later result in sexual dysfunctions in marriage that require sex therapy [106]. Sexual problems may also destroy a marriage. Divorce is one solution for some couples as incest has been for others.

Sexual tension normally occurs and recurs from cradle to grave (even during sleep) and requires either learned control or expression for relaxation and relief. The natural outlet of masturbation may provide release of sexual tension, without harm to child, married or single adult, or senior [129, 184]. However, when masturbation is so laden with learned guilt about wrongdoing or shame or fear of discovery, sexual needs may instead be suppressed or may finally take unacceptable outlets (the incest pathway).

In the modern West, sex education (both in the home and in the schools) is still minimal or absent [127, 128]. As mentioned, what little sex education parents give may be negative: "Don't touch, don't look, don't enjoy down there, and don't get pregnant!" Most persons have been reared and rear their young as sexual illiterates. For most persons, therefore, sex education (much of it inaccurate) is still acquired from peers.

Children have a natural drive toward learning and will explore the world around them with all their senses: touch, smell, vision, hearing, taste. By age three they know "I'm a girl" or "You're a boy" and quite innocently explore their own and each other's bodies. They watch Miss Piggy pursue Kermit the Frog. From the sixth intrauterine week, there are sexual organs and hormones, so infants have sexual and other body sensations from before birth onward. Childhood sexual curiosity and exploration is called normal developmental sex play or "playing doctor" (with self, peers or siblings). There may be looking, fondling, mutual masturbation, or attempted coitus, even in prepubertal peers.

What is the difference between normal sibling sex play and incest? This is unclear, but may be a matter of degree. Persistence, recurrence, and exclusivity may be key factors. Outside peer relationships are then avoided. Sibling incest or sex play may occur in total privacy, be pleasurable, and cause no distress to the children at all. However, discovery by adults may release a crisis of rage, tears, fears, and threats of damage to self and to future generations. "You will burn in hell," "You will not be able to have children," or "Your children will be abnormal" are some dire predictions reported. Shame, punishment, sexual inhibitions, guilt, and anxiety may result.

Therefore today, especially when both parents work and children have greater responsibility for self-care, and with so many reconstituted families, a comprehensive sex education must have more ingredients than only birds and bees. A healthy home sex education must explicitly teach that

Body privacy is a right.
Sexual feelings are natural and normal.
Sexual knowledge is a right and a responsibility.
Sexual parts have names in each sex.
Sexual intercourse is the way a baby is formed.
Sex questions may be discussed openly at home.
Sexual expression in public is inappropriate.
Masturbation is natural, normal, and needs privacy.
Not expressing sexual feelings is also a healthy option.
There is sex with love and sex without love.
Love without sex but with loyalty is part of family and friendship relationships.
Some people try to force sex on others and must be avoided.
Police and parents will protect a child from sexual pressure.
Certain partners are forbidden to marry by law.
Future marital sexual partners are to be found outside the family circle.
Some people get mixed up about their sexual feelings; it's all right to ask at home.
Different families have different ideas about sex.
A parent believes that sex is for marriage only or for a special relationship (or any other belief).
Sometimes infectious diseases are transmitted sexually.

Teaching and learning marriage partner prohibitions

Negative parental reactions to discovering siblings at sex play usually target the *sexuality* as bad, not even mentioning the sibling as an unacceptable partner. Therefore, "sex is bad" or "the genitals are bad" is the only message learned by the startled children.

What responsibility do parents have for teaching the proper or appropriate relationship within which sex play and marriage may occur? Dad may be flattered that his five-year-old wants to marry him when she grows up or mother pleased that her little boy compliments her in the same way or that their son and daughter say to each other: "We want to get married and live happily ever after." This is a wonderful opportunity to say to the children that loving each other is great, but some things are impossible—such as people in the same family marrying each other—because the church and the law do not allow it, not even first cousins. Then directive reassurance may be given: "You will find a good partner of your own later and start your own family."

It has been said [97] that something is amiss in a family's structure when there is a need to evoke incest prohibitions consciously or explicitly. With the changing structure of today's family, that may no longer be accurate. Affinity ties make conscious incest education mandatory for incest prevention. Although the adults may know about kinships, children may not. A new adult sexual or marriage partner in the home may not have made any parental commitment within himself or herself, and therefore may be totally unprepared and without defenses when affectionate play with a child in the privacy of the home surprisingly sparks normal sexual feelings. The sexual arousal is natural and normal, but the sex object is forbidden by custom and by law. This is what must be understood, learned, and taught so that appropriate control and desexualization of the new relationship can occur. Therefore, conscious education regarding both sexual appropriateness and the law is needed as an active preventive measure against incest or child molestation.

Peer romances were surprisingly common in healthy 4-year-old nursery school children who were studied by Broderick [19]. They "adopted a coy, giggly archness . . . for all the world as though they had a crush on members of the opposite sex at four." They talked about getting married one day. He found child romancing continues between 4 and 12 years. This was considered a (sexual) latency period by Freud, whose postulate of sexual dormancy between 6 and 12 years has not held up to observation of boys and girls of this age group today in the United States [115]. Children also normally try romancing with parents and mimic television scenes.

Ethologists observe that many species of young animals rehearse and mimic the sexual movements of maturity in their peer play in much the same way as they rehearse the maneuvers of hunting for food during early play. The Harlows' [72] baby monkeys on film are seen to play at sexual mounting behavior, with the male gradually becoming more skilled at grasping the female's ankles and making thrusting pelvic movements, while the female adopts the correct posture for copulation. In the mammalian world, father-daughter copulation is common, whereas mother-son contact is determined by the dominance hierarchy. For years, the son is smaller physically and does not challenge father, the leader of the troop [56, 63].

Sexual play in children, including pelvic thrusting, is part of the early play and learned ritual dancing of some primitive African tribes in which puberty is recognized with circumcision, sex education, and purification customs for both girls and boys (usually aged 10–13 years). Since the prewesternized Zulu economic system revolved around *lobola*, or bride-price, the young woman was more desirable and higher priced if fertility was proven, so a prewedding pregnancy was not always a negative factor. In this particular African culture, learning the skills of mature sexuality has a positive value [29].

From Africa and Australia to the United States, play is the work of the child. Since mating is accepted and desirable behavior for mature men and women, when will we reach a threshold of recognizing and accepting that sex play and romances of childhood are, therefore, necessary tasks in the growth process? If enlightened parents realized how important their positive verbal feedback is to the growing child's general sense of self, confidence, and sexual self-esteem, they might be more willing to provide such messages as "Those are good, strong legs," "You have pretty hair," "Your eyes are stronger than mine," "That's a good healthy penis; girls have a clitoris," "That's a clitoris, and it's good to know where it is. Boys have a penis." A "why" question ("Why doesn't Mary have one?" or "Why does John have a penis?") can be answered, "The Lord made boys and girls a bit differently to make them more interesting to each other," or "Girls can become mothers, and a baby is formed deep inside to protect it as it grows."

Brother-sister sex play is often undetected and mostly unreported [40]. It is quite normal, and its significance is similar to that of non-family peer play, namely, it is part of developmental sexual learning. When sibling sex play is noted, then it would be optimal for a parent to say to the children together and openly: "Now that you have explored each other's bodies, you know that you have differences— green and brown eyes, penis and vagina. Both of you make bowel movements from the same place, but Mark, you urinate through the penis, and Jenny, you have a special tiny opening below your clitoris. Playing with each other's sex parts feels good, but it is not acceptable for brothers and sisters to keep doing so, because it is impossible for you to be like boy friend and girl friend and get married one day." It is also important for parents, although upset and embarrassed, to teach respect for each other's privacy and the age of consent: "Billy, although you're 3 years younger, you have the right to say no to John who is 12 and should not pressure you to do things that may confuse you. Your penis is private and John's penis is private and both must respect that. Also, like we all have different-sized fingers and feet, so there are different sizes for the penis. Don't let anyone tease you. Everyone is curious about growing up, but it really is no big secret. What you do with your penis, each of you, is private." The parents must be open to further discussion: "Do you have any questions?

There is a book all about the body on this shelf that you can read if you want to. Please come and ask me questions or talk about it any time. I'll answer as much as I know."

Loving parents, comfortable with explicit discussions, reinforce sexual understanding and appropriateness through every growth phase of the child. Children need to be imbued with parental and cultural moral values. "Sex and marriage between brother and sister is not allowed. Affection, loyalty, caring, and sharing, yes, but not sex and marriage. That's against the law and the church. You will find sex and marriage outside of the family." If such teaching is not provided or if there are intellectual limitations in the child such as mental retardation, learning will be slower and incest breaches more likely to occur. Patient repetition and extra protection will then be important until understanding occurs. "Sexual feelings are normal and part of you and every person, but your brothers and sisters are not your sex partners." Why not? must still be answered by "It's against the law." Just as a very young girl or boy or a retarded child must learn that taking another's property is against the law, so the concept of "wanting and not taking" or controlling impulses must be learned for sexual desires also.

Exploratory sex play between siblings (and peers) is expectable, nondamaging, and part of normal childhood development [40, 45, 120, 127, 135, 170, 173, 176, 184]. Homophilic peer play is normal and does not mean the children will be homosexual adults. Child sex play occurs in all social classes. Mostly it is unknown to parents or discovered accidentally. Although such sex play has been broadly labeled sibling incest, it is advisable for professional and parent alike to seek clarity of definition. For example, consanguineous or affinity child-child noncoercive noncoital sex play may resemble consanguineous, consensual, adult-adult coital incest where outside discovery is accidental in that "help" may be unwelcome when both partners consent and are content.

Teaching and learning the right to privacy and refusal of inappropriate sex

An important part of all sex and incest-prevention education is the concept of a right to privacy for self and others. This can be maturely and quietly done without blame and depreciation. Separate male and female sleeping quarters, taking turns in the bathroom, and a minimal dress code at home all reinforce that each member respects the other's privacy. It may take more time, effort, and repetition to teach this concept to mentally handicapped family members, but kin may thus assist them to learn responsibility for their own bodies.

Also to be taught and learned is the right to refuse any inappropriate and coercive sexual advances outside or inside the family: "That's private, I don't want to take off my clothes" or "I don't want you to touch my breasts," or "Your penis is private. Please put it back." Just as self-protection is part of growing up, so sexual self-protection is one dimension of sexual growth, while sexual expression is another. At the time a child is taught to cross highways safely and to refuse rides from strangers, refusal of inappropriate sexual advances can be taught. All may be lifesaving.

Avoiding secrets

An open approach provides sex education, and it avoids problems of secrecy. Injecting both parents' values is not unduly negative or traumatic and reduces the possibility of an "exclusivity bond" (just-us-two) or "excitement bond" or "anxiety bond" or "blackmail bond" of secrecy developing between family dyads. Secrecy breeds anxiety about discovery, punishment, and wrongdoing. When a parent discovers incest and is severely punitive, tearful, hysterical, or upset, all the child may learn is that "sex is terrible," unless the forbidden kinship context also is explained, and permission is given to come and tell the parent if incest recurs. Normal sexual feelings may later become extremely upsetting owing to unresolved distress about secrecy or discovery of incest. It is not uncommon for such guilt-ridden children to experience repression of all sexual fantasy or to develop an attitude of sexual distress, dysfunction, or disinterest years later, even when sex is appropriate, legal, and possible in matrimony [106, 155]. In effect, the "secret" becomes blocked and a secret even to the self, until opened up in later treatment. Anxiety, withdrawal, depression, or other stress symptoms may result. The best parental approach is calm and open: "Sometimes feelings get mixed up. In a family, sex is for mother and father only and that is the law. Like it's against the law to steal. Sex between father and child is against the law, which protects children."

Desexualization of affection

How do parents desexualize their own strongly positive attachment feelings toward attractive vital children? With more or less difficulty, depending upon the strengths and weaknesses of their own conscious controls and their less conscious defenses. The desexualization of affection is central to incest prevention. An essential ingredient of desexualization is a clear recognition of personal sexual feelings and fantasies so that these may be controlled consciously when they are inappropriate because of kinship, age, or nonconsent.

Feelings feel, they do not think. Intellect evaluates and mobilizes control of actions so that sex behavior may come under the same personal scrutiny and control as other appetites and impulses. Another ingredient of desexualization is recognizing the boundaries of affectionate touch and an honest acknowledgment that prolonged affectionate touching soon leads to sexual arousal. In fact, the latter is foreplay, a customary prelude to intercourse. The sequence of prolonged touching leading to incest is even more probable when a parent is sexually needy, in conflict with the marital partner, or under the influence of alcohol or drugs.

It is postulated that the use of the terms *mother* and *father* in itself establishes and reinforces protective parental responsibility and therefore maintains the necessary generational desexualized boundaries within a family [171]. The practice of suggesting that a minor (or adult child) should not call the stepparent by a first name may thus actually help to prevent the risk of inappropriate sexual familiarity. Although the United States in the twentieth century is a place of social informality, in a newly constituted family first names may be misleading to both the stepparent and the stepchild by preventing the development of parent-child boundaries. The respectful terms *sir* and *ma'am* are now archaic in families and even in the working world.

It was mentioned in an earlier chapter that a custom allowing cross-cousins to mate prevails in southern India. These cousins use first names to address each other. Parallel cousins are not allowed to mate; they are forbidden to use first names, but must address each other by the formal terms *brother* and *sister*. This desexualizing practice establishes and reinforces over many years the accepted and forbidden mating customs not only between cousins but also between brother and sister.

There may, therefore, be much wisdom in using and repeating "your new father," "your new brother (sister)" as reinforcers in newly constituted families. To learn accidentally and only after emotional involvement about prohibitions can cause much pain and even, in extreme cases, psychosis and as Shakespeare portrayed in *Hamlet*, suicide.

Years of being a parent provide the experience of rearing a child as a helpless, crying infant, with wet and smelly diapers or messy face, with illness or tantrums, and in need of constant motherly or fatherly attention. Siblings similarly have years of stress and conflict. Such experiences lead to desexualization of affection, according to a theory that excess familiarity is countererotic [178]. This theory has not held up to clinical studies of incest.

The boundary between affection (altruistic, nonsexual caring), prolonged affectionate touching, and strong sexual attraction on the one hand and possible sexual action on the other is not wide. It becomes narrower when either or both persons involved are physically attractive, wear scanty clothes around the home, are impulsive, and have a strong sex drive, poor self-control, or low regard for consequences. A few drinks may increase the incest risk.

Very special and consistent ongoing awareness and redirection of sexual feelings must occur within a parent (or surrogate parent) who must protect the more vulnerable minor. A child's capacity for consent is not recognized legally for any contract, sexual or otherwise. Even if a child is seductive, provocative, very sexual, or even pseudomature, a minor is a minor. Adult-child sex play (although consensual and noncoercive) places father (or surrogate father) at risk in any court of law of a charge of incest or criminal child molestation. Intercourse (even if a child consents) turns father into a criminal guilty of aggravated incest, which is a felony in most states.

Unfortunately, too few persons are aware of these severe legal consequences until after charges are brought. What then follows is a series of even greater problems—exposure, shame, guilt, loss of job, loss of trust, anger, destruction of the family when father is jailed and the daughter (or son) is placed in an institution or a foster home. Social consequences for a child may mean not one but many foster homes and other placements. With a sexual history a girl is labeled "difficult to place," and there is also a risk of further sexual abuse for her in placement [60]. This is an unfortunate clinical reality. Over the long run of years, therefore, desexualization of affection is an important incest barrier between family members and is a family task to be learned whether it is a family of birth or a regrouped stepfamily or foster family.

INCEST PROMOTING FACTORS

Disrupted marital sexual relationship

A disrupted sexual relationship between marital partners may be noted in many incest families with or without other incest promoting factors. If there is a clash of sexual attitudes, expectations, and satisfaction between marital partners and an inability to discuss their private feelings about this, they will not explore differences, nor reconcile or change their way of affectionate or sexual exchange. One or both may then silently avoid or refuse sexual contact. This also may lead to open conflict and affectional withdrawal. Some partners may search for sexual satisfaction outside the marriage. Others will control sexual feelings and become celibate. Some may be comfortable with masturbating for sexual release. Some spouses find sexual outlets within the family, when there is a lack of satisfactory sexual expression in their marital relationship. This may be in the form of adult-child or adult-adult coital or noncoital incest. Why other partners with similar marital problems and available children or relatives seek sex outside rather than inside the family is an unanswered question. Do "adulterers" have greater social skills or more personality resources? Each individual incest situation must be evaluated to answer these questions.

Previous incest experiences

An individual who has experienced incest in his or her own family of origin may repeat the behavior or excuse or condone sexual expression in the present family. The person has not developed or accepted or internalized the values of the larger community that certain behaviors (like the incests) are unacceptable, wrong, bad, or sinful.

Relevant questions to raise where incest was accepted in a family's value system are these: Does incest beget incest? Are women who have experienced brother-sister coital consensual incest more likely to initiate mother-son incest (transference reactions)? Are men who experienced brother-sister incest more likely to try father-daughter incest (object fixation or transference reactions)? Are parents who themselves enjoyed incest contacts as children more likely to encourage sexual contacts between their own children? These are difficult, unexplored, and as yet unanswered questions.

Prevalent incest customs

In contemporary Mexico, Puerto Rico, Appalachia, and some Polynesian Islands, and among certain American Indians, many incest-accepting families remain today. One very important assumption is that inappropriate behavior is learned essentially in the same way that appropriate behavior is learned, since both are based on the same fundamental learning principles. Values and customs are learned by modeling. By engaging in incestuous sexual behavior toward a child or condoning sibling or other incest, parents teach that family sex is acceptable. Rewarding a child's sexual advances toward a parent or sibling by smiling, responding, regarding it as acceptable, or giving privileges, money, or treats will certainly promote repetition of the behavior.

When parents have similar sexual (incest) values and these are in accordance with the values of the larger community in which the nuclear family lives, there may be no family or social problem. It is when an incest-accepting individual or family emigrates to an incest-rejecting community that problems may arise. The family may be ignorant of anti-incest laws. Distress may relate more to discovery than to the sex. Incest education for the whole family will be essential.

Social isolation of rural families has been theorized as a cause of contemporary pockets of prevalent incest customs [10, 135]. However, incest occurs in urban families with or without actual social isolation [40, 56, 172].

Alcohol or drug use

Convicted incest offenders have often reported that excessive use of alcohol accompanied their incestuous activities [20,

22, 40, 56, 83, 99, 103, 104, 110, 165, 172]. What constituted excessive alcohol use is an important academic question. The implication, of course, is that chemical intoxication altered sexual behavioral controls, lowered learned incest inhibitions, or allowed a forbidden family member to be misperceived as a marital partner.

The possibility that heavy drinking was being used for exoneration, an excuse, or a mitigating circumstance in incest must also be raised. The question of disavowal of criminal intent by reason of intoxication is not new [107]. Also, excusing or forgiving a family member for incest may be facilitated by seeing the behavior as "caused by" drink. Occasionally, drug abuse and incest are correlated [110].

Psychopathology

Intermittently learned sexual controls may be overcome by psychosis, sociopathy, restricted intellectual or social skills, pedophilia, or other disorders.

CASE 4-1. The fifth foster home was the only one remembered of the five this patient had been in between ages 3 and 8 years. Almost from the start, the unemployed foster father had made lewd remarks to her alone or in the presence of her foster mother, who did domestic work. The foster father had a fourth grade education and had often been jailed for stealing or urinating in public. Despite his wife's yelling at him to watch his obscenities and to stop pilfering, he persisted in both. The foster mother had been sleeping on the living room couch, so the patient asked her to share her bedroom. The foster mother complied, and this pattern continued for years.

From about age 16, the patient worked outside the home; she learned to drive at school. She also joined the church choir, usually going with a girl friend who had a car. One evening at church, she realized she'd forgotten something, borrowed the friend's car, and went home. The foster father was alone and quite sober. He lunged at her, attempting to undress her. She struggled and ran to the car. He came after her. She closed the door on him, not realizing his head was partly inside. He screamed, and she pushed him out and drove off in panic, leaving him unconscious, concussed, and with both his ears bleeding. He was found by his wife some hours later. He recovered after two weeks in the hospital. At the time, the patient requested the status of emancipated minor, but her caseworker refused to believe that this was an attempted rape. She finally ran away, was not followed up by the Illinois Division of Children and Family Services, but made it on her own.

At age 41, the patient had severe migraine, the pain being in a highly unusual distribution across both temples and ears. It was only after incidentally reporting the foster father's pursuit of her that she was able to connect her headaches with the unresolved emotional trauma of his attack and her quite normal efforts at self-defense.

Her foster father showed the incest fostering factors of poor or no sexual contact with his wife (who slept with the patient), possible retardation, and unemployment (which lowered his self-esteem and provided more opportunities for private interaction with the patient in his wife's absence). Although the foster mother was concerned and protective, the home was chaotic. There was good judgment, strength, and maturity in the patient's unassisted escape from this home.

CASE 4-2. An inhibited, withdrawn engineer, this patient, aged 36, presented at a sex clinic with lack of interest in sex. His wife was nonorgasmic. He was reared in a stormy urban home with a passive father who worked in a bank. His earliest (and most frightening) sexual experience was when at age 12 his very obese mother, a Ph.D. counseling psychologist with the United States Army, herself stripped, sat him down, spread her huge legs, and showed him her genitals. She said it was time he learned about women. The patient ran out of the house and did not return till nightfall. The parents finally divorced when the patient was 17 years old, and he has not since seen his mother, who is now in Japan on an army base. The patient dated little, and did well at college and at his work. At age 30, he married a sexually nonthreatening woman.

The patient described his mother as an angry, needy, troubled lady with severe marital (and possibly sexual) conflict, who had made an aggressive rather than seductive sexual overture to him. He responded with fear to both the aggressive and the sexual elements of her act. This strange, inappropriate parenting behavior could be called exhibitionism and adult-child noncoital incest, although it is questionable that there was sexual intent.

CASE 4-3. A manic-depressive father who refused his needed medications woke his 12-year-old daughter at 5:00 A.M. with a full erection, saying "This is what a man is all about, feel it and learn." Terrified, she ran out of the house into the snow, hid in a nearby unheated basement, and was found the next day by the police. Her mother took the father to a psychiatric hospital for treatment. The girl remained afraid of him and slept with her door locked and a knife under her pillow. There was a definite possibility that her father's exhibitionism could forcefully continue to adult-child rape incest.

Hypersexuality or undifferentiated sexual urgency (as displayed by this father) is one of the symptoms of the manic phase of manic-depressive illness and may be controlled with adequate lithium medication, which the father used erratically. He suffered from a chronic psychotic process characterized by heightened drives (aggression, sex, and motor activity) and lowered controls; therefore, when psychotic, he might approach anyone (even a stranger) as he did his 12-year-old daughter.

Inability to accept masturbation

From cradle to grave, normal sexual tensions wax and wane. A normal and quite natural release for both sexes is masturbation. However, for centuries and still today, many cultures have had inhibitions and numerous myths about masturbation: that it is a perversion; that it causes venereal disease or homosexuality; that it reduces potency [129]. If for an individual, especially a morally upright person (of any socioeconomic class), the taboo or negative injunctions against masturbation are stronger than those against incest, then an available, legally forbidden family member may be selected for sexual satisfaction.

Sustained proximity with privacy

Learned personal privacy and the right to refuse inappropriate sexual advances are important incest-preventing factors for a child in the privacy of the home. Split shifts or unemployment may at times be incest promoting, e.g., when mother is away and father is at home in some adult-child incest cases, or when parents are out in many situations of sibling or kinship peer sex play or coital incest.

Darkness, covers, bed, bedroom provide degrees of privacy. Sometimes at family gatherings, by need, custom, or choice, these are shared, with pleasurable closeness. Sometimes incest results. Very recently three novels about incest between attic-confined childern simultaneously made the top ten mass market best sellers list [5, 6, 7]. Millions of teenage girls are noted as their most avid readers.

It is interesting that in the impoverished, crowded coal-mining area of northern Wales, there are very large families and little heat in the homes, and a high incidence of incest. Proximity provides at least body warmth; sexual arousal also markedly increases body temperature. Sibling incest is allegedly commonplace there and the most common form of incest. This is understandable physiologically (need for warmth) as well as psychologically (need for caring, closeness, and special attention in a large group). Also darkness gives privacy, being in bed is relaxing, and somnolence lowers voluntary controls. Eroticized sibling exchange differs from purely altruistic brotherly love [53] in that the sex exchange serves a definite personal purpose for each, although there may also be altruism in the relationship.

Proximity-seeking and touching-seeking behavior of children is a recognized part of normal human development and continues for life unless discouraged [75, 116]. It is described as similar to refueling [101] or regaining emotional security from the sight, touch, or presence of a parent or loved one [102]. This allows a child or adult once more to explore or negotiate with the world outside. It is the task of parents to override prolonged proximity seeking of a child in the interest of the autonomy of both child and parent; otherwise their interdependence becomes symbiotic and maladaptive. It is also the task of parents to recognize real sexual overtures from the child and set limits, such as "Only Daddy kisses me like that on my mouth. One day you will have your own wife to kiss like that." Later the child will internalize these verbal controls provided by parents. Unless this is done with awareness, such sustained proximity may become sexualized and result in incest.

Parents who promote a child's extended emotional or sexual dependence interfere with social development and psychological independence by keeping the child inappropriately within the closed family setting. This prevents appropriate peer play and proximity seeking with peers, which is the beginning of later, more mature psychosexual development.

Newly constituted families

A simple change of neighborhood, school, room, bed, yard may represent losses, despite material improvements. Death or divorce causes stress for all family members. Adjustment may take the form of irritability, anxiety, or crying for either adult or child. Realistically or not, the custodial parent may be perceived as having driven the other parent away. Resentments, rivalry, and attempts to replace the lost parent may occur on the part of a child. Sometimes hostility, temper outbursts, regressive behavior from thumbsucking to soiling, fearful clinging, or severe withdrawal may follow a foster placement, a divorce, or a remarriage. Disruption of a family is one of the most severe life stresses for each individual member [123]. Adjustment to changes takes time, support, and open, honest communication that provides as much information as possible to help each family member.

When a sexual partner is invited into the home by a single parent, there must be appropriate concern for restoring the concept and structure of a family, since this will affect each member. What is the message given to children, especially prepubescent ones flooded with hormones and sexual energy? "John is your new stepfather" (that is, we were married). "John is going to stay here a few days. He'll sleep in the living room. He is a friend" (that is, we are not married, it is a brief stay, and he will not have parental authority). "John is my boy friend, and he will live here for a while" (that is, this is not permanent, and it is unclear what his role will be). "John is a truck driver and travels six days at a time, so should be home weekends. He will sleep in my bedroom and maybe later we will think of getting married" (that is, a more permanent contract is pending, so adaptation must now commence). The message must be spelled out, whatever it is. Children are resilient and can cope better when they know what the situation is and may be. Secrets are difficult to keep in a family. Nosy relatives and neighbors often cross-question a child. Better they be told something like "and that information is private to the four of us in the family. If people question you, just tell them to ask me." This prevents needless painful assumptions and self-blame on the part of the child. Introduction of a new member, transiently or permanently, into a family expectably shifts the dynamic equilibrium of the group. The age, needs, and maturity of each member, the birth parent's protective stance and the capacity of the incoming adult to assume a desexualized parental nurturant role toward the children will all determine how the newly constituted family will adapt and fulfill its role of serving their physical, social, emotional, and spiritual needs.

A hypothetical stepfamily: John, Donna, and Sue. The expectation that a 26-year-old stepfather (John) should automatically and immediately have repressive defenses against sexual arousal towards an attractive, physically affectionate 13-year-old stepdaughter (Sue) when she teasingly wrestles with him may be unrealistic. Even to call their arousal feelings incest may be inaccurate and presumptuous. Maintenance of generational boundaries and awareness of the fine balance between parental affection and sexual or erotic feelings take years to develop. A prerequisite for the development of a parental coalition is that there be emotional and sexual satisfaction between the natural mother, Donna, and the new stepparent, John. Extra protection of vulnerable children by the natural parent is needed in the new family group. She must have realistic awareness of the inherent potential of heightened sexual feelings that normally flood every adolescent, including Sue, at puberty. Just as aggression breeds counteraggression, so sexual arousal quite normally sparks sexual arousal. Although fleeting, if there is visual or tactile recognition between Sue and her new stepfather of his erection during their wrestling play, both know an erotic spark has occurred. There may at first be immediate fright and withdrawal. However, there may also be the savor of a powerful sexual attraction that both may want to check out again. Despite theories of an anti-incest instinct, arguments for an inborn psychological deterrant to such sexual arousal even toward blood relatives have not been convincing—in animal studies or for humans [73]. John is not a blood relative and only just beginning to learn a stepfather role, which will entail protecting his stepchildren from sexual exploitation, including his own.

If the relationship between mother (Donna) and stepfather is healthy enough for them to talk as a couple about the (not abnormal) sexual feelings that occurred between John and Sue, the parents may appropriately consolidate to prevent unacceptable sexual behavior or flirtation between stepfather and the teen. If the mother is sensitive and unites well with her new mate, she protects both the overt affectional-erotic John-Donna bond between them as well as her protective mother-child bond and an emerging affectional desexualized stepfather-daughter bond. Also, Donna must covertly send Sue the message: "You must find your sex partner outside of this new family." To John, a protective stance by Donna openly confirms that Sue is sexually out of bonds to him. There is also the inevitable fact that the Donna-John relationship, in its newness, is strongly erotic and their embraces and overheard lovemaking may be normally arousing to Sue, who at 13 has more sexual feelings than sexual controls and may not only identify with mother but also compete with her.

Helpful and growth promoting to all three would be an open talk: "Many girls go through a phase of falling in love with their dad. I did too with my father. (Or, I didn't because he drank and yelled so much I couldn't wait to leave home.) You were only 5 when your father left and that was difficult. Now it's great but also a bit confusing to have a new dad in the house. You like John and he's also sexy. But he is your new father, not your boy friend. We all get lots of sexual feelings for lots of people, but we control them. Fathers are not allowed to be sexy with daughters and stepchildren, but only with their wives—otherwise there's a big problem, and it is also against the law. You're 13 years old, and as your mother my job is to help you learn about these exciting feelings so you don't get carried away and allow your body to have sex before your head and emotions are ready. Grown-ups (your new father John and I) express sexual feelings with each other but at other times we also must control our sexual feelings. Please trust me and come to me any time if you are upset or have sex questions, because that's my job as your mother. It would help all of us if you would call John father and save *daddy* for your daddy Eric."

If for stepfather John affectionate touch has been learned as synonymous with sex, then when 13-year-old Sue, who may have innocently learned to express much affectionate touching with her mother, uses this same way to relate to the new surrogate father, both Sue and John are at high risk for being flooded with sexual feelings. He will need extra special control since his body response may be touching equals erection. If wife Donna does not for any reason have a close, understanding relationship or mutual give-and-take with John or with Sue, and is unaware of the Sue-John sexual "kindling," then Donna and John may miss this opportunity to come closer and to help each other grow as parents. Then Sue and her stepfather will have a secret that may be both exciting and binding but also guilt-laden and anxiety provoking. It is not an exaggerated analogy to say that for such a newly regrouped family, the unfolding sexual dynamics may be a blindfold obstacle course for all unless deliberate suppressive defenses against normal sexual arousal are developed along the way with full conscious awareness, dialogue, and mutual goodwill to respect the anti-incest laws of their belief system and of the community at large. Stepparenting is a challenge to maturity and integrity [166].

CASE 4-4. A residual nuclear family showed an unusual "stable disequilibrium" that resulted from consensual incest. A 28-year-old married woman with one 3-year-old child, went once a week to have coitus with and clean house and cook for her widowed 64-year-old father as she had willingly done for the last 10 years. The coital noncoercive father-daughter incest was not known to her husband, who admired her filial devotion. She said she felt sorry for her father. She attained climax with neither father nor husband (both of whom were premature ejaculators). She and her husband thought theirs was a good marriage. They did well with seven weeks of sex therapy; their presenting sexual symptoms of anorgasmia and premature ejaculation were reversed. The wife was not at all guilty or distressed about sex with her father. She revealed the history comfortably and quite incidentally as part of a routine long, explicit sex history. She thought her husband would not understand the incest and therefore had not told him; she asked for this part of the history to be confidential. She had two years of college and was a well-adjusted person. She said she learned the meaning of the word *incest* in college. Reflecting at age 20 on her relationship with her father she felt it was not harming anyone. He was getting older and sometimes did not get an erection, so the sexual "obligation" would soon be over. As her son became more active, her father seemed to prefer to play with the boy rather than signal her to the bedroom.

An only child, she viewed family loyalty and her father's needs above individual needs. Her mother had been dominant, and on her deathbed had said, "Take care of Dad for me," which the woman literally obeyed. Her passive father had not restricted her socially, although he himself was almost a social recluse. He worked in a factory, watched television, and cared for plants and tropical fish. He accepted her dating and later her husband and dearly loved his grandson.

The woman interpreted her mother's last request as inheriting a wife's role to her father and simply redefined and reversed the generational boundaries in her own mind, as apparently did her father, both seemingly free of conflict. Parent-child coital or noncoital heterosexual or homosexual incest often shows inappropriate dependency and role reversal such as with this woman. She had no idea incest was a criminal offence. At age 18, she willingly became her father's overall and sexual caretaker. At that time, because of her age, it was a felony. When coital incest with a minor occurs, coercion is adjudged to have occurred, because a child's ability to give consent to the sex act is questioned. Most children are dependent upon and possibly afraid of a nurturant parent, or uncle, grandparent, or older brother. The passive inability of this woman's father to search for another partner evoked her pity and role reversal. She was quite maternal when she described him: "inadequate, uneducated, but a good and kind man."

Incest personality?

Is there a specific personality type who will predictably seek incest? There are three descriptive studies of jailed adults who commit incest. In the prison's social hierarchy, sex offenders are at low levels, with men convicted of child incest considered the lowest. Weinberg [172] reported on 203 offenders in Illinois; Maisch [103] described 78 offenders in Germany; and Gebhard et al. [56] wrote on 1356 sex offenders from Indiana and California, of whom 147 were convicted of incest. In the studies, there was a concerted attempt to analyze (1) the types of incest: father-daughter, brother-sister, mother-son, etc.; (2) how detected; (3) race, nationality; (4) age; (5) socioeconomic status; (6) education; (7) intelligence; (8) family size; (9) marital status; (10) birth order; (11) sex habits; (12) previous arrests; (13) previous hospitalizations; (14) divorce status; and (15) personality.

FATHERS. In 1955 Weinberg reported a pre-incarceration diagnosis of psychosis or retardation, then added a personality classification of his 203 subjects (fathers) during their prison stay: (1) egocentric, (2) inadequate, (3) emotionally unstable, (4) adequate, (5) psychopathic, or (6) sexually psychopathic. Only 11 of the 203 were psychotics: paranoid, catatonic, alcoholic, senile, and two unclassified. Maisch in 1973 mentioned the high percentage of chronic alcoholics in the group of 78 offenders in Germany and the low percentage of mental retardates or persons with evidence of emotional illness or supersexuality.

Lengthy personal interviews were done with 147 men convicted of father-daughter incest [56]. Of these, 56 (group 1) had sexual contact with children under 12. Only 5 of the 56 had coital incest. Sixty-six (group 2) had sexual contact with minors (12 to 15 years old); there was coital incest in 46 of these cases. Twenty-five (group 3) had sexual contact with an "adult" daughter (over 16 years). There was no report of how many in group 3 had coital incest. The men in group 1 reported a high incidence of turbulent early life; much prepubertal sex play, chiefly with girls; a low frequency of premarital masturbation (2–3 times per month when comparative groups of boys had a frequency of 1–3 times per week). After marriage this group of men reported a high incidence of extramarital coitus (with up to four partners) and a high incidence of masturbation while married. Group 2 had a low frequency of marital and extramarital coitus and of masturbation. Group 3 was described as moralistic, restrained, highly fertile but with low frequency in all of their sexual activity.

Although these men provide an interesting and important study, it must be noted that convicted sexual offenders may not represent all persons for whom incest is used as a sexual outlet. They represent those who were reported and convicted of behavior contrary to the sexual mores of their community. Incest also occurs in the wealthy and well-educated family and may never reach the legal system. Also worth mentioning is that "worry about the effects of masturbation" was reported in a high percentage of the almost 3000 sex offenders (of all types) in the overall study [56], which was done between 1940 and 1955. Whether these men sought any sexual outlet rather than masturbation and whether this attitude may have driven them to incest would have been a relevant question to have asked the 147 incest offenders as well as the others studied.

The Gebhard group agreed that heavy drinking, unemployment, a working wife, a cultural tolerance for incest, and available daughters were important incest factors. No specific personality type was noted. Some of the men said their early relationships were good with both parents. The 56 men who were jailed for incest with a daughter under 12 years reported that before puberty they had enjoyed pleasant sex play with young girls. One may postulate that they sought to recapture that pleasure by regression to a child partner.

These three studies are thorough and painstaking but shed little light on the offender's personal capacity to relate to others as either a child or an adult. What feelings were they seeking in the incest closeness? The families of origin are described by Weinberg [172] as not incorporating restraints concerning incest. Again the questions arise, What are these restraints? When do they form? How do they develop? Weinberg also described (as do Gebhard, et al. for some of the 56 who chose a daughter under 12) fragmented and disorganized families, "loose sex cultures," or families "estranged from the larger culture." An important question, therefore, is, Were the early parent-child relationships for the offender *more* affectionate than usual?

Were there differences in erotic affection between the consanguineous adult-child and the affinity adult-child incest cases? What is there to learn from these relationships in their failure to desexualize the caring, affectionate parent-child bond?

In the foreward to the Maisch report (1973) Professor Hedwig Wallis wrote:

> Except in cases of attempted murder in couples living in intimacy, there is hardly any other set of legal circumstances which bind offender and victim so closely together in such a tight, often tragic network of affection and distance, fear and fascination, care and lack of consideration; in short all the ambivalence which is an integral part of the closest human relationship.

This excerpt once more emphasizes that incest partners may care deeply and sincerely for each other. Incest is not the same as child abuse except in coercive or rape incest. The latter does occur but rarely (e.g., 6% of the Maisch group). Many incest partners reportedly did not want to be parted from each other. Maisch concluded that most of the families in which consanguineous coital incest occurred were disturbed before the occurrence of incest and lists a full page [103] of factors that sustained the incest. Eighty percent of the men volunteered that sustained incest was due to a disturbed relationship with their spouse, which does not necessarily indict the wives nor exonerate the husbands. Of the "victims," 49 percent said they lacked knowledge of their rights (to refuse sex); 38 percent feared being removed from home; 31 percent feared breakup of the family, which was valued and protected; and 21 percent reported a sexual motive, so that for the latter group the term *victim* is questionable.

Could sex education have helped to prevent the incest? Together with teaching general responsibility and respect for authority and personal rights, parents must teach sexual rights. When parents are themselves aware, they may teach their children about closeness, particularly the differences among affection, touching, sex, and love. They will also emphasize values regarding respect of persons, of consent to give and receive touch. The pleasure of participation in sexual expression, its place in a relationship and in a marriage, and the roles of men and women in everyday living may be discussed at the same time [138, 184]. The right to refuse inappropriate affectionate or sexual touching is also to be taught. This is difficult when touching is so essential an aspect of forming relationships [116]. Even bumper stickers remind all of the need for touch: "Have you hugged your kid today?" To teach children to avoid all adult touching, at home and elsewhere, would be too restrictive to their developing a capacity to relate to others affectionately and later sexually. While children are developing, they are not appropriate sex objects for adults. Children at any age have a right to control or refuse sexual stimulation *before* the height of sexual arousal. They must learn that sex is optional for all persons of all ages and that refusal is quite normal and acceptable.

In a mental health clinic, nonprison study of 58 cases of incest [110], 25 cases (43%) were situations of stepfathers or affinity kin incest; 20 (34%) were father-daughter; 1 (2%) mother-son; and 16 (28%) were cases of incest with assorted relatives. In only 17 of 58 cases did coitus occur. Sixteen of the 58 male partners included four uncles, two grandfathers, and ten brothers. In some cases there were multiple partners. To have considered these cases legally and psychologically all as a homogeneous group is misleading. The duration of the relationship before incest and the age and dependency of the child participant are important aspects of each interaction. Meiselman states, "Sexual activity was defined as incestuous only if the participants had actually lived together in related roles such that a feeling of 'real' relatedness could have been achieved." Achieved by whom? Were both participants asked about this feeling of being related? How long must persons live together to obtain the emotional state of "real" relatedness? In the case of 13-year-old Sue and her new stepfather

John, aged 26, how long does it take to feel "real" father-daughter *desexualized* affectional relatedness?

A report of interviews with 183 women survivors of incest who responded to various magazine and newspaper ads was popularized in a book, *Kiss Daddy Goodnight* [8]. It sold well because of many pages of explicit sexual scenes—allegedly verbatim and in the first person. Although the author mentions that the women described are not losers or permanently damaged or prostitutes, but average neighbors, the main stated goal of the book is to prove that incest is always child abuse. Annabelle's story [8] goes on for 21 pages, describing a start with consanguineous consensual adult-child noncoital, then coital, incest with a pedophilic father who next sets up group sex with his boss, boss's wife, Annabelle, and himself. All this is "more joy" for Annabelle who plans to have her father's baby as she pursues her father and wishes to marry him. The vignette ends because she later leaves her father, saying that he wants only sex and that he lies when he says he loves her. She then propositions her natural mother for sex. The battered reader, after this sensational journalism, is given the redeeming comment "Can this be what anyone wants the wives and mothers of America to be?" In the afterword one comment is worth noting: "[Five women] did not want to be known as a victim. Better . . . to speak of the fathers as the victims of their own sexuality, their promiscuity with power. We were only incest objects. Chipped, maybe, or chipped and mended. But still with value and integrity."

Other descriptions of incestuous fathers have little consensus and include a range from sociopathy to rigid morality, from violent to introverted behavior, and from low coital drive to hypersexuality [22, 76]. Each individual must be carefully and objectively evaluated to understand his or her strengths and weaknesses, which are factors to be considered in treating the family.

MOTHERS. When mothers are involved in incest they may be fully participant or only peripherally or indirectly involved.

Mother-son and mother-daughter incest may occur as consanguineous or affinity adult-child, usually consensual, usually noncoital and sometimes coital incest. Generally mothers who are initiators of sex with their own children are described as severely disturbed, psychotic, immature, or mentally retarded [110, 173]. Some are, but others may not be any of these. Instead they may be lonely and emotionally needy. One woman wrote about mother-daughter incest to Ann Landers [44], saying, "My mother was a teacher and a churchgoer," a pillar of the community. An explosive protest by the writer's father who discovered the mother stroking the daughter's genitals in the bathtub when the child was 12 years old, traumatically ended the fondling which had occurred for several years, with much shame expressed by the writer. On the other hand, if genital fondling by mothers were culturally accepted, father would not have been enraged. Was it the open anger, fear of father, conflict between the parents, fear of harm to mother or self, or the shame of father seeing her genitals that upset the writer? Discovery added much complexity.

Clinicians have frequently noted that a mother, although not a participant herself, may be a more or less conscious third party in father-daughter incest [100, 110, 172]. Sometimes she may herself have been a child incest participant with her own father [124] and may therefore believe that repetition of this phenomenon is acceptable; she may even set it up for her husband and daughter. Some of these mothers, even when not aware of the husband's sexual activity with the daughter, are described as emotionally deprived and distant; some spent years in orphanages, institutions, or foster homes and were thus perhaps deprived of learning a protective mothering role [34].

These mothers did not learn the receiving and giving of desexualized family affection. They (and their husbands) may perceive that affection equals sex equals intercourse equals more children. Such a mother may, therefore, withdraw totally from both affectionate and sexual relations with the husband. The wife of an incestuous man may or may not be absent from home because of illness, pregnancy, childbirth, or an outside job before or at the time of the onset of incest between father and child [56, 88, 103, 110, 172].

The wife of an incestuous man has also been variously described as weak, tired, worn out, submissive, dependent, ambivalent, masochistic, maternal toward her husband, frigid, indifferent, and promiscuous [81]. However, many of these women are caring, protective mothers and do effectively intervene to stop or prevent incest. They must not be presumed to be in collusion and unjustly blamed, since this will damage the possibility of a therapeutic alliance.

Whenever the descriptive spectrum is so wide, it is safe to say that there is no specific profile of mothers involved directly or tacitly (by failing to prevent or stop it) in family sexual activity. Each woman must be given the benefit of an objective evaluation, for the purpose of documenting her strengths and weaknesses, important factors for further family therapy.

SONS AND DAUGHTERS. More has been written about daughters than sons because of the predominance of studies of father-daughter incest. As with father and mother profiles, any of a number of descriptions prevail for the girls. These contradict an old stereotype that girls involved in incest are of subnormal intellect, as one rural study in Japan found [88]. Although a child chosen as a sex partner by a parent may be retarded or deaf or mute, raising questions of double exploitation owing to disability as well as minority, this is not necessarily so. Daughters involved in incest are more likely to be of average intelligence [62, 103, 110]. Some may be above average, college educated and well adjusted [40, 132, 179].

Another stereotype of these daughters is that they are promiscuous, provocative, or Lolita-like. They may be described as attractive girls with earlier than usual prepuberty development [13, 14]; however, menarche was not found to be significantly earlier than for peers [103]. Some prison offenders interviewed claimed that their daughters' physical development was a factor in their attraction to them and that they were cooperative until a quarrel between them provoked their retaliatory reporting of the sexual activity [56]. Although this may have been so, many of these men began adult-child noncoital sexual behavior years before their daughters reached puberty. Therefore, searching for affectional as well as sexual contact must be considered as a possibility for both father and daughter. Each father had the responsibility to desexualize that affection. His failure to do so perpetuates his affection equals sex belief for one more generation.

Often it is the oldest daughter (described as reversing roles with her mother in domestic duties) who is chosen as father's incest partner [103, 110, 172]. Sometimes father will go down the age ladder to younger daughters as older ones leave home [27]. Other fathers choose a younger girl [110].

There are occasional case reports of mother-son or father-son incest [9, 89, 126, 139, 167, 179]. The sons are described by some reporters as effeminate and dependent, with guilt, poor social skills, and anxiety [39, 81, 126]. The total of the few samples in the literature is still very small.

There are also many clinical and nonclinical instances in all socioeconomic groups of sons and daughters who have experienced parent-child incest in some form, and who are average, well-adjusted, even well-educated and productive persons [8, 132, 184]. Their adult personality indeed must have been shaped by the experience, but not necessarily warped, nor wounded beyond healing. Open-minded, objective evaluation of each remains the essential clinical task.

FALSE ACCUSATIONS OF INCEST

Manipulations and destructive coalitions may occur in families. Conflict and competition between parents or siblings or extended family members may be severe around issues of status, privileges, or property. There have been occasions where inaccurate reports or accusations of incest have been made, either maliciously as blackmail, or in a misguided way as a result of misperception or ignorance of the term *incest*.

There are occasions when a child may falsely accuse a parent or sibling of sexual activity [64]. It is misleading to think of the term *incest hoax* as being jocular. It is always important to understand why sex is so much in the foreground of a child's thinking as to be chosen as a conflict area rather than violence. (There are also on record a few false accusations of child abuse by manipulative, precocious minors.)

A false incest accusation is different from withdrawal of a charge of incest when a frightened, threatened child changes stories. She may deny a previous report of incest after being punished at home or told by mother that father will otherwise go to jail and they will be deprived of income. An example of a false incest report follows.

CASE 4-5. The patient was 10 years old when brought by her irate mother to the emergency room at 2:00 A.M. for "a rape test." The gynecology resident examined her and assured the mother the child was virginal and undamaged. The mother adamantly insisted on a sperm search, saying that the child said her father had molested her. The psychiatry resident was called. The story emerged that this was a second marriage of one year's duration. The girl woke that night at midnight to a loud fight, with her mother accusing her stepfather of molesting the girl, and threatening to throw him out. Remembering similar fights before the first divorce and tearfully trying to stop the battle, the child intervened: "No, he didn't do that, but Daddy did last Sunday" (visitation day). This statement dramatically succeeded in polarizing the angry mother against her former husband. She suddenly realigned with her second husband. Together as concerned parents they then rushed the girl to a hospital to gain evidence to incriminate the innocent natural father. The exhausted child broke down and cried as she gave her story. She had absolutely no idea of what the word *molested* meant. She was humiliated at having her groin exposed by the examining male physician, not knowing why this was being done. The child had simply become ammunition in the war of an immature, insecure mother against men close to her. Predictably they did not keep the given appointment to the child clinic the next day.

CASE 4-6. A combatative 16-year-old who was on street drugs was hospitalized because of psychosis. He and his older sister were adopted at age 3 and 4 by his stepfather. His natural father, mother, and stepfather were all alcoholics in a chaotic, conflictive interaction of regular crises. The mother was in the process of divorcing her second husband and wanted to return to the boy's unemployed natural father. However, the boy was on the stepfather's hospital insurance policy. Mother and stepfather continued to battle, oblivious to any attempt to intervene. Mother refused a conjoint interview, broke appointments, and would call often, shouting obscenities about all and sundry. One specific call was of note. Totally unexpectedly, after the boy was discharged and the follow-up appointment broken, I received a call from the mother: "He won't give me my divorce! I'm going to press charges for molesting my daughter!" I asked when and how this had happened, since she had moved out with her 19-year-old daughter to the maternal grandmother's apartment. "She was 13 years old and he did it five times!" I mentioned that such a matter should have been dealt with at the time, if it had occurred. If it had not, then lying under oath was perjury. Predictably, she hung up with a slam. True or false for the incest? Certainly rage and retaliation were evident.

Intentional blackmail may incorporate many types of threats. At times, "leaking" a false incest accusation may be done with deliberate intent to harm a reputation, a career, a political opportunity, or a property claim. This is a highly malicious and unscrupulous act since it is so difficult to disprove incest because of the involvement of others, especially children, and the private nature of sex.

If children and family service agencies are prematurely and erroneously informed in these cases, there may be a destructive course even for the innocent. A careful, unhurried professional evaluation must be made; this may take more than a single visit to avoid violation of the Hippocratic oath's injunction, "Do no harm."

CONCLUSION

The family, despite its changing structure, remains the place that breeds us, feeds us, and shapes our personality upon our given biological attributes. The capacity to make close, good, indifferent, or poor relationships takes time to learn and occurs, from birth onward, in the context of early and ongoing primary family experiences. Here consistency and trust are learned; affection is learned; touching is learned. All are aspects of close relationships that enhance an individual's capacity to cope with life stresses.

Most persons have four opportunities to learn trust, touching, affection, and closeness: our family of birth or rearing, our life partner, our children, and our grandchildren. Too few persons learn closeness, affection, touching and trust until the fourth opportunity as grandparents. Yet these are all lifelong human needs.

Somehow, through the centuries, caring, sharing affectional family nurturance has had to be desexualized. Apparently this has been achieved unconsciously by heavy inhibitions against all sex other than procreative sex in marriage. Privacy was taught and separate sleeping space provided for male and female children. Incest avoidance was apparently expected to be learned by osmosis under this same general sexual prohibition. Legends, literature, medical practice, and the courts attest to the failure of such an assumption. Vague incest prohibitions do not eliminate incest.

Although our culture still (although less vehemently) teaches that sex is for marriage partners only and that extramarital sex is wrong, families no longer or only rarely teach partner prohibitions. With today's small, mobile nuclear family units, cousins are not usually geographically close by, and parents may not mention which relatives are inappropriate romantic playmates and later marriage partners.

Like other vital human functions, sex is also learned behavior. Yet the vast majority receive no sex education in the family and mistakenly learn that sex is bad or wrong, that masturbation is perverse or worse, that love equals sex equals intercourse or touching equals sex (because that is the only time real or screen adults are seen exchanging sustained touch), and that affection is mainly shown to babies or as a sexual overture.

Many confused Victorian sexual attitudes remain today as they did when Sigmund Freud, product of his own nineteenth century rearing, formulated his libido and oedipal theories. Dreams or fantasies of sexual contact with a family member were not at that time considered to be part of normal growth and learning. Instead of being considered sinful, persons who incidentally, as part of a life history, reported sexual thoughts regarding family members were now labeled neurotic. For the first half of the twentieth century, incest became a target for lengthy years of individual psychoanalysis, without definition of the word or of its specific behavioral aspects in family relationships.

In every case of consanguineous or affinity parent-child incest, at any age, the husband-wife relationship must be the core area of clinical scrutiny. Their affectional *and* sexual relationship is primary— literally the very heart of all secondary family relationships. If their human needs for affection and sex are met within their relationship, it is highly unlikely that either will turn to a child to meet them. Rare exceptions would be the onset of a psychotic process because of which the child is misperceived or in which hypersexuality, consisting of undifferentiated sexual urgency, incorporates the most available sex object—child or other. Chemical toxic distortions caused by alcohol or drugs might also produce exceptions.

Therefore, to reverse incest, the essential first target for treatment must be efforts to restore a healthy, sexualized affectional bond between the parents (natural, step, or adoptive). Brief sex therapy may on occasion be of value when indicated to reverse an existing sexual dysfunction. Next will be family therapy to prevent secrecy and encourage appropriate protective desexualized affectional relationships between other secondary dyads in the family.

Although there are many factors yet to be understood in the incests, it is clear that they are sexual learning disorders. Within the incestuous family, essential learning regarding desexualizing touch and close affectionate relationships has not occurred between siblings, parents and children, or within other dyads (e.g., uncle-niece, grandfather-grandchild). Therefore, teaching about touching, affection, relationships, and sex must be incorporated into family therapy so that desexualized affection may be taught and learned by the family.

Professionals realize that there are some cultures and individuals who evidence no distress even when they participate in consanguineous coital incest. They may merely report this fact incidentally as part of a solicited life history. The protection of minors should be a concern. The professional can ask whether the incest participant is aware that the behavior is contrary to the law of the land. There may be ignorance of this fact, so the education could be helpful incest prevention.

There is also the possibility that incest participants know that incest is wrong yet choose to sexualize family relationships. For some persons, such violations of values may at times result in withdrawal, depression, psychosomatic symptoms, or severe anxiety. Others deny distress about the love and sexual aspects of their relationship; this occurred when a brother and sister married in Salem, Massachusetts, in 1979. Both asserted that they were adults harming no one, and that their mutual consent deserved recognition.

Incest behavior can also be considered in terms of a choice of alternatives: gaining extra closeness, exclusivity, and sexual pleasure with one relative while perhaps losing personal peace of mind and risking loss of closeness, trust, affection from other family members. The parent who has recurrent incest with a child prefers such sexual opportunities to relating sexually to his or her spouse. The child who has recurrent incest with parent or sibling may lose out on normal psychosociosexual developmental peer contacts.

Academic focus has up to now been mainly on fathers who initiate incest, but these may numerically be a skewed sample owing to the fact that only reported and convicted men have been studied. Brothers, sisters, mothers, grandparents, and uncles may also initiate incest. They seem to be less readily reported and rarely sent to jail.

The initiators of incest may be the least likely to report the incest even incidentally. Usually, in clinical history taking, it is the partner who was approached, not the initiator, who describes the activity. Conscious fear of blame or loss of regard may account for the observation that the initiator remains silent. This impression requires further research.

Parent, child, and family may all become incest casualties upon discovery of incest. Our contemporary struggle to understand and eliminate child abuse has mistakenly launched an overzealous crusade to regard all incest as criminal child abuse. In a minority of cases, rape or coercive noncoital incest presents a crisis of both physical and sexual abuse. But incest may be tender, affectionate, consensual, nonabusive, and noncoital. Full information must first be gathered to avoid premature case closure and police reporting with damage and injustice in situations in which a malicious or capricious false accusation of incest is made.

The family within which incest occurs is rationally the unit of choice for incest education and treatment. A family session is also the best and only place to complete an evaluation of incest to determine the impact upon each member and the family's present equilibrium. Assumptions and speculations are inadequate in evaluation or treatment. The universal need for touching and affection that so many want and so few receive in their birth or rearing families or from their chosen marriage partner must be explored in history taking as a possible factor in the presenting incest case. The fondling and touch described explicitly in the first person may be highly erotic to the clinician who may become anxious and avoid completing the history taking. The same erotic component may arouse staff curiosity. Confidentiality must be respected and professionally protected.

Of significance to professionals is that although most families today continue to avoid thinking about or discussing and teaching the sexual aspects of touching and affection, hoping that incest will go away, there are a few voices *promoting* incest as a final avant-garde of sexual adventure [67, 118]. Expectably, there has been a backlash of attack on this so-called pro-incest lobby. All of this has generated much more heat than light [28].

What is important to note is that an objective academic forum on incest is much needed today, especially with the proliferation of step-families and newly constituted families. All family members must find a way to learn explicitly about desexualized touching, affection, and closeness; the time it takes to build altruistic family relationships; the right of each person to control and protect his or her own body; the age of sexual consent; protection from exploitation, even within the family; lawful and prohibited marriage partners; special understanding of step-kinships; and the limits of normal sibling sex exploration and play that may quite naturally yet illegally continue into recurrent incestuous activity. Such explicit communication may seem cumbersome, mechanical, or impossible as noted on paper. In practice it need certainly not be so. The comfort of each parent at home and each professional in a therapy situation will determine the comfort of each family member in discussing incest in the depth needed to understand, prevent, or reverse it.

5

HOW INCEST CASES PRESENT

HOW does a case of incest come to professional attention? Usually in one of three ways: in crisis, incidentally, or by a specific search as part of academic research, journalism, or other investigation. Incest crises present because of pregnancy or physical or emotional distress. Incidental incest presentations occur during history taking or discussions. A specific search for persons who experienced incest is made through a sociological survey or an advertisement in the media for persons with either positive or negative experiences with incest.

INCEST PRESENTING IN CRISIS

Most incest crises involve a child or a teenager. Only very occasionally does adult incest become a crisis, and then sometimes the crisis is not in the participant but in the observing other, such as a family member, neighbor, or professional. If a third person discovers or becomes distressed about sexual contact between family members, the outcome varies from silence to telling a parent, a sibling, a teacher, a school nurse, a friend, a neighbor, a school counselor, a social worker, a minister, or the police. Today almost every hospital has a child abuse hot line that persons can phone to report suspected or actual cases of sexual abuse and be directed to the nearest helping facility. If there is physical damage or a concern about pregnancy, the young person is usually brought to a family doctor, a pediatrician, or the emergency room of a hospital. The police may or may not be told [54].

The child partner in an incest case may tell someone when he or she experiences confusion, pain, fear, shame, guilt, depression, physical harm, or pregnancy awareness. When the child no longer responds to the adult incest partner's reassurance, injunction to secrecy, or threats (which at first may have maintained secrecy), then the child partner may tell someone. The adult to whom the incest is reported usually perceives a crisis of child protection. Professional or police help may be sought. Private citizens may report suspected incest involving a minor to a school principal or teacher or anonymously call the local child service agency, which will commence investigations immediately. If there is a report of a threat to the child's life or concern that the incest family may leave the area and be lost to follow-up, child abuse laws provide for instituting emergency investigation in the home. Otherwise, each incest report must by law be investigated within 24 hours.

A concerned person may avoid the law enforcement bureaucracy for a variety of reasons. Shame, protecting the family name, financial concern if a father is accused or arrested, and fear of retaliation to child or the reporting person are all possible barriers; there may also be some doubt as to the accuracy of uncorroborated allegations. Also there may be ignorance of the law or knowledge of the demoralizing reality of the long-drawn-out, stressful repetitive cross-questioning of the child by the bureaucracy.

Professionals in most states are under legal obligation to report when they have reasonable cause to believe there has been physical or sexual abuse. In Illinois, the Division of Child and Family Services (DCFS) has the charge to follow up on the reporter's belief that there is sexual abuse by immediate investigation. Objective evidence that such abuse has indeed occurred is then to be obtained.

In long-standing adult-child coital incest there may be no crisis for the child unless there are changes, for example, the occurrence of forceful rather than consensual entry with resultant genital or anal bleeding or pain, or cessation of menstrual periods. For the adult incest partner, there may have been stresses such as a job loss or alcohol or drug excess that increased sexual demands and lowered sexual controls to cause such sudden progression from fondling to force. There is also the possibility between the incest partners of conflict, broken promises, deceit, threats, fear, anger, and violence. Help may then be sought by the injured partner. This immediately and often permanently changes the previously private, exclusive, dyadic incest relationship.

When there is a crisis of pregnancy or physical injury, a physician is usually the first professional sought. When there is emotional trauma, a psychiatric evaluation is requested, usually after a physical examination is done. It is rare that the psychiatrist is seen first. At times the incest is secreted within the family for many months or even years—a case of "everybody knows but nobody says."

In some cases, a child incest partner may tell a parent or guardian about the first incest contact and be met with disbelief, an angry accusation of lying or having malicious intent to destroy the marriage, and an injunction not to mention the subject again. Sometimes the child incest partner is yelled at or slapped. Then the incest may continue unless the child is resourceful enough to protect herself or himself by telling someone outside the family.

CASE 5-1. One pattern of a crisis presentation of incest is outlined in this case. The patient's natural mother was alcoholic, and her natural father was a drug addict. They divorced when she was two years old. She had an older brother and a twin brother. Her mother had remarried and was pregnant when the drunken stepfather raped the girl at age 4 years. Her mother found her bleeding and took her to a hospital emergency room for vaginal repair. At this time the DCFS was called by the hospital rape team social worker. In this case, the adult-child affinity rape incest was also violent child abuse with a physical diagnosis of vaginal lacerations and a psychiatric diagnosis of withdrawal or avoidant reaction. All three children were taken into protective custody by the DCFS and separately placed in foster homes. The patient's twin brother had healing fractures of both ulnas received in a beating from their natural mother. Allegedly she was later declared an unfit parent. It is unknown what happened to the stepfather.

After two years in four different foster homes, the patient was cleared for adoption. She was taken on a trial pre-adoption placement at age 6 by a couple in their early 30s and unable to have more children. They had one natural son a year older than she. The adoptive father was college educated and the adoptive mother worked part-time as a computer operator. Initially for two weeks it was a stormy adjustment, with negativistic, challenging behavior on the part of the girl as she tested to see whether this fifth new family really meant to keep her permanently.

The adoptive family was quite unprepared and courageous in risking the task of rearing the patient from the age of 6 years without much knowledge of her early formative experiences. She is reported by both adoptive parents (after the first stormy weeks) to have been pleasantly cooperative for the trial period of six months, until the court appearance of the family to sign the final adoption papers. In the judge's chambers she asked, "Is this forever?" The adoptive mother said, "From that moment, even in the car on the way home, she started to demand and argue and mimic what I said. For a year she nearly drove us crazy! I myself was a rebellious kid and maybe that is why it was even harder for me, but the power struggle was terrible. I know she was a battered child. We don't spank anyway, but often she nearly drove us to it."

A social worker was voluntarily approached for family counseling, which brought about little change in the negative behavior. Then, at age 7 years, the patient started sexual exploration and play with her adoptive brother aged 8 years. He was a follower and a pleaser, and the girl threatened she would not play with him if he "told." He complied and kept their secret for some weeks but was overcome by anxiety and guilt and finally told his mother. She reacted with panic. Later she could say that the panic related to (1) her own restrictive Baptist rearing, (2) ignorance about normal childhood sex play, (3) terror about the girl's "sexually contaminating" her own 8-year-old son, (4) anger at the daily conflict over "everything" with the girl and now this was "the end," (5) the feeling that the adoption was a big mistake and a wish to undo it, and (6) worry that she was harboring a prostitute.

General family upheaval, yelling, and tears followed the boy's disclosure of the sex play. He loved his adoptive sister (as she did him) and was agonized that his confession not only did not relieve his anxiety, but brought an open threat by his parents of "getting rid" of her and a retaliatory response from her: "I hate all of you. I want to leave." This made the boy even more upset.

Then began a painful six-month attempt to get in touch with the adoption agency (1000 miles away in another state) to ask them to take the girl back. The agency caseworker assigned to them had left two years before. Long-distance calls brought no information. The family then went to a local private child agency who assigned them a caseworker to collect data. Miles of words, many weeks, reams of paper, and no less than 31 professionals were involved in this case. The parents' expectation of adoption reversal was given support, without legal consultation, by the caseworker's attempts to have the DCFS assume custody of the girl. That could not be done without a court order, a long procedure.

Meanwhile, in the adoptive home, there was total emotional withdrawal from the 7½-year-old child. She maintained a tough, angry silence. Touch was forbidden between the two children. "Somehow I just couldn't get rid of the thought that she looked like a prostitute," said the adoptive mother later. The girl became severely withdrawn. She ate (in silence) but had sleep problems. "I would check on her at night and there she lay with her eyes wide open." She refused to play with her adoptive brother or other children or to work at school.

Eventually she was brought to a psychiatric clinic for an emergency evaluation for depression and a perceived suicide attempt (her mother said that she had wrapped the chain of a swing around her neck). There were no marks or bruises upon examination. Her mother came prepared with a large suitcase with all the girl's clothes and toys, saying the child was a danger to herself. She was hospitalized in a closed mixed psychiatric unit in a general university hospital. For four weeks, the adoptive parents refused to call or to visit, saying, "We've said our good-byes." They now hoped to "unadopt" her through the agency and the courts and return her to the foster home circuit. This fortunately did not occur.

Observation of the patient on the psychiatry unit showed a healthy, chubby, freckled, selectively friendly 7½-year-old. She was quite able to perform at the second grade level; she read at the third grade level. Schoolwork, however, had sharply declined in the past six months (from the time of the family's threat to send her away), and the school had suggested she be kept in first grade because of her apathy. In the hospital, she at first refused to talk about her experiences between ages 4 and 6. She did not know she was a twin, nor what the word meant. She knew all the names of her consanguineous and affinity relatives and explained at amazing length who was who. On occasion she would describe her natural mother as pretty, then quickly say "I don't want to talk about it" or "I'm not going to say." "Don't talk about yukky things" she would say when the therapeutic hour was directed to sex education, using paper doll cutouts of boys and girls. She clearly remembered her stepfather and his drinking and the rape. She refused to talk about the first hospitalization or the many foster homes. "I'm not talking today" was a favorite response. However, the ploy of a tape recorder in therapy had her at least listen to the therapist, and sometimes she would respond or sing. She seemed to welcome the replay, which she could control by pressing the buttons.

She was neat; self-sufficient about her clothes, hygiene, toilet, and food; business-like; self-willed; not at all seductive; selectively guarded or open or cooperative; and appropriately careful to avoid adult psychotic patients and seek staff. She was "Little Miss Helpful" to old, senile, and wheelchair patients. Only twice in four weeks did she cry. Once it was a mixture of anger and relief. The second crying episode was in sadness when I spoke of her adoptive home and adoptive brother. She was an interesting child.

A program was set up for her on the psychiatric ward: schoolwork, limit setting, and earned privileges. Adjustment was a week-by-week effort owing to the DCFS's delayed communications and the adoptive family's standoff. No long-range planning could be done because of the family's ongoing efforts to cancel the adoption. The child agency social worker said that the girl was in the difficult-to-place category because of her past history of affinity adult-child rape incest. It was as if within the system of child care the three-letter word *sex* was branded upon the girl. One day the worker called to say that they had a very special foster couple in a rural area whom they would approach. The next day I was told, "Sorry, they would, but they have an 11-year-old boy and couldn't risk or handle sex problems."

Finally, after four weeks, there was some resolution. In a special court hearing for annulment of the legal adoption, the adoptive parents were told "in no uncertain terms" by a State's attorney that this was not legally possible: "She is your child in the eyes of the law, as much as if she were born to you." Furthermore, the State's attorney allegedly told the parents that the courts take guardianship of a child from parents only in cases of severe physical child abuse, since the cost to taxpayers for maintenance of child placement in 1980 was $35,000 per year.

The chastened adoptive parents were then, with assistance, able to become re-engaged with the girl. Both parents seemed ready and relieved to do so. The girl was extremely hesitant at first. However, she began to giggle as soon as she saw her adoptive brother. They were essentially good friends, and he really had missed her. Intensive daily family therapy was done with the four. This incorporated open, explicit sex education and discussion of sex play and the difference between affection and needed desexualized touch. A few times we talked about the meaning of adoption: that it was, like marriage, "for better or for worse." Sometimes people want to divorce. Sometimes adoptive parents want to give back their child, but they find this is too difficult. Her adoptive parents had now changed their minds and wanted her back home. The child's depression lifted. She earned a home visit. There was some expectable normal anxiety for all four persons in the family about "what now?"

A week later, the patient was discharged from the hospital. There was a five-week testing period, with some recurrent negative behavior that was dealt with at home by open recognition: "You're angry. That's OK. When you get over it we'll talk." And they did. The mother would call for support and advice. Family therapy continued for six weeks; then finally all of them settled into a comfortable adjustment with an occasional phone call in time of doubt. The suggested first grade holdback did not occur, and school became an area of achievement. The adoptive father is a quiet, gentle, and concerned man who is supportive without being threatening. Both parents are aware that the girl is the dominant child, but the older brother is learning to assert himself.

Will there be problems later for the patient? Of course there may be. She is understandably sensitive but has strengths to overcome the many hurts, separations, and losses that have forged her little life thus far. Puberty may represent a special stress, as may the ups and downs of dating and losing idealized friendships and teachers. We will have to wait in the wings to see the long-term outcome and be available in times of high stress.

CASE 5-2. A different crisis presentation was the case of a plump, pretty 8-year-old girl brought by a school social worker and the girl's mother for a hospital emergency room child abuse evaluation. A friend of the girl had spontaneously told a school social worker that the girl's "daddy took his clothes off, lay on top of us, and put his thing between our legs." On inquiry, the patient quite openly said, "Yes, he lies on top of us and gives us candy and he always wants me to bring [two other friends] home." This allegedly had gone on for almost 12 months. The girl's mother was called in by the school. She was quietly cooperative, but said she could not afford to lose work hours since hers was the only family income now. She worked the night shift while her husband watched the two children. It was a second marriage for her and a fifth for her husband, the natural father of the patient and her 2-year-old sister who had not yet been sexually approached by him.

The history emerged from the mother that before this marriage, her husband had had two convictions in other states for child molesting plus a number of nonprosecuted complaints against him for the same charge since he was 17 years old. He was now 39 years old but looked 49. He had worked in a factory job for the 10 years of this marriage, experiencing the most stable adjustment of his life. Since her last pregnancy, the patient's mother had withdrawn from her husband sexually. They were not openly affectionate with each other. She talked little about her first marriage, birth, or family. She was 5 years older than her husband. A year before, when he had lost his job, she began to work nights. She was a tired woman, concerned but not visibly distressed at this sexual report. She at first did not believe the accusation of sexual contact with her daughter and only did so after her husband's confession in the emergency room. Her reaction was stolid silence. The girl had not told her mother. Later the mother said, "Yes, she always has been Daddy's girl." She was also his first child and sat on his lap as often as possible. The mother viewed her husband as a good father and husband upset at his recent job loss. He did not drink, nor was he abusive. Both were from rural areas and neither had completed high school.

This was clearly a case of consanguineous noncoital adult-child noncoercive pedophilic incest. There was no evidence of physical injury. The hymen of the girl was intact. She was conveniently available (as were her little friends) at a time of stress (his job loss and discontinuance of marital coitus).

The father came to the hospital at the request of a social worker on the the hospital's child abuse team. At first he denied the charge of sexual abuse; then he broke down, cried, and talked. The pediatric social worker was sensitive and supportive to him, saying it was difficult to ask for help and that here now was an opportunity for him to get help. The resultant emergency court order (obtained by the social worker through the DCFS) ordered him out of the home pending investigation of the case. This was not perceived by the father as help. In panic, he made a suicide attempt that same night, using over-the-counter sleeping pills. He was taken to the emergency room of another hospital, treated by having his stomach pumped out, and released. The court then recommended psychiatric treatment for him.

There were severe financial problems, and his wife's job provided very restricted hospital insurance coverage. He was unskilled and had not for a year been able to get a job. Before marriage, he admitted to his present wife his long-standing compulsion to fondle children of both sexes (there was no coitus with any of them). His previous marriages all ended when his pedophilic activities came to light. This present marriage seemed stable. He thought that after the birth of their first child (the patient) that his pedophilic compulsion was gone. At that time, he was working 14 hours a day.

His wife was a quiet, nondemanding woman. They respected each other, had intercourse once a week, and she accepted him although she knew of the pedophilia. She decided to stop having intercourse because she didn't want a third child. No contraceptive options were even discussed. They could not talk about sex. At the same time the patient was an extremely affectionate and active little girl very partial to her father. The mother and the second child seemed to pair off. Then he lost his job. The mother went to work nights while the unemployed father was left to babysit.

His old drive to seek solace and excitement from touching a child's genitals surfaced again (after about seven years of remission, he said). He stated that he was feeling depressed. He was gentle with his daughter, and she was not upset by his fondling her generally and genitally in the shower. As months went by and he couldn't get a job, he wanted variety and asked her to bring two younger neighbor girl friends into the house. He wrestled with them on the floor and fondled their genitals. He denied being nude himself or undressing the girls. Later one girl friend told the teacher, the school social worker, the principal, her own parents, the DCFS worker, and the patient's mother.

After her friend's report, the patient had (at the very least) twenty occasions of cross-questioning in the hospital from emergency room staff, nurses, the pediatric resident, the social worker, the pediatrician, medical students, and ward nurses on the pediatrics unit. Then there was a transfer to a psychiatry floor. There an explicit history included questions like "Why are you here? Did your father hurt you? Did he touch you? Did it feel good? Did he lie on top of you? Did he take your clothes off? Did he take his clothes off? How long has this been going on? Did your little sister join in the game? Did mother know? How come you didn't tell Mommy?"

The hospital routine was frightening to this physically healthy child because of (1) separation from home and family, (2) the endless leading questions, (3) being told her father was in another hospital (after his suicide attempt), and (4) the power of her evidence to affect her father and the family. Of course at age 8 she had no way of knowing the possible consequences of her report. Stressful and necessary as an explicit history is, it must not overemphasize the sexual aspect of the behavior without assisting the child to understand the following: (1) Her father's choice of a minor child (her friend) or herself (a daughter) for sex play is not appropriate. (2) In the family, sex is between father and mother. (3) Sex organs are very private, and even as a child she has a right to say no. (4) Her father is a good person, but his behavior is confused between affection and sexual feelings and therefore is unacceptable, wrong, and against the law. (5) Grown-ups should know better, and this was her father's responsibility. (6) Now that she knows all this, it is her responsibility to avoid sexual contact with her father. If it happens again she must tell her mother, the school social worker, or her teacher.

In retrospect, it may have been better to tape-record the girl's second report for reuse by the family and concerned professionals. This would have prevented overemphasis by endless repetition; possible anxiety, self-blame, and guilt for consequences; and real fear about what would occur next. All too frequently, informed professional reassurance is difficult in these circumstances, because the child and family await a court order. The outcome is only sometimes influenced by professional recommendations, and inaccurate predictions may be perceived as double-crossing at worst or with hostility at best. Better to state there is no way to predict what the court order will say.

In practice, family and health care professionals are effectively hostages to the court system, while the child, defined as the patient, is hospitalized at a cost of almost $2500 per week, an incredible burden for a family or to a hospital when there is limited or no health insurance, contested custody, and the family cannot pay the bill.

During 14 days in the hospital the patient showed minimal symptoms. She was affectionate and manipulative but accepted limits. Except for constantly saying she wanted to go home, she was cooperative and seemed energetic but not overactive. She was an average 8-year-old, quite at ease for her two-week observation in the hospital. Her father visited, as did her mother. She sat on their laps and talked to them a great deal. Both parents were quiet, inarticulate people. The girl was an average student, helpful at home, normally rivalrous with her 2-year-old sister, and well liked by the neighbors, as was the family. The father was seen for a few visits alone for his reactive depression. He was placed on one year's court probation. Mother and father were seen together a few times. The mother agreed to change to the day shift. Contraception and restoration of their sex life was discussed with them, and both seemed to understand the importance of appropriate sexual expression.

Shortly after discharge, the father got a job, so mother and daughter were seen by a psychiatrist. Their relationship improved, but numerous appointments were cancelled by the mother, claiming cost and inconvenience. They finally arranged to have family therapy through the probation division of their local police. Five months later we received another crisis call from the DCFS to see the girl. This time it was for physical abuse. She had some arm bruises. She denied that her father or mother beat her. Investigation is in process. This case shows the value (to the child at least) of ongoing collaboration between legal and health services—albeit tedious, time-consuming, and very expensive—when minors are in need of observation and possibly of protection.

A very large network of helping professionals becomes involved with crisis presentations of incest: emergency room nurses and physicians; pediatricians, gynecologists, residents, students; the hospital's child abuse team, which comprises numerous social workers and supervisors familiar with the legal element; a psychiatry unit, which includes a team of nurses, medical students, psychiatry residents, mental health workers, and at least two psychiatrists; plus school, child service agency, police, and probation officers. This is an enormous and complex group. An inordinate amount of time is required to coordinate all of the institutional efforts and financial responsibility for the high hospital costs.

Problems of pedophilia are usually long-standing and difficult to treat except temporarily by prison containment. The use of female hormones to reduce sexual drives and attempted aversion behavior therapy are controversial and not curative. Individual psychotherapy offers very little promise for control of this compulsive behavior. Family therapy alerts the whole family to the problem, and marital therapy attempts to encourage appropriate sexual expression between a couple in the hope that inappropriate child partners will be given up. In the second case, it seemed as if an accepting marital relationship, a stable home, plus aging may have been factors in the father's alleged temporary remission. The future may be stormy for all involved with this girl and her family. Her father's pedophilia is unlikely to stop spontaneously.

Both cases of incest crisis presented in a metropolitan university hospital emergency room. In rural or urban areas, family physicians would be more likely to deal with such incest crises. Family doctors say crisis cases present when a girl is brought for a pregnancy test and "she and her mother are silent when I ask who the father is. When they're really tight-lipped and I ask a second time, then I know it's a family member." What then? If the girl is physically intact without evidence of physical abuse, there is little the physician can do besides the requested examination and pregnancy test. It is the right of the mother and the girl to be silent. It may be worthwhile for the physician to ask to speak to each separately and confidentially for a few minutes. If the mother refuses to allow this (this is her privilege as natural and legal guardian of her minor child), it may be of help to reassure her that the doctor is on their side and wants to help the family. The doctor may then ask, "Is the father of the baby in the home? Brother, uncle, grandfather, daddy?" It may be a relief to have the doctor understand. He or she may then say, "Are you afraid he will hurt you if you tell?" If the answer is yes, then the physician must gently tell the mother, "Then it is your duty and mine to protect the girl and help your son (brother, father, husband) to get counseling."

This is difficult and complex. However, certain aspects of medical practice are complex and difficult, but must nevertheless be done, in spite of the expectable very great time expenditure. With or without physical damage or child abuse, crisis presentation of incest takes extra time, a great deal of extra time, which must be anticipated and allowed for by some schedule rearrangement. Without this planning, an easier course will be professional avoidance. The pain is great, the remuneration about nil in some instances. Professional integrity is perhaps the only reward when there is a real need for intervention and help.

Thinking about and discussing family sex causes quite normal tension and discomfort in the professional himself or herself. Instant recoil and a tendency to handle the incest by avoidance—giving superficial medical care with no explicit questions, no follow-up appointments, and no calls for broken appointments—all too often may be the easiest and most frequent approach to incest management in medical, court, and counseling practice.

If an incest case presents with a crisis of physical injury, minors must be treated in the same way a rape victim is treated: with reassurance, respect, privacy, careful repair, collection of sperm and other samples for forensic inspection, and VDRL and pregnancy tests [133]. Then, if possible, a tape-recorded history from child and parent or adult could be made as soon as is humane and feasible. Boys as well as girls may present with a crisis of rape incest, and a similar approach must be taken. Child protection laws must be invoked. Attacking the rapist is not enough. Picking up the pieces includes working with all family "survivors"—rape victims and other family members who are victims of shame and rage. Adaptation may be assisted by a few crisis family therapy sessions, so all may understand what transpired. This way the stress is shared and thus somewhat alleviated.

Another type of crisis presentation of incest occurs when there is accidental or incidental discovery of consensual incest. The discoverer often has a horror reaction, first of recoil, then of legal attack, as was the case in August 1979 when the Pittorinos of Salem, Massachusetts, filed charges against their adoptive daughter Victoria (aged 24) for marrying her newly found natural brother, David Goddu (aged 22). The crisis was not in the couple, but in others. This case was consanguineous consensual adult-adult coital incest.

At times there may be a personal crisis of distress, but long delayed, sometimes 20 years later. Under other life stresses, someone may react with anxiety, panic, or a clinical depression as part of which there may be guilt and self-blame. He or she may then target the incest as the cause of the depression, as did a 50-year-old man who had an agitated depression. He had a business failure, his wife had recently divorced him, and his son was killed in Vietnam. He presented in the emergency room after a suicide attempt, saying, "God is punishing me for sucking off my [twin] brother when we were 12 years old."

INCEST PRESENTING INCIDENTALLY

As part of taking a medical history, a physician asked, "How are things at home?" The doctor was told by a juvenile diabetic that her alcoholic stepfather tried to get into her room to molest her at night and she had the dresser in front of the door and a kitchen knife under her pillow. Her mother, who was brought in by the doctor, disbelieved the 16-year-old girl, saying her second husband was impotent. She told the doctor the girl didn't approve of this marriage and made up stories. The physician later reported, "I didn't know how to handle it. I have a busy diabetic clinic, I had no time. I told the mother to go to Alanon and Alateen. I didn't see them again."

How many such incidental reports are handled in the same way? Would a social work referral have helped, or would the mother have "run away" anyway? The mother was obviously aligning with her new husband in playing down the girl's story. Was this an incest hoax on the part of a hostile teenager? An attempt on the girl's part to get special attention for herself from the young physician and to discredit the drunken stepfather? Or was it true? We will never know. Perhaps a few tactful questions by the physician to the teen alone would have helped: "What do you mean by *molest*? Has he tried in any way to force or hurt you? What part of your body does he touch? How often has this happened? Is he drinking when he does this? Where is your mother at night? Have you told her or anyone else? Does your stepfather have a job? Does he try with your sisters or brother? How do you and your mother get along? How much do you see your natural father? How do you get along with him? What do you think caused the divorce? How does your stepfather get along with your mother? With you? How well do you sleep with this worry on your mind? In there a school counselor to whom you could talk?" All this before talking to the mother, who always must also be seen when a minor is involved.

Another incidental presentation may occur when someone is feeling discouraged and upset and seeks medical or psychiatric care or counseling from a minister, clinic, or private health professional. Then, simply as part of an in-depth personal history, there may be a report of incest experiences in the past. These may or may not relate directly to the present emotional problem [54]. When such material is incidentally presented, it is the task of the evaluating physician, psychiatrist, or other professional to establish (1) whether or not there was conflict or distress at the time the incest occurred, (2) how it was handled then, (3) what residual feelings there are currently about the experience(s), (4) what the present relationship is with the incest partner, and (5) what relationship (if any) the patient thinks there is between the present problem and the past incest experience(s).

Perhaps the most recent form of incidental presentation of incest occurs in clinics and with therapists who now offer "the new sex therapy" to couples or to single patients requesting help with a sexual problem [106]. A first step of sex therapy is a comprehensive history. This includes an explicit history of sexual experiences (positive and negative) from childhood to the present as well as questions about sexual knowledge, attitudes, preferences, fears, fantasies, aversions, and questions. Such a complete sexual history usually includes questions about possible incestuous experiences, eliciting details such as age at occurrence, identity of partner, type of sexual exchange, feelings and outcome at the time, and the person's current view of the experience. The following information emerged from a midwestern urban university medical school sex clinic.

A study of 106 cases of incest presenting incidentally

At Loyola Sexual Dysfunction Training Clinic, over a period of eight and one-half years, 505 couples were treated for a sexual problem in one or both partners. Their average age was 38 years (range: 19–83 years). Often both partners had a sexual problem; however, 22 percent of the individuals seen had no sexual problems but came with a sexually dysfunctional partner (Table 1). The great majority of couples seen were average citizens, well adjusted in their work, who had not received any type of psychiatric help—perhaps 10 to 15 percent had had psychiatric care. Many needed and received marital or relationship therapy as part of the intensive seven-week sex therapy program in a medical school teaching hospital.

Table 1. Incidence of sexual dysfunction
in sex clinic patients with and without history of incest

Group	With Dysfunction		Without Dysfunction	
	No.	Percent	No.	Percent
All patients (n = 1010)	788	78	222	22
Incest-reporting patients (n = 106)	63	59	43	41

Week 1 was a detailed 5-hour personal, medical, social and sexual history taking. One routine question concerned incest.

Trainees, in 15 hours of preliminary didactic workshops, role-played the clinical work so that they would be prepared for the fact that certain history taking, such as hearing details of incest, may cause them some unexpected personal anxiety, which could result in avoidance or judgmental behavior. Still, panic sometimes occurred. While taking a history, a medical student asked about incest. The male patient said, "Yes, with my father . . ." The student stood up in the middle of the sentence and said, "I have to go for supervision now." In supervision he admitted his confusion and apprehension: "I wouldn't know what to do." He was reassured and told to be aware of his recoil, anxiety, avoidance, possible outrage (attack), or even normal arousal (attraction) in listening to the history. Just allowing the patient to tell his story could be relieving, and therefore therapeutic, for him. It then became the task of the female cotherapist to obtain a more explicit incest history. In this case, initially, the neophyte male therapist was far more uncomfortable than the patient. The incest turned out to be genital fondling from the patient's father's brother, a single man in a wheelchair who lived with them on a farm. The uncle was always generous to the patient when his monthly disability check was cashed. They played checkers and he told war stories. No one was told, and there was no negative residue. Uncle died just before the patient left for college. This patient did not have a sexual problem, nor had he had difficulties as a child.

Probably 10 percent of the trainees reported, "I forgot to ask," when a supervisor asked about incest history. It is worth emphasizing again that the comfort of the professional always determines the comfort of the patient. Just as discomfort will prevent asking routine questions about menstrual cramps or constipation, so will it prevent taking a thorough personal and sexual history that includes a question about incest.

In general, because of time pressure medicine is problem-oriented, with an approach of "If it's not a problem, don't tell me." For a sexual history, it is important to elicit any early sexual trauma, such as rape,

Table 2. Types of incest reported by sex clinic patients

Type of incest	Men		Women	
	No.	Percent	No.	Percent
Coital	8	19	3	5
Noncoital	34	81	61	95
Consanguineous	36	86	49	77
Affinity	6	14	15	23
Heterosexual	26	62	57	89
Homosexual	16	38	7	11
Adult-adult	5	12	3	5
Child-child	31	74	41	64
Adult-child	6	14	20	31
With				
sister	18	43	4	6
brother	12	29	35	55
mother	4	10	1	2
father	1	2	5	8
multiple relatives	2	5	4	6
other	5	12	15	23

incest, or discovery of or guilt about masturbation. This is to evaluate whether there is unresolved conflict that may still be an inhibitory block preventing sexual enjoyment. In supervising trainees who took the 106 incest histories, I was impressed that many persons who reported incest experiences did not have sexual symptoms but came with a partner with a sexual problem (Table 1). In the first two years of the sex clinic, reports of incest were not followed up by a special history taking. This was later added. I was struck by the fact that many persons were quite casual and unperturbed by giving their incest history—despite academic statements to the contrary.

In this incidental incest presentation, some interesting figures emerged. Coitus occurred in a minority of incest cases: 3 of the 64 women and 8 of the 42 men (Table 2). Of the three women who reported coital incest, one had adult-adult coital incest with a brother; one, coital incest at 14 years with a new 16-year-old stepbrother; and the third, coital incest at 12 years with her stepfather. Two women had adult-adult oral contact, one with a stepfather, the other with a brother. For the eight men, coitus was as follows: one, child-child and then adult-adult with twin brother; one, child-child with a girl cousin; four, adult-adult with a sister; and two, child-child with a stepsister.

The majority of incest contacts were consensual, child-child, noncoital, and consanguineous (Table 2). Thirty-one of the 42 men and 40 of the 64 women reported child-child contacts (which can be more accurately called sex play or sex exploration). The age breakdown of the child-child contacts for the men was 12 at 10 years or less, 7 at 11 to 13 years, and 12 at 14 to 21 years; for the women the age breakdown was 20 at 10 years or less, 8 at 11 to 13 years, and 12 at 14 to 21 years. With the exception of a report of anal penetration between twins that continued from age 12 to 28, when the reporting twin married, the same-sex contacts for both men and women occurred when they were younger than 13 years, were noncoital, and therefore were in the category of homophilic sex exploration and play.

Table 2 also presents a breakdown of the relationship of the incest partner. The subgroup other included uncle, grandfather, aunt, niece, nephew, and brother-in-law. A small number of both men and women had an incest history of multiple family member contacts—some at separate times and two in a small group setting of mutual sex play as children at a family gathering.

Five men and three women of the 106 reported adult-adult incest contacts, not all of which were coital. Seven of the eight had two to five contacts only, and five of the eight stated that they had harmed no one because both partners had needed sex. Very few (5 of the 106) had told their spouse of the incest experience. Most considered it confidential and not relevant. Interestingly, the five who told did so after the death of the incest partner. Another woman, when asked if she had told her husband of her teenage sexual experiences with her brother, said "Why make trouble between them? It's all over and past."

Although 63 persons in the incest group had a sexual symptom, none stated that the early incest related to their sexual problem. None volunteered the incest history. In one man and three women of the 63, I considered their long-standing lack of sexual interest in their marriage partner psychodynamically related to (1) guilt regarding the incest, (2) denied longing for the early sexual arousal experience and partner, or (3) traumatic discovery and being beaten and repeatedly blamed for the sexual (not the prohibited consanguinity) aspect of the incest contact.

A comparison of sexual symptoms between the total sex clinic patient population and the incest subgroup (Table 3) shows no major differences. The number of cases of incest is small (106 of 1010 or 10.5%); however, of this group, 43 percent of the men and 39 percent of the women had no sexual problems but came to the Loyola Sex Clinic because of a partner who had a sexual problem.

CASE 5-3. A 42-year-old woman came to the sex clinic with sexual disinterest. She did not refuse her husband, but was not aroused sexually, refused his manual touch below the waist, and had never masturbated. Her story was extremely complex. Her father had died when she was 2 years old. Her mother became an alcoholic, had a number of illegitimate children, and was profitably promiscuous. When the patient was 5 years old, her mother's brother, who was a "strange sort of rover," undressed her, sat her

Table 3. Reported sexual symptoms of sex clinic
patients with and without history of incest

Symptom	Incest Group		Total Group	
	No.	Percent	No.	Percent
Men	42	100	505	100
No symptom	18	43	102	20
Secondary impotence	11	26	156	31
Sexual disinterest	5	12	86	17
Premature ejaculation and secondary impotence	4	10	40	8
Premature ejaculation	2	5	111	22
Primary impotence	2	5	10	2
Women	64	100	505	100
No symptom	25	39	120	24
Secondary anorgasmia	19	30	147	29
Primary anorgasmia	8	13	101	20
Sexual disinterest	9	13	106	21
Vaginismus	3	5	31	6

on the side of the bed, and began to play with her genitalia. He was gentle, she enjoyed the contact, and he offered her money to do this again. Her older brother walked into the room, saw the exchange, and rushed out to tell the parents. "All I remember was the fighting and the shouting. My mother was screaming, and my stepfather hit Uncle Eddie. I was terribly frightened and thought I caused it. It wasn't the sex, it was the fighting that scared me. My mother yelled at me, 'Don't ever let anyone touch you down there!' and kept saying that over and over for years. I didn't even touch myself after that except to wash, and I had these terrible nightmares about snakes, nothing special, just snakes. Now they're gone, since the sex clinic."

A previous therapist, who had not obtained the history of the incest episode, had presumed that her aversion to sexual arousal was caused by negative identification with her mother and suggested that she repeat twice daily, "My mother was a whore!" She said she did this for weeks, "But it did nothing. Besides, I loved my mother. She couldn't help her life."

In an open letter to the dead Uncle Eddie, the patient wrote: "You're a sick man, you should have been put away years ago [adult perspective]. . . . I was too small to really know better" (absolving herself of blame, since she was 5 years old at the time). She warned she might kill him if she knew he was still doing this to children, then said, "No, I don't mean that, because I can understand your sick mind" (forgiveness?), and ended, "Don't bother my thoughts again, because if you do, I'm ready this time to handle it all. . . . Your niece, . . ." [132].

This was one case where the para-incest turmoil and subsequent maternal injunctions related to the patient's long-standing block regarding her natural sexual desires. Her husbnad, who was considerate and loving, supported her attempt to overcome her early "negative programming." Had it not been for his altruistic concern for her sexual pleasure, she would never have sought help. He was the one who suggested that relief or release from disinterest was possible. And he was right.

SPECIFIC INCEST SEARCH

Within the past few years, the theme of incest has appeared in numerous books, masters' and doctoral theses, lay and professional articles, and media features. Sometimes the author openly admits being an incest victim herself and therefore undertaking the study of incest as a personal odyssey [8, 44].

The search for book or feature material may take the form of advertising in newspapers and periodicals for women (usually) who have had incest experiences. Radio talk shows have invited similar calls. Occasionally, researcher bias is clearly advertised: "Wanted: 100 women who have had positive incest experiences."

More objective is a literature search or a review of available patient records or court histories to study the incidence of, prevalence of, reactions to, and outcome of incest [54]. Between retrospective search and active research on ongoing incest behavior is an enormous contemporary block—the current criminal status of incest. The National Center on Child Abuse regards not only intercourse, but "any act" as intrafamily sexual abuse. This imposes a presumption that abuse or victimization, and therefore a crime that requires reporting, has occurred. The latter will alter the family, as may field studies, but honest research will make note of this.

Scientific ignorance about the incests remains because we have a paucity of longitudinal studies. Untested theories of minimal clinical help abound. Specific ongoing follow-up studies are needed of incestuous families treated clinically in various ways, of untreated families, and of families handled by criminal court. These must then be contrasted with nonincestuous families.

6

TREATMENT OF INCEST:
PHASE ONE

T H E clinical setting is remarkably different for incest cases that present in crisis and those that come to attention incidentally. Volunteers who are specially sought out to give personal information about incest are usually adults not in need of treatment. Professional management of each incest case does, however, show important similarities in the approach, philosophy, and personal reactions of each professional: teacher, minister, family physician, gynecologist, pediatrician, psychiatrist, health care worker, policeman, judge, or other. Although techniques of incest treatment ideally require the same basic principles, actual practice may vary in the intensity of professional involvement or avoidance, governed at times by the less-than-conscious internal emotional responses of each professional helper.

REPORTING ISSUES

In conventional medicine, treatment presupposes that a patient in distress approaches a doctor and requests (and waits for) relief or healing. The word *doctor* means both healer and teacher in its ancient roots. In the modern, literate West, all persons (except minors and those incapacitated by accidents) internally define for themselves that they are in distress or sick and find their way voluntarily to a physician or alternative helping resource.

Today, the health care system has expanded to include nurses, social workers, psychologists, counselors, probation officers, teachers, and ministers. Any of these persons may be the first professional to learn of incest-related problems and may therefore have to evaluate the situation. Referral to a physician may or may not occur. Under present Illinois child abuse laws, if a minor is involved beyond reasonable doubt even noncoitally in sexualized family contact, the health care worker has no option but to report this to the Division of Child and Family Services (DCFS).

It has been argued that because incest is grossly underreported it is better to overreport, i.e., report all suspicious cases. There is not a single follow-up study available on the social and individual effects of wrongfully accusing a family of incest. Nor are there statistics on how many reports of incest are thoroughly investigated and found correct or incorrect, so that it may be determined whether overreporting of incest actually occurs. Such figures should be reported annually to give a coherent understanding of the extent of incest as a social problem. The incest behavior (e.g., child-child, coital or noncoital) must be clearly defined in official statistics on substantiated incest reports, with the number of each specific type case given with due regard for confidentiality.

The patient-doctor relationship differs from that between a patient and any other health professional. A doctor is legally protected from mandatory reporting laws by the same special privileges of confidentiality as those between priest and penitent or lawyer and client. Therefore, a physician has the option not to involve legal machinery in incest cases. For an adult, only a court order may demand a doctor's confidential information. For a minor, a parent or legal guardian may also obtain such information. Either may cause a true dilemma for the physician.

If a priest hears *in the confessional* of adult-child incest, this information is similarly privileged and confidential. However, if the same priest works as a counselor, such information may have to be reported in Illinois under the Child Abuse Reporting Act. A lawyer as a neighbor or Big Brother is bound similarly to report incest but is protected if he has an incest partner as a client.

CLINICAL PRESENTATION OF INCEST

Crisis presentations
It is unusual that physicians or emergency rooms are used frivolously. It is the physician's task to establish why medical treatment is sought. A teacher, school nurse, or social worker may have been concerned that forcible rape had transpired in a family and therefore have convinced the mother to take her daughter to a hospital. The doctor in the emergency room is likely to call a pediatrician or a gynecologist to talk to the mother and, with parental consent, examine the girl.

If a parent refuses to cooperate with the school's suggestion to see a doctor, the school authority may then call upon the courts, who then may define the case as a child abuse crisis in need of emergency health care. Although incest may have continued for years, a midnight crisis presentation in an emergency room is not unusual in adult-child incest cases because an immediate medical exam plus a subsequent psychiatric and social work evaluation are legally required.

Discovery of adult-child incest may be accidental and the child not nearly as emotionally distressed as the adults who report it. On the other hand, incest may be reported by a very upset child to someone outside the family. Professional and legal concern, following the spirit of child abuse laws, is to protect the minor and prevent the recurrence of child abuse. However, implementation of the laws in incest cases may be a severe and recurrent trauma for the child. The devastation may be more extensive when a report of incest is not accurate.

When there is a report in the classroom of incest at home, the task for a teacher, school nurse, or social worker is to speak to a supervisor or principal, who will then call the parents in. The next step will probably be involvement of the local child service agency. It should be explained to the family that current laws mandate such reporting if adult-child sexual contact has occurred. Every possible personal support and encouragement should be given to the family and to the child if the adult admits such contact or if there is reason to believe that the child's report is accurate and in need of follow-up. This help from the school system can make all the difference between a traumatic and a therapeutic intervention or referral. Accepting the persons—child and family—is different from condoning their behavior problem.

Not all incest crises reach physicians through legal channels. A family crisis may occur when an incest pregnancy is suspected and a physician is sought privately or in a clinic. A family is an entity of itself, fiercely protected by its component members. Questions to a girl or her parent about who the father is may be met with silence. Suspicion is not fact. Someone other than a family member may be the father. Ongoing health care is primary. Within a trusting doctor-patient relationship, more history may emerge later.

As a professional protected by confidentiality laws yet also bound by law to report actual or suspected cases of child abuse or incest, the physician's role of confidant becomes blurred and difficult. Report a suspicion and lose the patient to care and the family to possible later help? Ideally, doctors will try to do both—give physical care plus persuade the family to get family counseling under the state's child services. Later, if it is admitted that this is an incest pregnancy, court supervision may be sought. Between ideal and real management may be a great gap. Nonetheless, each physician must responsibly do his or her best.

In Illinois, the nurse attending a child involved in coital incest is not bound by the doctor-patient privilege and is mandated to call in the hospital child abuse team (if any) or the DCFS. This report may set up tension between the nurse and physician, or the physician may be relieved that a report was made. These are all unpleasant and complicated realities resulting from the current criminal status of incest. Health care professionals thereby become willingly or unwillingly linked with the penal system and may be seen by some or all members of the family as adversaries rather than allies. Patience, time, and testing are preliminaries to their finally establishing a therapeutic alliance of trust.

Sometimes a crisis may occur in an adult who had been functioning without problems. This may be triggered quite dramatically by a stimulus such as a movie, television program, book, or class dealing with incest. Old memories or conflicts regarding family sex (coital or noncoital) may then surface and cause an intense emotional reaction.

CASE 6-1. The death of his mother allowed a successful 31-year-old business man to break down and tell his wife of his many years of mixed emotions toward his mother, who had insisted on bathing him until he was 12 or 13. She would always stimulate him under the pretext of good penile hygiene. Sometimes he would ejaculate and she would laugh but he was humiliated. On his own, he began to shower at school to avoid the bathing ritual at home. However, when he masturbated, he would think of his mother stimulating him, which made him upset and guilty. His father had deserted the family when the patient was 4 years old. The patient's only half sister was 15 years older and was out of the home from the age of 17. He felt sorry for his mother, who was attentive and generous toward him but socially isolated. She worked (up to her death) as a night nurse supervisor.

The man's wife became quite upset at hearing his story of semiconsensual noncoital mother-son incest and persuaded him to make an emergency appointment with a psychiatrist. He agreed, and the wife went with him. They might have chosen a psychologist, minister, or counselor. It was quite clear that he was protective of his mother. For years he had understood the loneliness and sexual neediness that had driven her to sexualize her affection for him. He grieved over her death but was close enough to his wife to share the sexual history now that there was no risk of shame or confrontation between the two valued women in his life. A few visits with the psychiatrist allowed both husband and wife to obtain perspective and deal with the incest crisis. No legal or other health services were indicated.

For any incest crisis, the traditional medical model is both useful and essential, since it provides a structured, logical, and thorough therapeutic approach:

1. Clearly delineate the chief complaint.
2. Take an explicit sexual history of the incest: circumstances, recurrence, responses, etc.
3. Record the history of both or all incest participants as well as of other family members.
4. Assess the mental status of each incest partner.
5. Determine why incest was used for interpersonal expression by some members of this family.
6. Explore and record the strengths and weaknesses of each partner and of the family.

7. Do a careful physical examination if a child is involved or if illness at any age is suspected.
8. Discuss diagnostic possibilities with the nominative patient(s).
9. Give patient and family an idea of immediate, intermediate, or long-term treatment plans, which should be flexible and reassessed regularly.

The goals in incest treatment are to protect those family members in need of protection, to enhance the growth of each family member while ensuring the integrity of the family, and to encourage their continued involvement so that long-term follow-up may be provided. Family therapy is therefore indispensable. This usually involves a collaboration of the school, the therapist, a social worker, and a legal supervisor—probation officer or child service agency caseworker if a minor is involved.

Health care workers who may be the first professionals to see incest cases in a crisis presentation can follow almost all of the same general principles and refer a patient and family members to a doctor as needed for a physical examination or a psychiatric evaluation. Detailed gathering of explicit information is essential to understanding and treating incest participants and their family. Techniques will be discussed in a later section.

Incidental presentations

Incidentally some cases of incest may need no treatment at all. When the history emerges factually without distress as part of an explicit, detailed personal sexual history, no more than noncondemnatory listening may be called for. This in itself is regarded as acceptance of the person and may enhance a professional or personal relationship. If the incest is still occurring and is adult-adult and consensual, no mandatory reporting laws apply in Illinois (nor in most states) for any health professional. However, reporting to the police by distressed persons will be accepted and duly investigated for infringement of state incest laws.

If an incidental report of adult-adult incest (retrospective or current) suddenly causes patient distress when volunteered, further professional dialogue is indicated (1) to understand why it surfaces now, (2) to resolve residual distress, (3) to change current incest behavior if so desired, and (4) to refer for individual psychotherapy if needed. If an incidental incest report is made by a child, child abuse laws apply in Illinois and many other states, so parents must be seen and told of the Mandate to Report Law.

Civic and professional responsibility require accuracy and completeness of each incest evaluation, protection of the human dignity and the right to privacy of each family member, constructive protection of a minor (when needed), and nondestruction of the essential nurturing family unit of that same minor. These tasks are complex and may seem impossible. An important mandate for the law as well as for all health care professionals is to help without undue harm to the child or to other members of the family unit. This is much more easily said than done.

Personal reactions of health care professionals to incest

Since the comfort of the professional determines the comfort of the patient, it is important for each helper to understand the normal responses and attitudes within the self when incest presents. Attitudes are a blend of beliefs and emotions that influence everyday behavior in all persons at any age. Emotional and behavioral reactions to incest may show a wide range and may fluctuate within minutes or months as incest is dealt with clinically and in depth. Awareness is a key to growth for all. Professional skill, confidence, and comfort will result from academic knowledge about the incests plus actual clinical practice in dealing with a number of incest cases over some years.

Entry into any new situation is accompanied by some expectable, normal anxiety about unknowns and personal adequacy and competence. Similar entry anxiety is noted by Peace Corps Volunteers arriving in a foreign land and by medical, nursing, counseling, social work, and other health care students in their early clinical training. Any health professional (young or old) who ventures into a first explicit incest history, or, for that matter, any person who unwittingly is told about incest activity, may quite normally react with sudden anxiety related to the incest and also to, "What am I supposed to do or say now?" This may be a good moment for a little silence to gain professional calm. Then a response like, "It is important that you brought this up. We will have to talk about it again in a few minutes" may be helpful. Allowing a short but needed break may also be necessary.

At this point, the anxious helper may use an immediate "curbstone consultation" with a colleague at hand or may call a supervisor and simply say, with honesty, "I got quite a shock when this woman told me she thinks her daughter is pregnant by her husband. I didn't know what to say or do. I said I'd be back in a few mintues." Distance (even being a few doors away) can lend some detachment. Also there is less emotional impact for the other professional, who may point out that it is normal to feel anxiety. Reassurance and directions to the therapist on how to proceed professionally will surely allay the immediate reaction of anxiety. However, immediate avoidance will not effectively deal with the incest case. Centuries of medical and other face-to-face clinical training have proceeded with this directive: "It's all right to be upset, but go right back there into the clinical zone and care for the patient." The professional must return and let the patient talk some more, giving details about the incest. The structured incest question-naire (Figure 1) is a clinical help, and it reduces any feeling of unique-ness. A form means that many others have had similar experiences. Self-administration of the questionnaire is possible but eliminates the opportunity to explore the patient's feelings beyond the facts on the form.

Regarding accessibility of incest data, this rather profound com-ment made by a comic could apply: "Ignorance is not the problem. It's knowledge of wrong facts." The scientific and clinical value of available academic material is lessened by condemnatory opinions and predictions. Confusion then occurs in professionals because incest literature has a tendency (1) to switch the frame of reference (even within the same sentence) from legal to social, moral, biological, or psychological aspects; (2) to lack clear definitions; (3) to presume that most incests are coercive adult-child; (4) to presume that all the in-cests are coital; and (5) to presume that all the incests are severely traumatic to both partners. Scientific data on ongoing incest (i.e., longitudinal study) is impeded owing to (1) legal entanglements in nearly all states, (2) flight or destruction of the family as a result of reporting and criminal laws, (3) professional ignorance of the fact that reporting laws apply only to minors, and (4) few scholarly researchers.

Pressure to provide clinical help may propel a search for more aca-demic information about incest. Applied knowledge will gradually im-prove skills and then lead to professional comfort. Direct professional experience may sometimes be the only education available. When large numbers of incest cases present, structured and supervised train-ing may be difficult to come by. Either direct experience or specific training may produce resourceful and gifted clinicians willing and able to understand incest and to help those patients who seek professional guidance. These clinicians may then educate other professionals in search of training.

CASE 6-2. A young physician in the emergency room treated the facial bruises and lacerations of a 58-year-old factory worker. The physi-cian then became very upset (fortunately after the facial repairs) when he was getting a history. The patient's 22-year-old son, who still lived at home, attacked and beat him when he unexpectedly found his father having inter-course with the son's paternal aunt, aged 60. (The attack response may have been to the incest or to the adultery elements or both.) Then the distressed son left home. The father had a sixth grade education and was raised on a farm (as was his divorced sister). She had volunteered to have intercourse with him when he said he was going to find a prostitute because he was horny. The patient said he considered masturbation "very freaky" and more abhorrent than finding a prostitute. His finances were low because of high costs for his currently hospitalized wife. The newly divorced sister told him to save his $50 prostitute fee for groceries and that she would oblige him. He said he was neither guilty nor ashamed of the sex nor did he think his sister was, since both had enjoyed the encounter. He was enraged that his son "dared hit me after all I've done for him." About the incest, the father

	Never	Sometimes	Frequently
Fantasy only			
Breast/genital fondling			
Deep kissing			
Masturbation of you			
Masturbation by you of kin			
Oral-genital contact			
Anal contact			
Intercourse			
Climax a) you b) kin	a) __ b) __	a) __ b) __	a) __ b) __
Pregnancy			
Fear			
Pain			
Force			
Shame or guilt			
Thoughts about incest			
Dreams about incest			
Reporting to another			
Police/hospital			

(Rels. = relationship)	Good	Average	Poor
Rels. between mother and father			
Sex rels. between mother and father			
Rels. mother and self a) past b) now			
Rels. father and self a) past b) now			
Rels. incest partner and self a) past b) now			
Relationship with teacher			
Relationship with minister			
Relationship with spouse now			

Kinship of person who made sex overtures: _____

Was he/she drinking at the time: _____ Threat? _____ Violence: _____

Did he/she have a) sex with other family? _____
    b) Psychiatric problem? _____

Your age at time: _____ Kin's age at time: _____

How did it end? _____

Did you like this person? _____

Do you see each other now? _____ Details: _____
_____

Told to keep it secret? _____ Feelings about the secret? _____

Did you tell? _____ Details: _____

Did someone else tell? _____

Details: _____

Pregnancy: _____ Outcome: _____

V.D. Yes/No Outcome (if any): _____

Preoccupations with incest (present)? _____

Preoccupations with incest (past)? _____

Dreams about incest (present)? _____

Dreams about incest (past)? _____

Reading about incest (past)? _____ Present: _____

Does your spouse know about this? _____

Reaction: _____

Need for psychotherapy (past) _____ Present: _____

Sex problems in past: _____

Sex problems now: _____

Details: _____

What helped you most to handle or resolve your feelings
    about the incest: _____

Figure 1. Incest history flow sheet for face-to-face history taking or for self-administration.

felt, "It wasn't harming nobody." He went on to say that his first sexual experience was at age 14 with a cow on their farm in southern Illinois, and that after all "sex is sex" except for masturbation, which aversion was similarly reported for less educated lower socioeconomic groups in the 1940s [84].

This patient and his sister were apparently incest-accepting; his son was not. The incest diagnosis was adult-adult consanguineous consensual coital incest; the physical diagnosis, laceration of the lower lip; the psychiatric diagnosis, none.

The startled emergency room physician simply listened and then sent the patient home without further comment. The doctor was learning by direct experience to control his own feelings and to think quietly on his feet. Later he said, "There were no minors involved. Surgical care was requested and given. I didn't have time for more than I did." He had no academic knowledge of incest but had come to ask for reading references. Did the incest continue? Yes, on two more occasions, it was learned later. The man's wife was discharged from the hospital shortly after the father-son crisis. The couple presented together a few months later at Loyola Sex Clinic for his selective impotence that had begun shortly after her illness. She knew from her son of the incest, but was far less upset about that than her husband's reluctance to approach her sexually after her cervical cancer treatment. He was able in treatment to disclose his fears of coital cancer contagion.

Three essential personal and professional reactions to incest may conveniently be listed under the headings *avoidance*, *attraction*, and *attack*. Underlying emotional responses of anxiety, sexual arousal, and anger may, however, be cloaked by various complex behaviors. Therefore, some of the guises of attraction are tabulated for ready reference to highlight positive reactions to the incests (Table 4). Also listed are the protective or defensive behaviors that may be used to cope with problems or negative feelings that result from incest thoughts or behavior.

For every health care professional, an essential distinction must be made between the person of a difficult patient and his or her recurrent problem behavior, e.g., prostitution, addiction, or incest. Whenever a patient's behavior is in conflict with the value system of the helping professional, an emotional response of moral outrage may quite easily occur. Then professional avoidance or attack behaviors may follow (neither of which may be in the best interest of the patient). Self-awareness and repeated reminders that understanding and helping the patient does not mean condoning unacceptable behavior are part of learned professionalism.

A feeling of emotional depletion is known to occur when clinical practice is intensely personal, is highly charged emotionally, demands constant availability, and offers many more frustrations than positive results. There may be a real sense of defeat and feelings of apathy and emptiness. This is known to occur in those who work continuously with dying patients or persons with recidivist problem behaviors: alcoholism, addictions, or the incests. This phenomenon of emotional (rather than physical) depletion is now popularly called professional burn-out [52]. Knowing that intensive incest treatment is emotionally

Table 4. Possible reactions to incest

Personal Avoidance	Professional Avoidance	Attraction	Attack
Recoil	Textbook denial	Sexual reactions	Personal reactions
Horror	Absence from DSM I, II, III	Mandated incest customs	Fighting off
Silence	Restricted research	Acceptance	Homicide
Anxiety	Withdrawal	Enjoyment	Suicide (enforced or voluntary)
Crying, fear, pain	"Lack of time"	Arousal	Prejudice
Running away	Lack of follow-up	Affection	Condemnation
Locking door	Avoiding learning to take incest history	Conquest	Religious reactions
Seeking protection	Ignoring	Novelty	Calling incest sin
Secrecy	Feeling overwhelmed, anxious, inadequate	Excitement	Legal reactions
Self-blame	Referring case	Challenge	Making incest a felony
Physical symptoms	Refusing to see	Hedonism	Arrest
Conflict	Closing case	Forming pro-incest lobby	Incarceration
Tension	Covering up	Making pornography with incest themes	Hospitalization
Hysterical seizures	Misperceiving	Nonsexual reactions	Foster placement
Panic attack	Disbelieving	Attention	Death penalty
Hyperventilation	Denying incidence	Affection	Psychosocial reactions
Vomiting	Trivializing effects	Exploitation	Telling a parent, sibling, teacher, friend, neighbor, physician, professional, police officer, press
Headaches	Burn-out	Gaining special status, treats, money, privileges, protection	Autobiography to expose partner(s)
Vaginismus			Psychotherapy to resolve residual problems
Depression			Sex education to prevent incest
Suicide			

demanding allows early use of sensitive preventive measures against feeling emptied out. This protective posture by health care professionals can prevent loss of valuable contributions just when clinical experience and therapy skills are at a peak.

The following points may help to prevent burn-out:

1. Realize that even the most brilliant and talented professional has limited (not total) responsibility for the patient and family. Patients go only as far and as fast as they are willing to go in treatment.
2. Patients define the problem and retain it or relinquish it. Except in life-threatening conditions, professionals stand by to offer help, with judicial injunction and legal supervision in certain cases.
3. Patients have a right to refuse medical help. They do not have a right to refuse legal intervention when the law has been contravened.
4. Remember that patients define improvement subjectively. What may be a millimeter to a helper may be a mile to a relieved patient. Do not set up excessive initial expectations that will lead to inevitable disappointment.
5. Anticipate extra time expenditure in incest cases in which family members must be involved, as you would in teen pregnancy, stroke, or cancer. Take care that excessive time commitments and case loads do not continue long after the crisis has been dealt with.
6. "Re-create" the self very regularly with fulfilling change and fun in order to renew patience, tolerance, and giving capacity.
7. Do not hesitate to join or set up a professional support group, time-limited or open-ended, even informally with two or three peers, to talk about each other's cases and personal reactions that arose in working with incest families. This reduces feelings of isolation. New treatment techniques may emerge and be shared. Such a support group can regenerate and even sharpen professional skills, and the peer exchange may provide perspective during the very act of summarizing a history verbally.

DATA GATHERING

Data gathering is the first phase of good incest management. Control of emotional reactions within each professional permits noncondemnatory listening to facilitate the objective collection of facts. An incest history that extends beyond the routine medical history format is usually obtained by more than one health care professional. Since adequate incest information must be both detailed and sexually explicit, questioning must be calm, thorough, yet not offensive or overwhelming. Special interviewing skills can be learned and enhanced by an incest questionnaire (Figure 1). A sensitive approach toward patient and family is always the basic ingredient for all clinicians. This allows supportive inquiry to become therapeutic rather than threatening.

History taking

When complete, a routine medical history has this customary outline:

I. Identifying data and chief complaint
II. Present illness
III. History
    A. Family constellation
    B. Family history
    C. Developmental history
        1. Infancy and early childhood
        2. Adolescence
        3. Education
        4. Sports and socializing
    D. Adult adjustment
        1. Vocational record and finances
        2. Cultural and recreational activities
        3. Religious orientation and participation
        4. Military history
        5. Sexual and marital history
        6. Relevant history of illnesses or surgery
        7. Problems with the law
        8. Other problems

A detailed medical, personal, sexual, and social history must be taken for all cases of incest—those presenting in crisis, incidentally, or by special search. Only in this way is dignity given to each person involved, so that all participants are viewed in the context of their family.

An incest allegation implies some type of sex between family members, so the family structure and function must be explored and an adequate sexual history taken on as many members as possible. Ethnic or regional customs and family sexual attitudes complete a competent professional evaluation. Many persons may be involved in incest activity, so the question, "Who else in the family is involved?" at times reveals a broader picture.

Both the father's and the mother's history will contribute to an overall understanding of how the family functions and what its strengths and weaknesses are. If siblings are incestuously involved, a thorough history for each child and for each parent will need to be done. No assumptions should be made. If attitudes are similar, a good history of each will confirm their concordance, but there may be differences to be noted and respected.

The frequency of intercourse; feelings and interest regarding marital sex; extramarital sex; previous marriage(s); early sexual experiences; masturbatory frequency and attitudes; whether favors, privileges, or special rewards were returned for sexual contacts; sexual dreams and fantasies; venereal disease; history of arrest for sex offenses or other; alcohol and drug intake; school, job, religious, psychiatric, and military history—all will give a total picture essential in formulating a prognosis and in management.

In assessing the severity of the problem it is important to remember that the patient defines internal reactions. These should not be imposed. They must be expressed, understood, and respected. They may relate to ignorance, misunderstanding, fear, or combinations of these. It is neither professional nor objective to use the self as an index of comparison; this may indeed compound problems. Either an overreaction to or the trivialization of a patient's history impede trust and therefore constitute poor clinical practice.

These aspects of history taking must be learned by today's physician assistants, and emergency room technicians who share with nurses and social workers the task of front-line history taking before a physician is called.

Rarely is incest given as a chief complaint. It is useful to list some of the ways adult-child incest cases may present as medical emergencies in a hospital or a doctor's office. This is what the first history taker may hear as the chief complaint:

From the mother
　　"Is she pregnant?"
　　"Is she still a virgin?"
　　"I want a sperm test."
　　"She's bleeding down there. . . ."
From the school authority
　　"Has she been sexually abused?"
　　"Check her for child abuse."
　　"The child service agency says she must be hospitalized and placed."
From the child service agency
　　"The home is unsafe. We have custody. Hospitalize her until we
　　　find placement."
　　"We need a full workup, a psychiatric evaluation, and psychological
　　　tests."
　　"Do a physical exam to see if there is any injury, venereal disease,
　　　or pregnancy."

In various states of upset, guardedness, and bewilderment, a child incest partner may sit in an emergency room for hours, not knowing what the grown-ups are talking about. What the child fears most is separation from his or her parents, even temporarily. Even exploitative attachments are familiar and preferable to loss of one or both parents. Hospitals are frightening, busy, impersonal places, so the child should be told as much as possible: "Everybody who comes here has a physical examination. No shots right now. If you need one, I promise to tell you. This is only a physical exam. Mother can stay with you." After that reassurance, a question is in order to the child: "What makes Mother bring you to the hospital tonight?" If there is an injury, "How did that happen?"

Avoid leading questions. One night, called in as a consultant to the emergency room, I walked to the corner bed where the child was, to hear a well-meaning resident ask the child, "Your father is a bad man, is he not?" I was appalled. This was how *not* to take a history. It was a closed question that showed observer bias and prejudgment rather than professional objectivity. Only a yes or no reply could be given to such a closed question. Sometimes these must be asked, but it is preferable to avoid them in history taking. Fortunately, the child could not understand the doctor and said, "What?" I rephrased the question: "Doctor was asking how you get along with your dad."

Malicious intent on the part of an angry wife has been known to produce a false accusation of incest. Therefore the physician must begin by constructing a clear picture from both the child's and the mother's history. The diagnosis of incest should not be made by inference. A subjective history taken separately from child and mother must be followed by an objective physical examination. In addition to verbal reports, nonverbal responses are important clinical observations.

If the child is anxious, is the anxiety or discomfort related to fear of the hospital, of being questioned, of separation from mother, of physical pain, of shots, worry about father, or some other factor? "I don't know" responses are very common and to be expected from children and even teenagers. "Think again. It happened to you. Help me to understand what brings you here." If the child doesn't respond, it is fair to say, "The school (or your mother) seems to think there are problems at home for you. Are they correct?"

Be alert to precocious sexual knowledge on the part of a child. Precocity is related to the age, social status, and intellect of the child. Many children other than incest participants know correct and slang terms for the genitals. Although the physician is not expected to be Sherlock Holmes, some coherent, explicit sexual details are essential (1) to protectively educate the child against inappropriate sexual contacts, (2) to inform the doctor about what occurred (if anything), (3) to protect the child from further harm if there were problems, and (4) to do (if needed) a careful yet considerate physical exam, so further trauma does not result.

If rape has actually occurred, the child may be in physical or emotional shock or both. The primary care physician may call in a pediatrician or gynecologist. "Do you remember who did this to you?" is a valid physician question when the child is comfortable enough to reply later on.

Rape is a legitimate and important health issue. Overall, 1 percent of rape victims contract syphilis; 3 percent gonorrhea; and 4 percent become pregnant. Although the law remains mired in its morass of complexities around rape issues, doctors are free to provide excellent medical care. Be understanding. Listen. Be aware that personal anxiety and professional irritation at the extra work and specificity needed with rape cases may make one angry at both victim and perpetrator. If it is a question of homosexual rape incest, the personal emotional impact is compounded because three taboos have been violated: violence, incest, and homosexuality.

The physician must now avoid the easy trap of becoming a prosecutor. Be on guard about stereotypes of the "rape precipitator"; these can make a physician accusatory rather than inquiring. Allow the patient to cry. Reassure: "This is difficult, I understand." Do not overly sedate with medication. This only delays resolution of feelings. Arrange privacy if at all possible, even in a busy emergency room, for the history taking as well as for the physical examination with a nurse attendant. More detailed guidelines for rape cases will be given in the section Physical Examination.

When a child incest case has been referred, much additional history may be available from the school principal, teacher, counselor, neighbors, police, probation officer, child service agency worker, and other family member(s). This information is usually gathered and collated in due time by the assigned social worker. This is time-consuming and demanding work because of the many personalities to be considered and the complex underlying emotional reactions of each to the incest aspect of the case. Social workers are often the unsung heroes of incest management.

A brief survey of a few cases may illustrate some "dos and don'ts" of incest history taking.

CASE 6-3. A 24-year-old male college student was extremely upset when his girl friend of three years confessed to him that her father had incestuously fondled her on and off from age 4 until college. When the woman was 21 and at home on vacation from college, her father allegedly had raped her in the den, with her mother upstairs and two adult brothers somewhere in the house.

The young man went to see a college counselor about this. "What freaked me out was that she laughed at me. She (the counselor) said this happens all the time, it even happened to her." He was angry that his distress was ridiculed and minimized but had enough self-assurance to seek another opinion. He also tried to read about incest in the library, saying correctly that he could not get a clear picture. He reported, "I've met her father. He doesn't drink, he's quiet, he works, he has friends. Her mother's a very bright lady and a nice person. One brother is a creep and still teases her and puts her down. The other brother is OK. I can understand the stuff with her dad when she was little and she didn't know. She never told her mom, says she didn't want to break up the marriage, even that I can see. But it's that rape at 21 that burns me up. I don't know how I can face her father after this. But there's something else that worries me. How come she didn't scream or run or kick him in the groin when he did that to her? She was 21 years old. There were three people in the house. How come she's so vague about that? She just cries and cries when I ask her. The other thing that bugs me now is that when I was at their house, her father made obscene jokes in front of her and both laughed. She kisses him good-bye when she leaves. Also she said that the day of the rape, she was wearing nothing but a T-shirt in the den. Why would she do that when she *knew* he was trying to be sexy with her all these years?"

This young man was tortured with some very real and relevant questions regarding the role of his girl friend in the adult-adult coital incest. He was worried that it was consensual rather than coercive. She told him that nothing sexual had transpired between her father and herself during the three years that they were dating. The story emerged when he asked her why she was unable to climax.

The college counselor assumed that the man's discomfort related only to the incest. Although it may have been an effort to comfort him, the counselor's trivialization and self-disclosure was clumsy and untherapeutic, besides being incomplete history taking. Yes, the man was upset to hear of the rape incest. He loved his girl friend. But the essential agony now was a crisis of trust. "Could she be making up the whole thing?" is one question he asked. Without waiting for a reply he said: "If she did, that would be even worse; then she'd by lying. I'm really mixed up."

Conjoint therapy with these two young people is the only rational way to proceed, but she has preferred to join a group of pre-orgasmic women to seek a sexual climax.

CASE 6-4. Exaggeration of the damaging effects of incest in a textbook of psychology precipitated one crisis presentation of incest. A 20-year-old college junior was brought to a community hospital's emergency room after a sudden panic attack in the library. She had begun to hyperventilate, cry, and scream. At the hospital, she was given a shot of a tranquilizer, told to breathe into a paper bag, and advised to see a psychiatrist. She kept repeating, "Let me die! Let me die!" but had made no suicide attempt.

When I saw her, she was upset, disheveled, tremulous, and sweaty, but able to respond. I asked, "What happened? When did it happen? Did anything specific seem to frighten you?" She had been in the library preparing an essay on sex deviations for her course in abnormal psychology. She saw a chapter segment on incest and read it. This was the first she learned of the word *incest*. The final paragraph allegedly stated that this "rare, heinous, and felonious crime" caused "irreversible damage, which is why the death penalty was employed in the past." It was at this point that she developed an acute anxiety attack with hyperventilation.

The woman was the youngest of four children. Her father, who had a sixth grade education and was born and raised in a rural area, had his own construction company that employed the three sons, all of whom had completed the eighth grade. The patient's mother, who had completed high school, was frail, quiet, and hard working. When the patient was 13 years old, her mother died suddenly of brain hemorrhage (possible berry aneurysm). There was available family to help, but without question or direction, the girl assumed all the maternal tasks: shopping, cooking, cleaning. She also continued to get good grades at school. She had school friends, but played no sports, did not date, and came straight home from school to keep house. The family had at no time been affectionate or verbal. All worked hard and for very long hours. There was little social life other than visiting grandparents twice a year. They did not attend a church.

About five months after her mother's death, her father came into her bed and had intercourse with her "without saying a word." She said that there was no foreplay and that he left immediately afterward. She was 13½ years old. She described no pain, pleasure, surprise, or shock. "I just did it"—as she did her other household tasks. From time to time he would return to her bed and so would each of her three brothers. "We never talked about it. I figured men needed it." When asked if she was orgasmic through any of this sexual activity she said she thought perhaps she had been on a few occasions. She reported occasional masturbation, usually the day before her period.

No pregnancy resulted (amazingly). She used no contraceptive and had no idea whether her father or brothers used a condom. "It all happened in the dark. It was always over quite quickly." It sounded like a scene from a Bergman movie, dark and quiet.

Business was good for the men and little changed until the patient finished high schcool at age 18. She decided to work for one year and then go to college. Her father did not object, but said he thought it was time to return to his home town, which he did with the sons.

In her freshman year, the young woman stayed in a dormitory for one semester, but did not enjoy the "noise and silliness." She got an apartment with two other girls, and that was satisfactory. All did their share of chores. She had a boy friend who was shy and a good student (as she was). There was petting, which she enjoyed, but no sex because "neither of us want to now." He introduced her to sports and music and art. She met and liked his family. In short, she was well adjusted and quite guilt-free—until she read about the "horrors" resulting from incest.

The patient had many strengths and talents, and was neither hysterical nor suggestible. She had shown pseudomaturity in her coping skills while in the home and had handled her college independence well. She became calmer and calmer as she talked.

After being quiet for a while she said, "How could I have been so stupid? Do you think my father didn't know it was wrong? And my brothers? What would my boy friend say if he knew? He'd never speak to me again." These were all real and important questions and comments. I was unable to answer all of them, but we explored them in the next few visits. This was in 1965. The incest questionnaire (Figure 1) was not yet constructed.

My professional task in gathering the history was to collect sufficient data to be able to answer clearly at least these questions:

1. What is the problem? For whom?
2. What is the degree of distress? For whom?
3. What is the actual severity of the current problem?
4. What are the current legal implications? For whom?
5. How can I best be of help now? Later?

For this woman, the presenting problem was emotional conflict resulting from the fact that her compliant sexual behavior (consensual consanguineous adult-child, child-child, then adult-adult coital heterosexual incest) was described by a textbook (she had a high regard for authority) as both psychologically dangerous and criminal. This was an internal problem of sudden and overwhelming distress, triggered by the external stimulus of a partially accurate academic statement. It was a problem for no one else at the time she was seen. Her male relatives, who were unlikely to do much reading, were not in apparent discomfort before, during, or after their sex with her. "How can I go and talk to them about this? We never talked much ever. There's no way I could. Why should I? For what purpose? They didn't mean to harm me. They were not bad people. We never fought or yelled. Sometimes I'd hear the neighbors yell, and I'd think they must be drinking. In our house, maybe there was a beer Saturday or Sunday. We had no TV, only a radio. Perhaps that's why I got my homework done."

What about the severity of the current problem? In the past, as the patient described, aggravated incest had occurred with her father and incest with her brothers (both felonies with different penalties). If this had been discovered or reported when she was a minor, her father and brothers could have gone to jail and she to a foster home. The severity of the outcome of incest in clinical practice sometimes relates to its criminalization, especially in cases such as this one. There was no violence. She and her father and brothers cared for each other and were law-abiding people. The men respected her assertion of autonomy. There appeared to be ignorance of incest laws. She and they apparently accepted intercourse as purely functional. This attitude was noted among blue-collar persons in the 1940s [84]. She had no idea whether they masturbated. Occasionally in doing the laundry she had noted stains on their underwear but did not question this.

The current legal implications were none, in my opinion, since this was all retrospective history. The way I could best assist the patient was to listen to her, allow her to express her doubts and distress, critique the inaccuracies of that and other segments of textbooks (the beginning for her of intellectual emancipation), help her gain perspective as an adult regarding her lack of explicit sex education and her father's responsibility in the given circumstances, and discuss with her her right to privacy and confidentiality regarding these experiences. She had experienced no great pressure to talk until the day of the anxiety attack.

Her current boy friend was a fun-mate rather than a sex-mate or possible life-mate. She trusted him but thought he might become even more upset than she had if she were to tell him about the incest.

There are clinical conditions other than incest that the law (external imposition) defines as a problem, even though the patient may be symptom-free. Examples include communicable diseases such as tuberculosis or syphilis. Under infectious diseases regulations, medical treatment is mandatory. Refusal of treatment makes the patient liable to apprehension for further tests and institutionalization until test results are negative and transmission of the disease is no longer a risk. Before the days of antituberculous drugs, minors were considered in need of protection if someone in the home had tuberculosis, and were removed by law.

The implications of laws requiring physicians to report tuberculosis, despite disastrous personal loss and distress for patients, were as difficult before the 1940s as they are today in incest cases. It is always easier for the professional to explain medicolegal realities when there are gross pathologic findings: bloody sputum, evidence of rape or violence. Cases such as 6-3 and 6-4 merely raise many questions.

Overquestioning or underquestioning a child

I have real concern about repetitious and sometimes excessive explicit questioning of a child about incest details. Quite unconsciously, the attractive, arousing aspect of explicit sex (Table 4) may impel this approach. This can be prevented by use of a tape recording, especially when legal and other authorities all have their protocol of questioning yet to follow. Potential for adult prompting, rehearsing, or intimidation exists. A child may be vulnerable, anxious, and suggestible, especially when deprived of home and eager to get out of the hospital.

In the medical care of children, too often the only history taken is that of the adult who brings the child. This is not an acceptable alternative to overquestioning. Personally, I need to know how the child views the problem, whatever his or her age. From about 1 year a baby responds to, "Where's the boo-boo?" by pointing. Even the way the child understands and responds to a question reveals intellectual capacity and cooperation. A verbal 4-year-old can respond to, "Why did Mommy bring you here? Did anyone hurt you? Who? Where? Show me. Did anyone take off your clothes? Who? What did he do? Where did he touch you? How many times did this happen? Did he take off his clothes? What did he do? Did you tell Mommy? What did she do? How do you get along with Mommy? With Daddy? How do Mommy and Daddy get along? Do you have brothers and sisters? (If there was an earlier affirmative response) Does Daddy play with them too? Did you tell anyone about Daddy and you?"

Questions must be kept short and simple so a child does not get confused. A rough drawing can be made of a nude boy and girl so the child can point to body parts. The examiner should avoid prematurely touching a child who may be shy and embarrassed. Paper dolls (one with a penis and one without) are easily made, and features can be added. These help in asking what happened. I used paper dolls to help the 6-year-old child of a pedophilic show what her father had done to her. (I also used paper dolls with her brother who was 4 years old.) We tore the paper together to make the dolls, talked at the same time, and gave names to each doll. She said her father had fondled her crotch and had requested that she hold his "wee-wee" (penis). There was no vaginal penetration, only mutual genital touch.

Paper cutting, drawing, and dolls are all familiar and nonthreatening. Also, since play is the child's way, it is an easy vehicle of communication.

Incest questionnaire

An explicit incest questionnaire (Figure 1) may be self-administered by a teenager or adult when there is time pressure or discomfort in the patient, the professional, or both. It is most valuable when used for face-to-face history taking by the professional, but self-administration is better than avoiding the taking of an incest history. The very fact that an incest questionnaire exists reassures the patient by giving evidence that enough people have had incest experiences for a questionnaire to have been drawn up. Anxiety may be alleviated simply by its use or by seeing it while the professional uses it to obtain more data. It is a brief form. Patients who self-administer it should be encouraged to write extra comments on separate pages if they so choose.

Whether incest presents incidentally or in crisis, the same questionnaire may be used, depending on the patient's cooperativeness. If an incest crisis occurs in a depressed, guilt-ridden adult who blames early incest for her current problems, the primary issue may be the depression, the possibility of suicide, and her safety. Use of the questionnaire may be delayed until later to gather needed data and help her deal with her residual feelings about early incest experiences.

When research involving a special search for incest participants is done, the incest questionnaire could be used with each member of either incestuous or random families for incidence studies. There are so many unknowns in this area that a great deal of incest data must be gathered for improved understanding. However, unless there is adequate (explicit) data gathering, proper definition of reported incest behavior (i.e., adult-child, coital, coercive, rape incest) will not be possible. Without clear definition, valuable hours of professional work may be nullified.

Noncondemnatory listening

In taking an incest history or in treating an incest participant, is it personally or professionally possible to be a nonjudgmental listener? I think not. Each human being develops a value system that evaluates incoming information. Upon such emotional and intellectual processing, a private judgment occurs: good, acceptable, neutral, fair, bad, terrible. The private internal judgment may differ from the verbal, nonverbal, or written response, but the evaluating process still occurs in all alert, thinking persons, however objective they may try to be.

The spirit of the much-used term *nonjudgmental* is really a plea to health professionals to be noncondemnatory. Objectivity attempts to separate clearly the setting, the behavior, and the person of the patient. Only this way can arbitrary rejection and condemnation be avoided.

Noncondemnatory listening and acceptance of a patient does not at any time mean condoning the behavior that brings him or her to professional attention, be this chain-smoking, drug abuse, or incest. Nor will noncondemnatory listening preclude giving an honest professional statement that the patient's emphysema is aggravated by smoking or that visual hallucinations may result from street drugs or that consanguineous coital adult-child incest is against the law.

The capacity for noncondemnatory listening will differ for each personality and with the time and place. When confronted with a crisis presentation of rape incest at 2:00 A.M. in a pressured emergency room, a horror reaction is not unnatural. The obvious child abuse entails immediate steps to protect the minor. Quite normal judgmental or even angry and condemnatory feelings may arise but must be understood and controlled. Expressing these feelings by berating the mother who brought the child or threatening to have the perpetrator castrated and hanged will serve merely (1) to ventilate a personal reaction, honest as that may be; (2) to humiliate and frighten both mother and child, who may still have to face that family member again and again, with possible further threat to their safety; (3) to interrupt or preclude ever obtaining an adequate explicit history of the event because of real fear of unknown consequences; (4) to frighten the child more—here is one more authority figure who is out of control.

For all these reasons, "keeping cool" externally will assist patient, mother, and other staff members. Good emergency medical care demands a calm, careful approach: rape care first, complete the history taking second. By that time, noncondemnatory listening may be more possible because of some professional dialogue between the time of the presenting impact and the data gathering a few hours later.

The evaluation of mother and child may be in process when the father is unexpectedly brought in intoxicated or beaten up by a neighbor or unconscious because of a suicidal overdose. These are all real possibilities. What then? Usually because of professional conditioning, the health professional's first reactions are to salvage life: start intravenous fluids, stop bleeding, suture lacerations, wash out the stomach, draw blood for tests. Only then may the second emotional surge be felt, at which time pure exhaustion may mute potential feelings of outrage against the father who now has been revived to face the legal consequences of his unacceptable incestuous behavior.

The medical task is to give (1) physical care, (2) emotional support, (3) psychiatric evaluation, (4) an understandable summary of the incest behavior, and (5) treatment recommendations. All of these call for professional judgments. Condemnation, if any, will be judicial.

Similar personal and professional shock reactions may occur when unexpected incidental presentations of incest history catch a physician unprepared. These may cause (even momentarily) a loss of control in connection with a juvenile diabetic girl or a depressed woman who just tell their family doctors one day. Sudden avoidance (leaving the room) and silence may be the defensive ways a physician responds. It may be the best he can do at the time. These are quite normal defenses against internal anxiety and moral outrage. Each patient, however, will receive an unspoken message that the doctor was not able to deal with the incest story. Will the patients feel judged by the silence or avoidance as being bad or tainted? Will they try to talk with another, noncondemnatory professional on another occasion? Perhaps when the distress increases.

Physical examination

Not all cases of incest require a physical examination. Those who respond to research studies certainly do not. Usually an incidental presentation of incest occurs during marriage counseling or individual psychotherapy, and no physical exam is indicated. A physical examination is more usual in cases of suspected or actual adult-child or adult-adult heterosexual or homosexual rape that may be consanguineous or affinity incest. Occasionally it may be for child-child (sibling) rape incest.

The most immediate concern for the physician is usually an emergency attempt to get a rudimentary history, then to stop any bleeding, examine, treat, and later to get more history. For all suspected rape cases, outside or inside the family, this is the medical protocol:

1. Be calm and gentle. Tell the patient what you are doing and why.
2. Carefully use a sheet to respect privacy.
3. Reassure and gain the confidence of the patient—boy, girl, woman, or man.
4. Although in incest the rapist is usually known and samples of hair, shreds of torn clothing, or skin left under fingernails from scratching may seem less pertinent for identifying the aggressor, they must still be taken.
5. Make a thorough and well-recorded examination generally and then genitally for trauma. Mark specimens very carefully (name and date); all may be subpoenaed later if the case goes to court.
6. For child rape cases, stirrups are unnecessary. Just raise the knees and have the soles of the feet on the table. A nasal speculum is quite adequate for vagina or anus. If the hymen is intact, a gentle recto-abdominal examination is sufficient.
7. Make smears of secretions around the vulva or anus.
8. Use a water-moistened (nonlubricated) speculum (with reassurance and a statement that this is done to check medically as well as to provide needed legal evidence later). (1) Make one wet mount from the vaginal fornix or the rectum for an immediate spot check for motile sperm or spirochetes. (2) Make two or three smears for the pathology department (and the police). (3) Do a Pap smear. (4) Take a scoop of secretions in the fornix pool, rectum, or throat. Place in clean, marked test tubes for an acid phosphatase check. (Acid phosphatase is an enzyme secreted in the seminal vesicles and found in semen. Since a man may be aspermatic, especially after a vasectomy, sperm may not be seen, but acid phosphatase will still be found if semen is present. There are diagnostic tablets that immediately show the presence of acid phosphatase. The vagina, rectum, or throat do not naturally contain acid phosphatase, which is therefore an important diagnostic test for semen in rape cases.) (5) Throat and anal swabs are indi-

cated if there was forced fellatio or anal intercourse. (6) Do a pregnancy test (for prerape pregnancy) and repeat two weeks later. (7) Do a culture plate for *Neisseria gonorrhoeae.*

9. For prophylaxis against pregnancy dilation and curettage may be futile, since sperm already in the fallopian tubes will not be caught. The use of diethylstilbestrol (DES) for pregnancy prophylaxis is highly controversial. It works optimally within the first 24 hours after coitus but 72 hours at the longest. It causes extreme nausea, dizziness, headache, and breast tenderness and does not always prevent pregnancy. In some rape cases, women are pregnant before the rape. DES poses a high risk to the fetus. If it is to be given, the dose is 25 mg twice daily for 5 days. It is, of course, contraindicated in pregnancy, in postmenopausal or premenarchal females, and in women who have had a tubal ligation or are using an IUD or contraceptive pills.

10. Prophylaxis against venereal disease could be started immediately if there is concern that the patient will not return for follow-up. Otherwise, antibiotic treatment can wait a few days for the results of the cultures or a few weeks for serology results. However, most physicians use 1 gm of oral probenecid and 4.8 million units procaine penicillin G by injection. If the patient is allergic to penicillin, 0.5 gm tetracycline 4 times a day for 15 days should be used.

11. Medical follow-up should be scheduled for 1 week and 3 weeks later to check for venereal disease and pregnancy and to evaluate emotional status.

12. Emotional support at presentation and later are essential aspects of management.

13. While the outlined procedures are in process, the hospital rape team or child abuse team (or both) can be mobilized by a nurse or assistant. Depending upon the availability of resource persons, the patient or parent can be told gently that a social worker, nurse, or chaplain will be coming to talk. The support of such persons may greatly lessen the stress of the long, lonely emergency room wait.

This usually completes the first phase of incest treatment: data gathering, including physical examination if necessary. Depending on child protection concerns, the child abuse or rape team may be involved. If neither exists as a formal group, then a community child protection agency may be alerted directly to send a social worker to see the family. Usually the next step in cases of adult-child incest will be to refer those involved to a psychiatrist for court-requested evaluations and recommendations or for psychotherapy.

7

TREATMENT OF INCEST PHASE
TWO: PSYCHIATRIC EVALUATION

W H E N there is no question of pregnancy, rape, or coital penetration, an incest case may not present for a physical examination. However, a case may still present in a hospital emergency room as a crisis of child protection, with a psychiatric admission sought until the family is evaluated (or investigated, if legal terminology is being used). Phase two, namely the psychiatric evaluation, must then commence after all the preliminaries of phase one.

The initial emergency room psychiatric interview may be neither thorough nor complete for a number of reasons: (1) patient and family guardedness resulting from the criminal status of incest and its possible classification as child abuse when a minor is involved; (2) lack of privacy plus time and space pressure in an emergency room; (3) incomplete coordination of the multiple professional reports, e.g., from school, child service agency, nurse, assistant, initial physician, and rape or child abuse team.

The use of a psychiatric unit to hold a child incest partner raises many questions. Most communities do not have readily available child psychiatry units. A mixed adult-child psychiatry unit can be a frightening place for a nonpsychotic child, just as a pediatric unit can be for a physically healthy child. A stable, nurturing foster home may be more humane for pre-evaluation protection of a minor. The court usually requires a psychiatric evaluation for possible emotional as well as physical trauma; some child psychiatrists may consider this to be more efficiently done by observing the child as an inpatient for some weeks. If there is concern about recurrence of alleged incest, then the child may be hospitalized for protection. However, adequate protection may be afforded in a good foster family. Much of a hospitalized child's distress may come not from the alleged incest but from (1) separation from home; (2) fear of other patients; (3) fear of unknowns and the hospital routine such as blood tests and x-rays; (4) fear of damage to a parent or to the family; and (5) self-blame, guilt, or anxiety regarding the discovery or telling of the incest.

A psychiatric evaluation considers mentation and emotions and those human activities that are considered to differ from socially acceptable norms (e.g., walking nude is acceptable on a nudist beach but not on a main street of a city). The artificial separation of psyche (soul or mind) and soma (body) occurs in textbooks but not in persons. However, medical or health care specialization today assigns the task of evaluating the psyche to a psychiatrist. The systematic clinical examination of mentation begins, for the most part, with alert observation during the detailed history taking described in the previous chapter. Since both speech and nonverbal behaviors may either express or conceal thoughts and emotions, physical reactions such as sweating, rapid breathing, muscle movements, and eye contact must all be noted while talking to a patient. These provide data in addition to verbalized thoughts and emotions, and can indicate anxiety that may be denied verbally to the self, to the examiner, or to both. Emotional distress objectively noted by others may not be conscious, it may be recognized but subjectively controlled, or it may even be exaggerated by any person, including incest participants.

The psychiatrist must then formulate an opinion—based on his or her direct knowledge of the patient and the family and the relevant reported circumstances—about why the incest occurred, whether or not there is psychopathology in any of the family members interviewed, what the diagnosis is, and what the outlook is for recurrence of the incest and for general adjustment of each individual. Within this framework, management recommendations are made.

Since treatment techniques (for those incests that reach professional attention) are still rudimentary and in the process of development, longitudinal follow-up of treated and untreated incest families and individual participants is essential. Only through such study can future psychiatric evaluation and treatment of incest be improved and can ways of preventing incest be suggested.

Mental status

With practice, ascertaining a patient's mental status may be done even though the patient is difficult, withdrawn, noncooperative, anxious, angry, or manipulative. It is important to expect numerous possible reactions to incest experiences, thoughts, or dreams (Table 4). The evaluating psychiatrist must anticipate, without foreclosure or condemnation, a wide range of attitudinal differences and must listen actively and alertly to pick up nuances such as discordance in voice tone, facial expression, and actual historical content. Ambivalence or conflict may thus be noted. Lack of evident distress or conflict must also be noted.

Be as open, objective, and calm as you possibly can. Recognize and accept *your own* (1) normal body response of tension or anxiety: tachycardia, sweating, tremor; (2) normal emotional responses: anxiety, tension, upset, anger, withdrawal; (3) behavioral responses: overactivity or underactivity; overtalking; overreassuring; irritability; speech that is too loud or too soft during the evaluation interview; and, later on in the day: insomnia; oversleeping, overeating, overdrinking.

Develop your own orderly routine to remember the key ingredients of a mental status evaluation, which is the core of a psychiatric evaluation. My mnemonic is JOIMAT, for *J*udgment, *O*rientation, *I*ntellect, *M*emory, *A*ffect, *T*hinking. These are essential components, with general appearance a normal lead-in.

General appearance encompasses age, sex, appearance, size, clothing (neat, torn); activity (slow, restless), alertness, consciousness (a person in psychogenic withdrawal may respond to being called by name), and verbal and nonverbal responsiveness.

Judgment is the patient's ability (relative to age) to reach conclusions based on facts so that appropriate action may be taken. The evaluating psychiatrist might ask, for example, What would you do if your car was stolen?

Orientation for person, time, and place all indicate contact with reality and the social surroundings.

Intellect is the individual's capacity to understand and use language and learning. When there has been no explicit incest education, ignorance about incest may not mean the patient is intellectually slow. A mentally retarded patient may be very aware that incestuous behavior is inappropriate because of general learning that sex is wrong and that it is shameful to expose the body to another. There may be no vocabulary to express details but knowledge (and emotion) about the incest activity. The flow of speech, general vocabulary, ability to read and calculate, knowledge of general information (for age and education), and grade level are all used for a clinical evaluation of a patient's intellect (average, above, or below). Actual IQ quantification requires psychological testing.

Memory is an essential aspect of intellect, since retention of knowledge comprises new learning and retrieval of stored knowledge. Immediate, intermediate, and remote memory are all separate components of recall. They may be affected to differing degrees by emotion and by illness, alcohol, or drugs. "I don't remember" is a common response, which may be accurate, but there may also be guardedness, fear of consequences, deliberate concealment, or unconscious blocking. The 24-year-old college student struggling to evaluate his girl friend's account of rape incest asked, "Could it be that she blocked it out so deep that now she doesn't remember?" Events or materials may be forgotten if they are considered unimportant or if they are emotionally threatening. Remote memory also fades as new learning occurs. This is a complex process complicated by the many emotions surrounding incest.

Affect, or feelings or emotions, may be objectively assessed by observing nonverbal expressions: anxiety, by facial expression, stuttering, muscle contractions, sweating, restless movement of small muscles of the face, hands, or feet; depression, by slowness of speech, slumped body posture, tears, sobbing. Some persons are more adept at articulating their emotions than others who can talk only about doing, not about feeling. Emotions of confusion, blankness, ambivalence, lability (e.g., swings from tears to laughter) sadness, grief, fear, flat expression—all must be noted. During history taking, a range from anger to smiles may be appropriate affect.

Thinking may be expressed in hand signals or sign language, on paper, or in words, drawings, or songs. Conveying thought may be disturbed by intellectual retardation; mutism; a speech disorder; absence of education (e.g., sexual and incest ignorance); emotional problems such as anxiety, depression, fear, or psychosis; or chemicals that alter alertness (e.g., drugs and alcohol). In assessing mental status, the clinician may also comment (1) on the patient's awareness or insight that there is a problem and how it came about (in incest cases, the legal consequences make admission difficult, which does not necessarily indicate lack of insight); (2) personal strengths such as charm, cooperativeness, accomplishments, or open-mindedness; (3) personal weaknesses such as negativism, severe or chronic anxiety, confusion or disorganization, intellectual retardation, closed-mindedness, or undue suspiciousness; and (4) motivation for treatment.

Psychodynamic formulation

The task confronting the psychiatrist is to assemble and integrate the historical and observational data, often from multiple sources in crisis incest cases: child service agency, teacher, probation office, school counselor, numerous social workers, emergency room nurse, gynecology resident, psychiatry resident, family doctor, family members, nurses, aides, mental health workers, and others, as well as from each alleged incest partner. From this long list of information, a hypothesis must be formulated regarding the personality of each incest participant, the uninvolved parent, and other family members; about the alliances or coalitions between family members; and about possible causes of pathology, e.g., pedophilia, exhibitionism, psychosis, or marital or sexual problems. There should be sufficient depth of understanding of the individual members and of the family interactions to explain factors that maintained and may perpetuate the incest: marital discord, mother working nights, recidivism in pedophilia, or cultural incest-accepting attitudes. Also, the degree of internal distress of each individual involved must be assessed regarding (1) the sexual element; (2) pregnancy concerns; (3) worries about preservation of the family unit; (4) feelings about nonprotective parent or siblings; (5) fear of pain or personal harm; (6) ambivalence or confusion regarding the incest partner(s), incest laws, sex, or the right to privacy and refusal of inappropriate sexual contact; (7) guilt or a sense of wrongdoing; and (8) shame or upset at the discovery or exposure. Enjoyment of the relationship, the affection, the touching and closeness, the privileges or rewards, and the sexual exchange may also be present. The possibility both of denial of distress and of actual absence of distress exists; these responses should be recorded if noted. Specific personal stresses (illness, depression, retardation, job loss, addiction) and social stresses (unemployment, financial pressure, retirement) must also be noted, since treatment may be directed toward these areas.

Many gaps in needed data may exist. This must be clearly noted in making a psychodynamic formulation: "It is speculative that x occurred. However, further information is needed from y. At that time there may be a reassessment." Such an approach is helpful both to the courts working from the psychiatric evaluation and to other professionals who must continue to work with the family.

Now a differential diagnosis must be discussed, as in any other branch of medicine. The psychiatrist's reasoning about each possibility must be given:

> Although the father may be correct that his 8-year-old daughter makes up many stories and may have invented one about his fondling her genitals, it is highly unlikely that this 8-year-old would manufacture a story about his taking off his clothes and lying on top of her and her 7-year-old girl friend whom he asked her to bring home. Since the father has a history of five apprehensions for child molesting in other states, and since pedophilia is known to have a clinical history of recidivism, adult-child consanguineous heterosexual consensual noncoital incest with a pedophilic father must be considered as a strong possibility.

If there were other reasons for thinking that the child's story might be untrue, such as hesitancy on the part of the child, the mother's talking for the child and putting words into the child's mouth, or a bitter conflict or divorce in process, these would need to be outlined. How can this be said on paper? Perhaps in this way:

> It is also not unknown that in interpersonal conflict between parents a child may be torn about whom to please. This child is ignorant of the meaning of the words *intercourse, sex,* and *incest.* She is distressed and confused about her mother's anger toward her father. I am unable to ob-

tain a clear picture from the child of inappropriate sexual contact. I am concerned about the destructiveness of incest accusations. Further observation and evaluation are essential in this case.

Then each involved family member must be sketched so that a clear picture emerges for therapeutic management of the family:

The *8-year-old* herself showed no personal distress about the sexual element. She is upset that she is separated from home (she is in a hospital placement now) and has corroborated her friend's story of her father's sexual activity with them. She is open and very affectionate with her father when he visits, preferring to sit on his lap rather than her mother's. She is not unduly seductive with him or male staff. She has no physical injury; the hymen is intact.

The *father* was anxious, remorseful, and acutely depressed on the night his daughter was brought to the hospital. At first he denied the sexual behavior. Later he broke down, cried, and admitted it, saying he loved his child and at no time harmed her. Although "remorse and getting religion" are well-known factors in avoiding jail in our culture, the man was sincere. The night of the child's admission, he attempted suicide with sleeping pills and was hospitalized overnight at another hospital. He is unemployed, and his wife works nights. There has been no sex in the marriage for three years. These are all incest risk factors. Additionally, there is the history of pedophilia, allegedly in remission for eight years. He is cooperative now but very anxious about his upcoming court date.

The *mother* is a quiet, tired-looking 52-year-old woman who responds only when addressed, at which time she is coherent and appropriate. Initially she refused to believe the child's story and was upset that the school had responded to the neighbor girl's story. She kept repeating that hers was now the only income and that she must return to work. Only when the husband admitted to the sex play (although he denied mounting behavior) did she, in a low, flat tone, reveal the premarital history of pedophilia that had broken his previous marriages. She is concerned for her children and also for her husband and the marriage, which she wants to salvage. She has not blamed anyone and expresses no anger.

Background material on each parent and on available family and community resources is helpful to mention:

Both the mother and the father are poorly educated. They moved to a different community when they married to make a new start. The wife was fully aware of the husband's history of child molesting. Money has always been a problem, although both proudly say they have never been on welfare. They have friendly and helpful neighbors but no relatives here. The school authorities regard them as good parents and have been helpful. Their community has a good family service agency which can continue to work with them in family therapy.

Then qualifying statements must be made regarding the further course of the case and potential helps and hazards:

> Although the father's confession, remorse, and suicide attempt may be seen as positives, there is the history of pedophilia and its present proliferation to friends of his daughter, who is at this age attractive to his pedophilic needs and available at home. She may indeed become less sexually attractive to him at puberty and his 3-year-old more so when she reaches 5 or 6 years of age. There are as yet no cures for pedophilia. Treatment with female hormones is experimental and controversial. The father will need extremely close surveillance at home by the mother, who should be with the children when he is at home.
>
> Every effort should be made (1) to assist him to find a job so that he will not be alone with the children while the mother is working, (2) to restore the marital and sexual relationship by marital counseling, (3) to institute long-term probationary surveillance to foster compliance and to prevent father-child sex from recurring inside or outside the family, and (4) to encourage occasional family therapy sessions in addition to weekly marital sessions to observe the family's interactions.

Any concerns about tendencies toward suicide or physical abuse are worth noting, always taking professional care to mention the time ("when last observed") or other qualifier ("both parents deny using severe corporal punishment with either child"). Also, when there is a new affinity relationship in a family newly reconstituted after divorce, this factor must be emphasized as being different from a long-standing consanguineous bond.

All relevant factors that may explain (not necessarily excuse) the incest behavior must be included: For example, the biological fact of twinship may provide an unusual mirror image of the self. For some twins, an extremely close bond, analogous to a lifelong marital partnership may develop [150]. Although many of these may be desexualized relationships, some are incestuous.

> CASE 7-1. A 48-year-old man presented for help under threat of divorce in a stormy marriage. He desired sexual intercourse about once each two months; his wife demanded intercourse nightly, which he consistently refused. He was a successful engineer and a monozygotic twin who married only after his twin shocked him by getting married at age 29. The twins had enjoyed consensual consanguineous coital (anal) and noncoital homosexual incest from age 5 or 6 years. The patient was the follower in this sibling relationship and had expected both would remain single but together. His loss of sexual desire related to marital conflict: His refusal to have intercourse represented a passive but deliberate retaliation toward his wife upon whom he was as dependent as he had been upon his twin. His wife knew nothing of the incest.
>
> After marriage he had had no sex with his twin and no other homosexual interludes or relationships. He was quite casual and not distressed about the incest history incidentally obtained. He masturbated 3 times per week without guilt. (This also was not known to his wife.) She enjoyed the battle, and

neither changed at all in brief marital therapy. She did not divorce him.

The twins' incestuous relationship, of course, combined both psychological and biological factors and is mentioned for completeness rather than to represent an expectable association.

Psychological factors in the psychodynamic formulation describe how each individual with unique biological givens learns, relates to, and feels about the social realities of rearing, e.g., by servants in a wealthy family, without real closeness to parents, or in a chaotic home with conflictive alcoholic or psychotic parent(s).

> CASE 7-2. A 32-year-old registered nurse came to Loyola Sex Clinic with her husband of six years, a premature ejaculator. This was his second marriage. She had no sexual problems. Her early history included chaotic social and family upheaval yet produced remarkable personal strengths and coping skills. An only child, she was 4 years old when her parents divorced and she went to a foster home. She was later adopted by a loving elderly couple who were both killed in a car accident when she was 12. Two foster homes later, she willingly participated, beginning at age 15, in noncoital and then coital affinity incest with her foster father, aged 40. "He had had a vasectomy. He was so gentle and loving, my foster mother wanted nothing to do with sex, and I was so ready. She never found out about us." There were three other younger foster children. She went to college, was quite active sexually, and displayed no conflict about any of her sexual activity. She had made no attempt to seek out her parents or foster parents, but since her marriage had related warmly and well to her husband and his personal losses. She was a remarkably mature and well-adjusted person.

From all of the gathered data and deductive conclusions, in clear language with as little jargon as professionally possible, the psychiatrist provides an understandable psychodynamic formulation of the entire incest case. A diagnosis for each person evaluated must then be made.

DIAGNOSIS

Coherent evaluation and exchange of helpful information between professionals is assisted by a clear, coherent descriptive diagnosis of (1) the actual incest behavior, (2) the physical diagnosis, and (3) any other psychiatric diagnosis.

From Chapter 2 the following classification of incest is outlined:

1. Incest Diagnosis
   a. Consanguineous (blood relative) or affinity (related by marriage) incest
   b. Consensual, coercive, or forceful incest
   c. Coital or noncoital incest
   d. Heterosexual or homosexual incest
   e. Adult-adult, child-child, adult-child, or group incest
   f. Rape incest
   g. Pedophilic incest

    h. Exhibitionist incest
    i. Multiple deviance incest (e.g., exploitation, prostitution, trans-
       vestism, child pornography, sadomasochism)
    j. Fantasy or dream incest
    k. Incest craving or envy
    l. Incest-accepting family, culture, or religion
2. Physical Diagnosis
3. Other Psychiatric Diagnosis

Some examples may facilitate the use of this classification.

CASE 7-3. A single 20-year-old woman from a community in which incest was socially, although not legally, acceptable, was tearful, angry, and upset that her father had bestowed his sexual favors on each of her five sisters, three older and two younger, but not her. She saw herself as the ugly duckling and was exhibiting rebellious tantrum behavior at home.

> *Incest diagnosis*
> Consanguineous adult-adult incest envy in an incest-accepting family and culture
>
> *Physical diagnosis*
> No abnormality noted
>
> *Other psychiatric diagnosis*
> Undersocialized aggressive conduct disorder

The following diagnoses could be made for the pedophilic father of Case 5-2 (page 79):

> *Incest diagnosis*
> Consanguineous consensual heterosexual noncoital adult-child pedophilic incest
>
> *Physical diagnosis*
> No abnormality noted
>
> *Other psychiatric diagnosis*
> Pedophilia (past: heterosexual and homosexual; current: with daughter's friend), acute anxiety disorder

For the child involved in Case 5-2:

> *Incest diagnosis*
> Consanguineous consensual heterosexual adult-child non-coital incest
>
> *Physical diagnosis*
> No abnormality noted
>
> *Other psychiatric diagnosis*
> No abnormality noted

For the mother in Case 5-2, who was not involved in the incest, there was no abnormality physically or psychiatrically. Her concern was quite appropriate to the events that brought her to the hospital.
For many patients tortured by incestuous longings, dreams, and

fantasies for father or brother, consanguineous adult-adult hetero-sexual or homosexual fantasy or dream incest may be the only appro-priate incest diagnosis. There may be another psychiatric diagnosis for such persons: obsessive-compulsive disorder, conversion disorder, atypical dissociative state, or hysterical seizure state. Any of these dis-orders may be due to distress about fantasies, which are neither un-natural, abnormal, nor illegal, about sex with family members. Such distress is not trivial and should be recognized as real. It must also be graded: moderate, severe. The possibility of suicide must be con-sidered if the patient finds the thoughts so ego-alien that self-destruc-tion is the only solution seen. Then, of course, immediate psychiatric hospitalization is indicated and lifesaving. In such a case, the other psychiatric diagnosis would be panic disorder or major depressive dis-order. Intensive psychotherapy and medication would be necessary to prevent a tragedy such as described in *Hamlet*.

PROGNOSIS

The prognosis is still a part of the psychiatric evalua-tion and is given importance by a separate heading. It encapsulates the professional's gut feeling about the outlook for this case:

Prognosis
Guarded owing to the father's pedophilic history

Prognosis
Good with treatment because of strengths and stability of the patient's personality and her family's concern

Prognosis
Poor owing to combined drug and alcohol abuse

RECOMMENDATIONS FOR MANAGEMENT

Recommendations for management, the final segment of a complete psychiatric evaluation, are important guidelines for the courts and other professionals. Although they may err on the side of the ideal and be impossible to attain given the realities of costs, avail-able facilities, and compliance of patient and family, they should nonetheless be as complete as possible. For example, in Case 7-3, the case of consanguineous adult-adult incest envy in a 20-year-old who was having behavior problems at home, the treatment recommenda-tions would be (1) family therapy to help modify unacceptable be-havior at home and reduce scapegoating, and (2) individual psycho-therapy to enhance autonomy and improve self-esteem.

For the family with the pedophilic father (Case 5-2), treatment recommendations would be as follows:

For the father
1. Court probation with close contact to prevent recurrence.
2. Weekly marital therapy with wife.
3. Vocational assistance to regain employment.
4. Individual therapy for self and sexual growth.
5. Possible use of medication (tranquilizers or anti-androgen hormones).

For the mother
1. Attempt change to day shift work.
2. Weekly marital therapy with husband.
3. Her close surveillance of both children to avoid extended times alone with father. Educate mother regarding a pedophilic's compulsive drive to repeat this behavior.

For the school
Teacher or social worker to stay in regular weekly contact with parents in supportive role, to give opportunity to build trust and prevent harassment of child concerning incest.

For the courts
Involve child service agency or probation officer for sustained monitoring of the family.

For the child
Monthly family therapy to (1) allow open dialogue, (2) teach the child her right to privacy and right to refuse sexual overtures, and (3) provide ongoing sex and incest education.

Longitudinal study

There are a dozen studies in search of careful researchers who might attempt the arduous (sometimes impossible) odyssey of finding and following families who received treatment for adult-child or adult-adult incest. Relevant questions will be, How did each member fare? What did each person know about the "family secret?" Was there professional care? For how long? What value did each place on treatment? Did treatment stop the incest? What of those whose "treatment" consisted of jail? Did they reunite with their incest partners? Did the family reconstitute in spite of the jailing? What life adjustment has each family member made since release of the father from jail? What of the child incest partners treated by court placement? How is their adult sexual adjustment? Were they sexually molested by adults or older peers in institutions or foster homes? What life adjustment did each incest partner make? What role do each think the incest experience played in his or her life?

Many unanswered questions remain. Reports that describe a search for 100 women who experienced "positive or negative incest" may perhaps be regarded as follow-up studies. However, longitudinal studies have greater scientific validity because of adequate early documentation of the incests. One follow-up study is available [14]. Many more such studies need to be done and in greater detail. Comparative studies of incestuous and nonincestuous families may be an ideal beyond current actualization because incest is still a crime in our culture. However, until we know why incest does *not* occur in families, we will continue to extrapolate, in a hit-and-miss way, from problem families. The health sciences must become more literate about the incests. Longitudinal comparative studies are an excellent pathway to understanding, treatment, and prevention.

8

TREATMENT OF INCEST:
PHASE THREE—TECHNIQUES

THE clinical approach is remarkably different when an adult presents alone for help with incest and when a child in need of protection is sent for professional assistance. Therefore these situations will be considered separately. In both circumstances, a child may be the incest partner, which will considerably alter the clinical management. Chapter 6 outlined general treatment principles. Now a few specific and explicit incest treatment techniques will be discussed to highlight the kaleidoscopic complexity of incest.

ADULTS AND INCEST

Treatment in adult-adult consensual incest cases may be requested voluntarily by an individual who usually is distressed and therefore assumed to be in need of help, motivated for treatment, and upset because of the reported incest. Whereas to the health care professional *motivation* may mean "no more incest," the patient may really have no desire to change his or her sexual behavior. Regular explicit inquiry about the incestuous relationship is, therefore, an essential aspect of responsible incest treatment: "What has happened sexually between you and your brother this week? Who initiated it? What was your response? Were you orgasmic? Was he? How do you feel about it? And he? Does either of you talk about it? Will this become an indefinite sexual partnership?"

Resistance to therapy or to change may not initially be evident either to the patient or to the professional, unless regular explicit discussion as treatment proceeds discloses the pattern of recurrence. Adult-adult consensual coital incest may continue despite some anxiety, guilt, and even negative social or legal consequences for the patient, whose treatment goals may not be congruent with those of the therapist.

It will then be the task of the health care professional to consider whether the patient's theme is, Help me but don't change me. Is there a hidden agenda? If so, what is it? What purpose is served by being in treatment? What other choices (besides therapy) does the patient have? Is therapy being used to pacify a spouse or a probation officer or to assuage a sense of guilt? Is the distress from a cause other than the incest? What does the incest relationship prevent the patient from doing, e.g., relating to peers? How equal is this relationship?

If the incest is not current but past history, why is the patient distressed now? Could or should some or all of the foregoing questions be raised directly in therapy? Usually, the answer is yes. It is important that the patient understand the many facets of his or her incest behavior and how these influence feeling and functioning.

A physician or other health care professional may resist recognizing incest distress because of difficulty in dealing with the incest content of the complaint.

CASE 8-1. A young family physician shared details of this case: "I was treating a 39-year-old married woman who had a lot of symptoms but no abnormal findings. She seemed down, so I put her on antidepressants and told her to return in two weeks. She came back on a busy afternoon. When I asked how she was getting on, she started to cry, saying it was the anniversary of her father's death, which she had not gotten over because he had molested her when she was 12 years old. Well, I got out of there so fast saying I had to make a phone call! I don't know what hit me. When I returned, she had stopped crying. I upped her antidepressants. She came back but never brought up the incest again."

This was an honest report of professional avoidance. The physician was later able to say he feared his lack of knowledge about incest. He had professional "performance anxiety" and used avoidance as a defense. He followed an old motto: When in doubt, do nothing.

How many such incidents occur daily in emergency rooms or doctors' offices? Shocked withdrawal, avoidance, ignoring the subject, feeling anxious and overwhelmed, disbelief, covering up, panic, silence, no follow-up of somatic symptoms or depression? All of the above would surely apply to many nurses, emergency room technicians, physician's assistants, interns, medical students, and attending doctors. The patient in this case realized that the family physician was unable to deal with her problem and did not again ask. How could he have handled it differently?

Any of the following responses might have helped (even if there was really a phone call to make or a beep on the beeper or 20 more patients):

1. "That's something we must discuss after I take this call" (acknowledging the incest problem).

2. "That's a topic we must get back to when I have more time. What about Thursday at 4:30 P.M.?" (acknowledges the importance of the incest problem, gives hope of help).
3. "That's an experience that may occur in more homes than you think. It also may happen with boys. We will have to talk some more on Thursday at 4:30 P.M. Can you make that time?" (reassurance, acknowledgment, and promise of help).

These responses show acceptance of the patient and indicate that her problem is not an overwhelming one. A calm professional response allays fears in the patient that the incest topic is too awful to talk about. If the doctor honestly states that there is time pressure now but promises follow-up later, it is still therapeutic because the incest has been acknowledged as the topic for that visit. In addition to giving acceptance and hope, it is helpful to give the patient informed reassurance (saying that incest is not that uncommon). This immediately reduces her sense of isolation or uniqueness.

If at the time of her first incest revelation there had been even 10 minutes for a few questions, these might have been asked: "How old were you when father died? You said you were 12 when he molested you? How long did it continue? Did he hurt or force you? Was there intercourse? Did you get pregnant? Whom did you tell? What kind of a man was your father? What kind of feeling do you have for him now? Have you had psychiatric or counseling help? Does your husband know? How long has this been distressing you? How much do you think about this? Do you dream about it?"

This line of questions allows the patient to open up. If it is the very first time she has ever talked, her relief at the emotional abreaction will be analagous to having an abscess lanced and the pus evacuated— painful yet essential. Healing of the incest wound may be rapid, or further follow-up discussions may be needed to relieve residual negative feelings [132].

What would the professional's personal reactions be to asking these questions? Possibly some hesitation. Yet these are not overwhelming questions; they follow good medical practice—when in doubt, get more relevant history to obtain a better perspective. Then the patient may be given informed reassurance: "Many persons make satisfactory adjustments although there was incest. What do you think of your own life adjustment? What part did the incest play in your overall adjustment?"

At best the patient will have done remarkably well, and recognition for that fact can be given. This will reinforce her strengths, which may have weakened temporarily because of a clinical depression that is causing her to see only the dark side of things. Perhaps she may cry and say she has felt lifelong guilt because of telling her mother who went to the police and had her father sent to jail. What can the doctor do then? Relax and again follow the same procedure you would in taking a medical history: get more history. If a patient had breast cancer and tearfully reported that her father died of lung cancer at 39 years of age, the physician would need more explicit details to assist her by determining how the family history related to her present diagnosis. Only then could the physician give the patient a helpful perspective. Similarly, for the depressed woman reporting incest, this cluster of questions will be needed: "Do you think your father had a psychiatric problem? Did he ever have trouble with the law? Did he drink? Take drugs? What kind of relationship did he have with your mother? What kind of relationship did you have with your mother?"

From this it is easily possible for the professional to assist the patient with something like the following retrospective reassurance: "You were only 12 years old, and you trusted and loved your father and didn't think anything he did was wrong. You couldn't understand why mother yelled at him so much for his drinking. When he cuddled you on his lap it felt good. Only this one time he was really drunk and tried to stick his finger into your rectum, and that hurt, and you screamed. So Mother came, and it was right that she protected you. She yelled at Dad, but he tried it again another time so she went to the police. You felt bad, and you felt to blame. Feeling bad was normal, because you loved your dad. Feeling to blame was not accurate. He was a grown-up and a parent and was responsible for his behavior, not you for his. Mother was also responsible for protecting you. Alcohol lowers a person's self-control. He was affectionate you said. Affection and sex are closely related. With alcohol he went beyond affection and also beyond sensitivity because he hurt you."

This technique of looking back into the past with an objective explanation helps to give the patient adult perspective toward her childhood self. This may be sufficient to relieve her feelings of distress. Further resolution may be assisted by explaining to her that conflict may be the main reason she has not resolved the problem: "You loved your father but were hurt by him. Those are two opposite feelings. Also the cuddling felt good but you felt upset or bad that he touched your genitals and rectum, and you blamed yourself. Feelings get mixed up."

If the doctor feels uneasy, he or she will not obtain a detailed history. One family physician expressed the concern: "I don't want to play amateur psychiatrist," implying that harmful effects could result from an explicit incest discussion. Thus far the suggested responses and questions are practical, straightforward, and concerned. Since the patient herself raised the issue, talking about it may bring relief.

For this 39-year-old depressed woman, one additional task could be of benefit, namely, forgiving her father so that her conflict may resolve. A few more questions may be required: "Did you see your father before he died? Do you think he forgave you? Did you forgive him? Forgiveness is an old-fashioned word, but it is a way of making peace." The patient may or may not be able to do this. One woman said, "I can understand him better, but I cannot forgive him. Not yet anyway." Does she have to? Not necessarily. At least she has gained some perspective through understanding the sexual behavior of her now dead father. She may then possibly accept his person while quite normally rejecting his behavior. This approach is useful. Adaptive behavior, as well as relief of distress, often follows from self-awareness.

In some cases, however, habitual, seemingly self-defeating interactions may continue for years. The difficult task for every responsible therapist is to analyze what specific gratification reinforces behavior that the patient knows is inappropriate. Since the incests provide sexualized closeness in a valued relationship, the reinforcement is strongly positive—physiologically as well as psychologically. The fact that incest is socially, legally, and morally unacceptable may not be a deterrent, unless negative effects (pain, shameful discovery, arrest) have been experienced.

Voluntary engagement in individual psychotherapy

Traditional techniques of psychotherapy include a supportive phase (accepting the patient and gathering data), followed by an insight phase (understanding the symptoms, conflicts, needs, and defenses), an action phase (with definite changes in maladaptive, unacceptable behavior), and finally an integrative phase (relearning, sustaining change, and attaining personal growth). The last of these phases begins during therapy and should continue after the termination of psychotherapy with relief of personal distress [183].

Rapid resolution of emotional symptoms may occur with the help of brief psychotherapy for some fortunate individuals who have adequate ego strengths, namely, an ability to tolerate anxiety yet face difficulties; adaptability; and a capacity for self-reflection, for relating well to others, and for change. These characteristics allow the individual to utilize psychotherapy optimally. However, the ideal resolution of incest problems may be blocked by pitfalls: severe anxiety or depression, which lowers or reduces ego strengths; resistance to change resulting from fear of unknown consequences; excess defensiveness that precludes self-reflection and constructive change; marked dependence upon an incestuous relationship; an unwillingness to move on to other, more appropriate relationships.

Just as the patient, consciously or unconsciously, defines his or her internal reaction, so too the patient determines the goals of therapy. For some guilt-ridden patients, simply getting psychotherapy may be sufficient effort and cost to assuage the guilt, while at the same time allowing the incest behavior to continue. Such a mechanism is analogous to using, in a circuitous way, the religious confessional, penance, and a professed resolution to change to temporarily improve internal guilt feelings regarding morally unacceptable behavior, and then repeating the same behavior within days. An alert, involved, ethical therapist will note such patterns, and point them out to the patient repeatedly until finally both insight and change may occur. Repetitious confrontation may be frustrating to a therapist yet is an important ingredient of psychotherapy. The therapist must be patient and able to tolerate ambiguity and the need for repetition, both of which are common human weaknesses.

CASE 8-2. A childless woman of 37 years came to the Loyola Psychiatry Clinic for an evaluation for depression. She was neither suicidal nor in severe distress. She had recently gone through a traumatic divorce after 10 years of marriage. Her husband had left her to marry another woman. No medications were prescribed for the patient. In psychotherapy it was revealed that she, a highly successful career woman, had drifted away from her husband emotionally for some years; the divorce stress related more to her sense of being rejected by him: "He was the dumper and I was the dumpee and that hurt. I'm not used to that." They had not fought and had had no sexual difficulties. They had both agreed that children would interfere with their careers, so she had had a tubal ligation at age 30.

Within one month of her divorce, her brother, a 35-year-old lawyer, also childless and divorced, moved in with her. "He was also a dumpee. We had not seen each other since college. He took the first job transfer he could get out of Minnesota. I said he could stay with me till he got a place." Both drank quite heavily at a party one night and also smoked marijuana. "It was a good party, and I was higher than he was. I walked into the bathroom when we got home. There he was in the shower. We giggled and I got in too. Next thing we were in bed."

This consensual consanguineous adult-adult coital incest had been occurring for many months when she came for psychotherapy. She and her brother both knew it was unacceptable and against the law. She kept saying that they must stop. They did not. She protested to the therapist: "We're adult. It isn't harming anyone else." However, she had discomfort, guilt, and fluctuating anxiety about it.

The therapist asked that her brother join the therapy. She refused. "He'd never come. He's a lawyer, and it might show on his record." Possibly, but this may have been resistance on her part.

The therapist then asked if her brother was as upset as she was about the incest. She was uncertain. Then another challenge: "Who is getting the most out of this relationship?" At first the patient snapped, "What do you mean?" The question was repeated. Slowly she picked up the lead. For the past eight months or so, the brother had received free room, board, and sex. She admitted that she needed his company and came back with the cliché misery loves company. Next the therapist asked if she would like to have this as a permanent, lifetime arrangement.

Suddenly she sat up and said: "No! He's untidy, he chain smokes, I've been doing his laundry. I have to be crazy. Next thing he'll find a woman and I'll be a dumpee all over again. No way." However, although the sexual aspect of the relationship slowed down because of a vaginal infection, coitus continued a further six months before she (indirectly) asked him to move out. The interdependence was intense. She was upset and very lonely. She was hesitant to commit herself to another close relationship, but began to attend some evening college courses.

Gaining perspective regarding the incest

In traditional psychoanalytically oriented psychotherapy, connections may become apparent to the therapist years before they dawn on the patient, although sometimes the reverse is true.
Improvement may occasionally occur without the patient ever verbaliz-
ing what the therapist considers critical links between the presenting
incest problem and antecedent causes. There are also situations in
which the patient knows and says exactly what occurred, what his or
her role was (e.g., coerced, misinformed), yet retains distress, guilt,
or incest dreams and longings [117].

The vital relationships between intellectual and emotional insight
still await discovery. However, therapists empirically use rational-
emotive pathways to assist patients to gain perspective regarding ongoing or earlier incest experiences that have led to the discomfort that
brings them to therapy. For example, in the case of the divorced 37-
year-old woman engaged in an incestuous sexual affair with her 35-
year-old brother, the woman was fully aware that her depression related to this liaison, although she avoided dealing with her feelings for
many months while she rationalized that both of them needed a sexual
outlet. The therapist repeatedly attempted, by incisive questions, to
assist her to gain perspective regarding her needs for acceptance and
affection after having been rejected by her husband. The patient knew
that her brother loved and accepted her with or without sex, but
thought that a sexual bond would be stronger. With the sexualized
affection, she obtained physical closeness and tension release, and
hoped to hold him permanently. Rationally, she saw he had much
more to gain from the arrangement than she, and that she was setting
herself up for being emotionally overly dependent on him and feeling
hurt and rejected a second time if he went off with another partner.

This approach in the treatment of incest was no different than it
would have been had the exploitative liaison been with a random partner. What was different was the therapist's obligation to point out
that the incest relationship was totally self-defeating, since the law
precluded their making a valid, lifelong marriage commitment. There
was no hope that time, death, or divorce might bring freedom to
marry. Few countries in contemporary society other than France allow
close consanguineous marriages.

Techniques of assisting a patient to gain perspective are ① talking,
② analyzing dreams, and ③ letter writing to the incest partner.

TALKING TECHNIQUE. The talking technique was used in
most of the cases already presented. It has no fixed format. Active
listening and incisive clarification questions allow the patient to search
the self for answers: "Do you want John as a permanent, exclusive
life and love partner? What are you getting from this relationship?
What is he getting from it? What are three positive and three nega-

tive aspects of this relationship? Write them down so we can discuss them."

All patient leads deserve follow-up: "It is the anniversary of my father's death. He molested me when I was 12." Comments like "When did he die? Do you get upset every anniversary? Do you visit the cemetery? Do you think your mother knew?" are all ways to help her look back in a different way, with less distress.

DREAM ANALYSIS. "Have you had any dreams that you remember? Do any of these relate to you and John" (or uncle or father, if the incest was in the past)? After the patient relates the dream, ask what it meant. The answer is usually in the patient and surfaces with surprisingly few questions such as, "Who did the bird remind you of?" or "Where were you in the dream?" or "Who was the man with the keys?"

Dream interpretation is far from an exact science. It is neither mysterious nor always a "royal road" to insight. It is often a hit-and-miss association of ideas. However, clinically it is neglectful not to ask about dreams, since sleeping is an altered, uninhibited state of consciousness. Recurring dreams of incest experiences or fantasies are of diagnostic importance, since they inform the clinician that, during the unconscious state of sleep, the patient is attempting to obtain resolution of residual incest distress or fulfillment of consciously forbidden incest wishes.

Most persons dream about three to five times per eight hours of sleep, yet few remember more than one dream and that may be occasionally rather than daily. Individuals can train themselves to record their dreams. Some keep a dream diary with note pad, pen, and flashlight at their bedside. For most persons, dreams seem to be a meaningless, mixed-up story. This is due to "dream shorthand," which at times may be decoded only with effort and review. At other times, dreams are vivid and relate to "day residue," problems currently preoccupying the sleeping mind, e.g., the winner of a horse race, exam questions, solving a problem, or making a decision.

One woman in therapy reported years of being blamed and shamed in her family of birth after age 6, when her maternal uncle was "caught playing with me down there." Her older brother told her mother, who berated her daily, "You're a whore! Don't touch yourself there." There was marked loss of self-esteem. She dropped out of school at age 15 and went to work. At 18 she married a stable, hardworking, caring man. She had successfully repressed the consanguineous noncoital noncoercive (the sexual contact was not upsetting or unpleasant; the discovery was) heterosexual incest until she came for sex therapy for her sexual disinterest. The routine questions on the incest questionnaire (Figure 1) elicited the childhood story. In her marriage, she refused any sex play but always participated in intercourse with her husband. "I give it to him, so why isn't he satisfied?"

Fortunately, her uneducated yet sensitive husband realized she was not enjoying their sexual exchange and altruistically sought help. She told her husband her incest story for the first time during sex therapy. He was supportive and noncondemnatory.

About two weeks later she lit a cigarette and said, "I dreamed about him, just falling and falling in the sky." "Him" was her uncle. Asked what the dream meant, she said she didn't know but, "I know he ain't going to give me no more trouble." There was no one else in the dream, yet she saw the descent. No further interpretation was given, yet she was correct. Her uncle was no longer a block, nor was the blaming mother. This was the week she had finally emancipated herself from about 46 years of conditioned suppression of her natural sexual feelings. For the first time she went to bed without night-clothes, accepted genital sex play, and became orgasmic.

LETTER WRITING TO THE INCEST PARTNER. Letter writing to the incest partner (alive or dead) is another technique that is therapeutically useful. The letter is not for actual mailing but explained as a "pretend" letter, totally honest, "as if you were brave enough to say what you really feel about it." If there is time, a blank sheet of paper is given in the therapy hour; otherwise the task can be assigned to do at home. In the case just described, since the husband now also knew of the incest, he was also asked to write an open letter to the uncle. This proved most supportive of his wife, since he rebuked the uncle for the act and excused her as an innocent child. This was of therapeutic value in reinforcing his concern and care for her.

Her letter to her uncle was a surprise to the therapist and revealed why her feelings about the incest had remained unresolved for so many years. She really loved her uncle! He had been kind and gentle, good and important to her as a child and had given her the only treats and money she had in an impoverished welfare home. With her mother's daily condemnation she had for years needlessly blamed herself for the adult-child sexual contact. She had then generalized that all sex is bad, not understanding that her uncle was a forbidden partner. Her uncle had been banned from the home after discovery of the incest, so she lost him then "all because of sex." The resultant conflict led to long-lasting anxiety and distress around any expression of sexuality. The letter-writing technique revealed her residual feelings of conflict and began the process of resolution. Thus she finally attained not only adult perspective regarding the incestuous fondling but also forgiveness of both her uncle and her mother in the circumstances. She said, "They didn't know any better, no schooling or anything."

Resolution of incest distress

All health care professionals must learn that incest may occur without any distress to either partner when both are incest accepting. When a whole culture is incest accepting, there may be pleasure and satisfaction at retaining the family status, name, property, or wealth. In many instances, religious dispensation for marriage between second-line consanguineous relatives (first cousins, uncle-niece, aunt-nephew) resolves any conflict between the legal and moral incest code of a community. Distress may relate not to the incest but to the legal red tape needed to obtain clearance to be married. In some situations, persons may drop a religious affiliation and even leave a country of origin in order to legitimize an incestuous liaison. It is rare and incidental that an incest-accepting individual is seen clinically. It is more likely that such persons would be found in demographic research by anthropologists and other social scientists. Observation, not intervention, is the task of the researcher. Incest distress or its absence should be recorded but not assumed.

When incest experiences of any kind come to clinical attention because there is emotional distress, then the therapeutic task is to assist the patient to attain relief. It is usually in retrospect that this will be called for. Some of the internal mechanisms or psychodynamics that will help heal incest distress are

1. Sharing the secret with an understanding, concerned person (relief from opening up without being rejected)
2. Cognitive evaluation of the actual events and the responsibility of each family member (gaining perspective)
3. Objective consideration of the history with feedback from a professional or respected authority regarding the possible cause-and-effect relationships (gaining further perspective)
4. Obtaining information regarding affection and sex (education about sex and feelings)
5. Learning that conflictive feelings toward the incest partner, such as love and anger or love and fear, are quite normal (further education about feelings)
6. Obtaining information regarding incest laws and practices (incest education)
7. Understanding in retrospect, with feedback from a professional or other authority, possible family dynamics leading to inappropriate sexualization of affection toward the patient (family perspective)
8. Possible forgiveness of the incest initiator, the self, and the nonprotective parent (*Forgiveness* means "to understand and pardon; to stop being angry with; to give up efforts to punish." An old French saying, to understand all is to forgive all, explains how final resolution of recurrent guilt feelings can occur through cognition of "why.")
9. Letting go of the past, that is, past regrets, remorse, blaming, guilts, envy, or upsetting fantasies
10. Tolerating ambivalent feelings toward the incest partner and other family members.

CASE 8-3. A woman in her late fifties sought help for confusion and agitation of about seven weeks' duration. In taking a thorough personal history, a woman medical student was amazed at this segment: "I had a wonderful father who really cared about me. My mother was in a wheelchair for as long as I can remember. She had multiple sclerosis and hardly talked. He looked after her, and so did my grandmother. I had one older sister who got pregnant when she was 18 years old and had to get married. Everyone was upset. I was 16 years old. Father came to my room saying he wanted to teach me about sex so I would be able to resist boys and not be trapped like my sister. He wanted to help me and I know he did."

The patient excused her father's noncoital consanguineous incest contact as altruistic and matter-of-fact. He had rubbed her genital area by hand, and she had had her first orgasm. Before this her occasional masturbation had been nonclimatic, but this changed. He was a quiet man. Neither father nor daughter had mentioned or repeated this sexual exchange. There was no distress in telling this early history, which was difficult for the medical student to understand. The story was detailed and given quite voluntarily and spontaneously. The woman had at no time received counseling or psychotherapy. This was the first time she had ever told anyone her life history, and she told it all quite honestly and completely.

Her immediate distress related to an agitated depression after a series of losses: Her eldest son was killed in Vietnam; her husband suffered a stroke and required total home nursing for two years until he died a few months ago. The final blow was the sudden death of her sister. When she told of her sister's adolescent turmoil, the woman revealed her own unusual sex education by her father. The incest was not a problem now or earlier. She understood it at the time (cognition and perspective existed at age 16) and was not distressed by it. There was no resentment, and no forgiveness was needed.

Her most acute current concerns centered around coping with aging and fears of death, sorting out her husband's complex estate, and entering the job market now at age 57. She had questions about a 41-year-old blind niece who was in a nursing home: "Is MS hereditary?" There was also some unfounded anxiety that she herself had multiple sclerosis. She was assisted with delayed normal grieving for the many close, important relatives lost during the past 10 years. She was given recognition for her strengths in coping so well (1) as a teenager with the early home stresses, (2) with the sex education given by her father, (3) with her husband's illness, and (4) with the deaths of her son and husband.

It is worth analyzing how this woman dealt so comfortably with her reactions to the single incestuous exchange. (1) Her secret was shared with her father who was concerned. (2) She understood her sister's crisis and her father's wish to prevent its recurrence. She trusted him. (3) She respected her father and his method. (4) She realized that this was a deliberate, one-time sexualization of her father's affection. Moreover, it was unilaterally sexualized, since her father was not aroused nor was he affectionate but rather very serious and calm at that "instruction." (5) She had no conflict about her relationship with her father. (6) She was blissfully ignorant of incest laws—then and when seen. (7) She clearly understood her family interactions even at 16. (8) She did not need to forgive her father. (9) She had no guilt or regrets. Letting go of the past was not an issue because she had not become overconcerned about the father-daughter sex contact then or later. (10) At no time did she have residual ambivalent feelings to be understood or resolved.

Occasionally an author in a published "autopsychoanalysis" reveals prolonged, almost lifelong preoccupation with incestuous longings [117]. At times, lengthy case analyses describe tortured unresolved guilts about incest fantasies [155].

Incest themes abound in erotic literature in which, until very recently, the redeeming social value was maintained by including punishment by death or worse [111]. These are often dismissed by clinicians as fiction rather than fact. However, an occasional person who reads about the "forbidden fruit" of incest may not only become aroused but may also relate these feelings to his or her own early, perhaps suppressed, incestuous thoughts or behavior. For some, anxiety, guilt, or distress then propels a search for professional help.

Accused or convicted adult initiators of incest

Accused or convicted adult incest initiators have not been studied longitudinally to understand their fate and future. Court procedures often take one to three years before sentencing. What happens in the interim to personal and family adjustments? Then there are the stresses of publicity, social shame, job repercussions, legal costs, and endless waiting. Upon conviction comes entry and adjustment to the penal world, where sex offenders invite great scorn from hardened nonsex criminals. Who has written or told of the shock of reentry into a life without bars for released incest offenders? Have they in the interim had regular family contact, letters, or visits? Do they return to the family? If they do, much will have changed in the years away. Some have been divorced while in jail. Do some remarry? Does the incest recur? Do they seek out and threaten or harm those responsible for their conviction?

Profiles of incest sex offenders that give history and a possible diagnosis present only a small and static segment of the complex course of their lives [22, 56, 110]. In the past few years, some specialized outpatient programs are providing family therapy and include convicted incest initiators on probation. Valuable data may yet emerge on the processes leading to the incest behavior, its discovery, possible recurrence, and perhaps on how to change it [59].

If there are any autopsychoanalyses of the thoughts and feelings of convicted incest initiators, I have not seen them. Is there remorse, indifference, or sustained desire for their lost forbidden partner? Do they receive psychotherapy in jail to help them understand what caused their affection to become illegally sexualized? Perhaps forensic psychiatrists could consider research on such questions.

ADULT-CHILD INCEST

In some instances, a parent may request post-incest treatment for a child from a private psychiatrist or counseling professional. This may occur in emotional crisis, upon incidental discovery of the incest, or long after the event. A child in emotional crisis may have symptoms of acute distress, without a parent realizing that incest is the upsetting factor. A psychiatrist may sometimes be the first professional seen, but figures are not available for the incidence of adult-child incest presenting directly in private psychiatric practice.

The first step in treatment remains the careful data gathering described in Chapter 6. Then the phase two psychiatric evaluation described in Chapter 7—mental status and psychodynamic formulation with proper and rigorous incest diagnosis—takes place. The next concern is for how the child has reacted to the incest and what negative effect, if any, there has been, namely, other psychiatric diagnosis and physical diagnosis if any. Concern for child protection is always primary, no matter where the child is seen.

In Illinois, the capacity for sexual consent of a girl or boy under 16 is considered by law to be absent, no matter how precocious the child is. Mandatory reporting laws in Illinois make it criminal for a psychologist, social worker, counselor, or nurse not to report, after a thorough evaluation, to a child protection agency. A psychiatrist has doctor-patient privileges under the law and may maintain confidentiality unless a subpoena is served. Not reporting does not mean not protecting a minor. Therapeutic protection may proceed quite successfully with concerned intervention.

The presenting parent's capacity to believe the child, protect the child, and challenge the incest partner (spouse or child) must be openly discussed with the child as the history unfolds, with the parent who brought the child, and then with both parent and child. This assists clear communication between them without undue blame or shame. Dialogue can reveal hostility, rejection, concern for the child, the attitude of each toward the other incest partner (helplessness or fear), and resources for safety and change. This approach is both supportive and begins to provide some insight.

CASE 8-4. After an interview with a 10-year-old, Mark, this was said to both mother and boy: "Mark is withdrawn, crying, and talking about wanting to die because his stepfather is forcing him to do oral sex every evening when you go to work, Mother. He has threatened to beat both of you if Mark tells. It is all so upsetting that Mark doesn't know how to get out of it. He thinks if he dies things will get better. I told Mark that he has a right to his own privacy of body and that sex should not be forced. I also told him it was rough to be 10 years old and want to protect Mother and himself. I don't understand why his stepfather's sexual feelings are so mixed up. Mark says he drinks at least six cans of beer every night. Mother, can you tell us what you think?"

At first, the mother shook her head and said she couldn't understand either. Then she looked at Mark and said she was sorry it had happened. The next statement was, "He's never hit anyone, you or me or anyone. He maybe is missing me in the evenings. I didn't realize he's drinking so much. I can switch to day shift from next week. I'll call in sick this week, so I'll be home." On her own, her maternal concern for Mark had immediately pushed her into the action phase of therapy—she made immediate plans for changing things in order to be with Mark and her new husband. She was a bright, well-integrated lady who asked for a few minutes alone with the therapist.

She revealed that she had gone off the pill six months earlier. Since then she had feared pregnancy and had decided that abstinence would be a temporary contraceptive. Her second husband, aged 36, was in his third marriage; she, at 28, was in her second. She felt sure that he was neither homosexual nor pedophilic. "We had a great sexual relationship. I was foolish, and he didn't pressure me for sex. Working different shifts, I avoided even knowing what he was feeling and what was happening. He's not a drinker either. Poor Mark. How damaged is he? Can we see you all together, soon, tomorrow, so we can try to straighten this out?"

Stepfather, mother, and Mark came in together the next afternoon, all three looking pale and tired but holding hands with mother in the middle—significant body language. In the family therapy session that followed, Mark started by saying, "We played Scrabble till 2:00 A.M." Who's we? "All of us." When did the game start? "After midnight." What did you do before that? "They talked." And you? "I heard it all." Where were you? "In the bathroom" (next door to their bedroom). What did they say? "They both said sorry, about three times." For what? "Jake's drinking and what he did to me." Anything else? "My mother said she was sorry too." What for? "That she didn't know he was lonely and that I was upset." Anything else? He shook his head, and both his mother and his stepfather smiled. Mark had overheard correctly. Mother had been correct, there was no beating.

Mark had emerged from the bathroom as his parents went down to the kitchen for a snack, to which he was invited. Then the stepfather had said what about a round of Scrabble since they were all up anyway? Late but relaxed, they finally all went to bed. No authorities were involved other than the therapist and the revitalized parental authority. In later sessions, the stepfather spontaneously said to Mark, "That was bad news. The beer really messed up my behavior. I feel ashamed that I frightened you and made you do stuff you didn't want to." He rationalized that alcohol lowered his controls but was uncomfortable using explicit sexual words. I asked if it was difficult to talk openly about sex? "Yes." Sometimes sex and angry feelings get mixed up, especially for some people when there's alcohol. "Yes." Oral sex is one of the ways of expressing sexual feelings. "Yes." In a family, expressing sexual feelings is between the mother and father only. "Yes." The law protects children from sex with grown-ups, so they can grow up themselves and make up their own minds privately about sex. There was a long silence as this education about sex and incest had an impact on all three. It was also teaching the rights of a child and parental responsibility.

In six months of treatment, there was no regression to incest, drink, or night shift work. Many times Mark came to therapy with Jake, having gone elsewhere first, and the mother met them at the psychiatrist's office. All three had adjusted and integrated well. The reconstituted family was now a nurturant one for all of them.

Engaging the family in therapy

The criminal dimension of incest sets up an inevitable contradiction between the professional and civil duties of a therapist. When legal coercion propels an incest family to a psychiatrist for a court evaluation of child and adult, the adult may comply externally. Internal attitudes and drives, however, are much more difficult to assess and perhaps impossible to predict. Although reforms of the incest laws have been recommended in Canada and in England, there has been no recent change in these laws in those countries or in the United States. Reporting adult-child incest is still required by Illinois law and possibly in all other states. Not reporting is a misdemeanor. Therefore, the dilemma caused by the criminal status of incest becomes how to engage the family in treatment.

Being both an advocate for the family and an adversary (legally) is an uncomfortable and conflictive professional position, which violates the privileged doctor-patient relationship. Referring the family for care to a social worker, knowing that he or she must report, is one way for the physician to handle this personal dilemma. Another way is to be quite honest: "I want to do my best to help you as a family and individually. Since Mary is a minor, I must inform the agency who sent you of the results of our talk. It is awkward, but I am bound by the law" or "It's hard for you to believe that first and foremost I'm on your side as your doctor, yet I have to obey the law, too."

Important questions in the initial phase of adult-child incest therapy will be

1. Will you come as a family for therapy? I recommend family therapy so you can all understand and get help.
2. Will the father (adult incest partner) come in to talk to me? I would like to let him give his side of the story.
3. Will you be able to ensure that the incest will not be repeated? I must make a statement to the court about how you can protect Mary from her father (incest partner).

They may say all the expected and acceptable things on evaluation, yet leave the state as a family in the next 48 hours.

Supervision by both a helping professional and an arm of the law, together, has been postulated to be an optimal therapeutic combination [59]. However, what may be perceived by professionals as good management of incest, namely, regular family therapy or individual or marital therapy, may be very differently experienced by the various family members involved. They may consider therapy an unwelcome invasion of privacy. It may be therapeutic to mention, "Treatment may seem like an intrusion but there are incest treatment centers that have worked closely with the courts and with families and so provided an alternative to putting father (adult incest partner) in jail and breaking the famiy up. This alternative treats the whole family as outpatients and gives regular reports to the Courts." This is factual and gives some hope.

Family therapy is an alternative to (1) recurrence of the incest, (2) disruption of the family by jailing one member, and (3) disappearance of the family, who may flee from the state before the evaluation is done. Therefore, the initial post-evaluation task of the health professional is to persuade the parents and child to remain in therapy and to use it regularly. The intruder image carried by helping professionals is inescapable initially. With concern and goodwill, a trust relationship may evolve so that a voluntary therapeutic alliance may develop later. Impending court dates, feelings about waiting, and fears about consequences of the incest need to be discussed.

The incest allegation may proceed to a court trial. One family member will be the accused, and others will have to appear as witnesses. Either position is highly charged emotionally and severely stressful. The legal system cannot be accused of being warm or supportive. The letter of the law must be upheld, and those who do not abide by the law must be apprehended, given a fair trial, and punished if condemned. Guilty or not guilty? How does each family member handle the fear, the panic, the pain, and the shame? Who is able to sleep the night before? Which parent is able to comfort and console a child witness before, during, and after an incest trial?

A child's testimony may be critical in the proceedings. Is the incest story true, consistent, and concordant with other data received? How upset is the child? How severe are the loyalty conflicts? Will the story change, or is there some pressure or adult coaching? It is an exceedingly difficult double bind to give evidence that incriminates a parent, possibly a loved family member—brother, uncle, or stepfather—and that may jeopardize the security of self and of the family. The implications and consequences can never be fully explained to child or family.

Integrity, sincerity, a noncondemnatory attitude toward the parents as people, and a willingness to understand and stand by them in their pain are all important qualities in a health care professional that will allow engagement of a family in a therapeutic alliance despite all of the difficult realities.

"Losing" the family

We have no idea what happens to the family that handles the incest crisis by "escape" from their given address. They simply do not show for the next appointment, and the phone may be disconnected.

There are many stereotypes about disintegration and disorganization in incest families. Some do—maybe those that are in legal custody. Many more have sufficient cohesion and collaboration to mobilize and leave after the discovery of incest and the initial legal inquiry. They pack up their belongings, maintain secrecy, sacrifice rental, property, school, and simply disappear suddenly.

Does the outside threat integrate the family and stop the incest? Does the child incest partner lose the affection of father and get blamed by both parents as a liar and troublemaker? How much do other siblings really know about the incest? Will the mother or a sibling become more aware of the child's vulnerability and now protect him or her? We have no idea, since there has been no follow-up of such families.

The responsible professional must immediately inform the referring legal authority that the family has failed to come for an appointment. Reporting must not be delayed until the agency calls the doctor or health professional. To protect a vulnerable child, the child service agency must be called, and a brief written statement must be sent to ensure follow-up. Phone messages may be misplaced, so a written note is necessary.

Timing of legal involvement

When the courts refer incest cases, the legal machinery has preceded the request for evaluation or treatment. In emergency rooms, child abuse laws mandate immediate involvement of a child protection agency for rape incest or for any adult-child sexual contact. The emergency room nurse will usually alert a social worker as soon as the physical crisis has subsided. The social worker may be on the rape or child abuse team and proceed to involve the child service agency for child protection.

In self-referred cases in private medical practice, the individual or family must first be carefully and completely evaluated to find out what actual behavior has occurred. Then the family members must be informed of the doctor's obligations and special privileges under local incest laws. It may be of help for the physician, psychiatrist, or other health care professional to seek legal counsel from a judge in children's court (anonymously to preserve patient confidentiality) or from a lawyer. When the legal position is clarified, it must be explained to the family as supportively as possible: "I wish we did not have these laws, but they still exist. I will do my best to back you up through the process." This may or may not prevent alarm, anxiety, or flight from treatment.

No health care professional is able to predict the course of an official report to a child protection agency. It may be pro forma, that is, a simple phone statement that there is alleged incest, reporting who was involved and saying that the family agree to treatment. However, there will most probably be a follow-up contact from the agency involving child, incest partner, and parents. No matter how tactfully all of this may be handled, it is stressful, anxiety provoking for family members and professionals, and time demanding. The therapist can only assure the family: "I will stand by to help you through the legal machinery" or "We can get our hospital child advocacy team to be of help to you." It is hoped that this organization can remain objective enough to be supportive to both the family and the minor in need of protection.

Currently in nearly every state, legal involvement remains an inevitable consequence of incest.

Contact with legal authorities

For a professional who has not regularly had dealings with the courts and legal agencies, contact with them is quite a learning experience. If the helping professional anticipates a totally different orientation from his or her own, the level of frustration may be lessened.

Once telephone contact is achieved, write down the name, title, and phone number of the child agency official. Expect about five transfers of your call and five repetitions of the facts, which will make you more objective and clear by the time the correct official is finally reached. Also anticipate that the person contacted today may be transferred or gone by the next time you call. One way to deal with the change is to write the child's agency case number clearly on the chart and use this when calling or writing, so that a newly assigned official can easily locate the needed information.

For adult-child incest cases, the Illinois Division of Child and Family Services in recent years has become crisis-oriented. There is a 24-hour child abuse hot line in most cities and towns, and the agency will move rapidly for minors in need of protection from violence or "any sex act" between adult and child. A report to the agency is followed by a home investigation, which usually means immediate removal of the child from the home. In cases of violence, this may be lifesaving. In cases of sexual coercion, placement elsewhere may halt the alleged incestuous sexual activity; however, the separation from home, family, neighborhood, teacher, friends, pets, and private belongings may represent equivalent or greater emotional stress for the child. Guilt and self-blame are not eliminated by placement alone. It will also take time and testing to build enough trust for valued, affectionate new adult-child or child-child relationships.

Resistance to making new relationships in a placement may be long and strong. There may be fear that (1) making new friends means disloyalty to his or her own family; (2) placement is very transitory so engaging is not worthwhile; (3) nonfamily are not to be trusted, no matter what they may say; (4) losing these new relationships will hurt if they become important; (5) the self is unworthy of being cared for because of the incest and resultant family upheaval or (6) the family will retaliate and punish when seen again. The more numerous the placement transfers, the more emotionally traumatic it will be for a child to relate to guardians and to new peers. Professionals should not expect a child to be grateful that he or she has been "saved" from an incestuous home, with or without violence or force. It is quite normal to love and fear the same person. It is known that children, even physically abused children or children who have been incest partners, run away repeatedly from a placement to seek their own home and family. They are not bad or ungrateful or degenerate. They are seeking to salvage important family relationships.

Therefore, all professionals, including courts and probation officers, may benefit from considering their management only just begun—not finished—with a placement. It is a holding pattern, analogous to that of a plane above a busy airport. A time of landing back in the family for the child must occur—3 weeks, 3 years, or 13 years later. Returning home is a strong instinct. The adult incest partner may or may not be jailed, but he will also later return to the home, sometimes having threatened to kill those who reported him. Ethically, every individual health professional must consider these facts and ask, What will the immediate, intermediate, and long-term outcome be? Optimum help with minimal harm is the essential edict of the helping professions. Immediate fragmentation of a family may cause severe, even irreversible, damage, including a lethal outcome of suicide or homicide.

Without any communications from home—cards, letters, or phone calls—a child in a temporary or permanent placement may become withdrawn, anxious, or depressed or show a variety of grief and stress symptoms: sleeplessness, loss of appetite, vague pains, school problems, aggressive behavior, crying, agitation, suicide attempts. Individual psychotherapy may be of immediate help. Family therapy must later be recommended if there is to be a return to the original family.

The use of tape recordings

The use of tape recordings has much to recommend it, and today's portable cassette tape recorders make it easy. A coherent summary of the case by the evaluating psychiatrist can be recorded; this then can be heard by each new health care professional involved in the case (and there will be many who will need to learn the child's story). Also, guardians—foster parents, teachers, nurses, and other professionals who need to know—may use the tape to avoid overquestioning the child about the incest details.

For the child involved in abuse or incest, there is a thin line between therapeutic, integrative recapitulation of history and stressful endless repetition. Self-blame, negative attention, and confused details may result from the latter. I have used the tape recording technique myself with child agencies and the courts. I keep an original tape cassette in the chart and send a copy. Just as medical records can get lost, so too a tape may be misplaced. To hold the tape, I have used a 6- by 9-inch envelope with *do not lose* written on it in red. The envelope with the cassette inside is easy to clip into a file or chart and is not awkward to retrieve or to mail.

The child's initial history is quite easily obtained on a tape recorder. Sometimes talking into a microphone is easier for a child, who is intrigued by the machine and its ability to replay, which can be under his or her fingertip control. (So little else is in the child's control!) Professionals responsible for the child may also communicate by tape cassette between cities or states. Many can express themselves better in spoken words than on paper, so valuable information about the child's behavior, feelings, and needs may be transmitted. The child can also take the familiar voice of a caring person, a natural or foster parent, along to a new setting. Then the tape becomes a "transitional object" for the child. An occasional tape recording from the birth family can be sent to a child in placement and vice versa. This is another valuable, inexpensive, and therapeutic use of this twentieth-century mechanical device and one that is particularly helpful in long-term placements on birthdays and holidays.

For briefer contacts between child and family of origin, telephone calls may be effective. However, these may also be quite painful and traumatic for all involved when unpredictable blaming, recriminations, threats, rejection, or rage are exchanged. Without professional supervision of the child during and after such a call (to deal with negative reactions), the pain may be greater than the reassurance that all loved ones are alive and unchanged. Absence may indeed produce a tendency to idealize the home situation. A negative telephone exchange may assist adjustment to a placement home, although denied hurt may persist. For some children, self-blame is more likely than the painful insight that a natural parent is uncaring.

The delayed feedback time of a tape cassette (compared with a phone call) recommends it, since professional screening and supervision can be done before a tape is given to the child.

The use of dolls

Children (as well as adults) may have a limited sexual vocabulary. In order to be clear, to avoid assumptions, and to assist meaningful communication, explicit nude drawings of males and females have been used. These help the dialogue but are less useful when explicit sexual activity is being described. Handmade, anatomically correct rag dolls have also been used. These have been featured on national television.

I have used small blue and pink pipe cleaner dolls, with penis for the boy and breasts for the girl. They are flexible, easy to manipulate, and as toys are well accepted by a child. They are also three-dimensional and allow for a simple yet clear demonstration of what happened.

However, neither kind of doll may be handy when an evaluation or therapy is in process. What then? Simply fold two sheets of paper (Figure 2) and with your fingers tear out two crude paper dolls, leaving a penis for one. Then draw in facial features, hair, nipples, and "belly buttons," telling the child what you are doing as you go along. Knees and arms of the paper dolls may be folded to give some flexibility. No matter about their artistic value, they serve the purpose well and may also be used with clothes for play therapy, adding family members when appropriate. Write names on each, and let the child

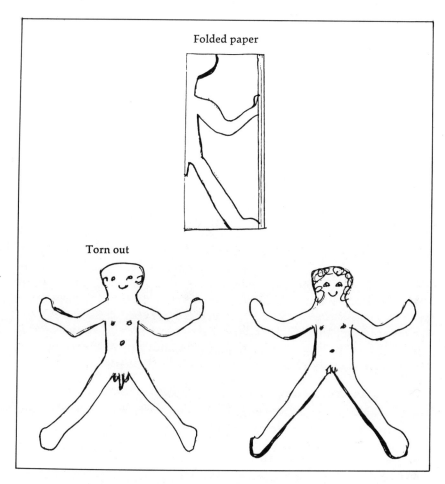

Figure 2. Torn out paper dolls used to obtain an explicit history from a child.

help. "If this is Uncle and this you, what did he do? And you? Anything else? What do you call this part?"

Family therapy

It has been suggested that since incest is essentially a family problem, rational treatment is family therapy [27, 81, 131]. Some therapists put pressure on both parents to apologize to the child for exploiting him or her [81]. I question how sincere such an apology will be under coercion of a therapist. If it is spontaneous, this is fine. Gentle repetition by the therapist might alleviate a child's self-blame or prevent scapegoating of the child incest partner: "Dad said last week his sexual feelings got mixed up. Also that he and Mother were having arguments, so he went to you instead of to Mother. He also said he was sorry." This approach in a nonreproachful but factual manner reminds the mother that she also has a role to play in the incest drama. This may be reinforced by saying, "Mother has changed to day shift so she can have more time with the family. Dad is trying to find a job (and to stop drinking)."

Then ask each member how the week has gone. After that essential status check, family interactions will usually proceed. Long silences may generate anxiety, even in the therapist. "It's difficult to talk tonight" may be sufficient to allow someone to say why. Some may resent coming to family therapy, missing sports or other activities. This must surface and be dealt with, by explaining, sometimes over and over, why they are here and how the whole family can help each other.

Some child psychiatrists use family therapy only if the child is in distress, otherwise doing marital therapy with the parents to strengthen their bond. This may work well in some cases, but what if incest is secretly still occurring? Certainly this is possible even with family therapy, but is much less likely when a whole family is alert to the problem, having open discussion of sex, and making an effort to differentiate between needed desexualized affectionate touch between members and mutual genital touch that is reserved for the parents.

One program that claims high success prefers to do counseling on site at the juvenile probation department, utilizing this strong legal reminder to change the incest behavior [58]. They also use modalities of therapy other than family therapy as needed.

The stages of family therapy are the same as in individual therapy: the initial engagement and support, then for each member the gaining of awareness and perspective regarding the problem of incest and why it occurred. Next needed is a phase of growth, change, and improvement. Termination of treatment should not occur until child protection is no longer a concern. Therefore, infrequent (monthly instead of weekly as in the crisis phase) follow-up visits are an essential part of therapy.

The final phase is the most difficult. Frequently the course of treatment involves numerous cancelled or "no show" appointments. A phone call elicits, "Someone sick," "No money," "Forgot," "No problems now." However easy it may be to use avoidance and drop unrewarding therapy, the family must be given a follow-up appointment. If that is broken, the probation officer or child agency must be called to assist with legal leverage. Only in this way can the needed child protection proceed.

Family therapy involves not one patient but as many patients as their are family members, plus the family itself, a nebulous yet very real and essential entity that must be preserved for the nurturance of all. Experience, supervision, and consultation all help to enhance the comfort of the health professional in family therapy, which is often a demanding and complex task. It is group therapy with family members providing the winds and the currents and a therapist managing the sails to keep the therapeutic ketch afloat, directed, and going. The final goal is for each member, including the incest partners, to obtain perspective regarding the different dimensions of incest and its meaning in this family and to resolve residual distress about it.

Other therapy

Other innovative modalities of therapy have been used in addition to family therapy or when family therapy is not feasible for some reason.

MARITAL THERAPY. Marital therapy with or without sex therapy has been used for couples motivated to work on a relationship that has become problematic. There may be personal or sexual distance or conflict that has turned a spouse toward a child. Marital therapy may in some cases be quite successful. Forgiveness of self and partner assist resolution of mutual resentments. Then, with time and testing of each other, trust and closeness may be developed and strengthen the relationship.

If there are sexual dysfunctions, sex education and self-help at home through reading or implementing suggestions given by therapists have been of marked benefit [106].

SUPPORT GROUPS. Support groups such as Parents United and Daughters United have been reported to be valuable to participants [58]. Where a big enough population of families are in treatment for child sexual abuse, as in the Santa Clara County Program in California, community understanding facilitates acceptance of program suggestions.

Support groups serve very real functions. By their very existence, they reduce the feeling that a problem is unique. For example, Alanon teaches that there are many families who have a member with an alcohol abuse problem. Parents United, Fathers United, and Daughters United help to reduce the sense of isolation an individual incest participant may feel. Acceptance by the group helps to heal the distress. Talking and listening can provide perspective and resolution of residual questions and distress.

Support groups also educate members about helping resources. They provide an important additional social and potential friendship circle, thus reducing the isolation evident in some incest families.

INDIVIDUAL THERAPY. Individual therapy may be indicated or requested by the child or adult incest participant for internal distress that the person feels unable to share in family therapy or a support group. Individual therapy follows the stages of engagement, insight, action, and integration as previously described [183]. It is always preferable to intersperse individual and family therapy for adult-child incest to keep a clear therapeutic perspective upon the interactional dynamics.

Confidentiality must be promised and maintained for what is revealed in individual sessions. I preface such individual sessions with, "I will keep everything confidential that you tell me with these exceptions: pregnancy and if there is danger to someone's life. Then I will ask you to help me help you to tell the family, since we'll need to work together." This has worked satisfactorily.

If there is a worry about being pregnant, I contract to wait to see results of a pregnancy test and go from there. Threats of suicide or thoughts of homicide are serious and must be carefully evaluated. The misconception still prevails that those who threaten to commit suicide do not do so. *They do.* Therefore, these questions are indicated:

Have you had thoughts of harming yourself? How (pills, gun, etc.)?
What kind of thoughts?
Have you ever tried to harm yourself?
Whom did you tell?
What happened then? (Were you hospitalized? Was it ignored?)
Did you see a psychiatrist?
Have you had thoughts of harming anyone?
Whom? Why?
What kind of thoughts were these?
Have you ever tried to harm this person before?
How (weapons, poison, plans, etc.)?
What happened then?
Did the person realize you were trying to hurt him or her?

Usually there is relief at unloading the secret burden. Most often, these thoughts are vague and unplanned and have low lethal potential. If they are serious, hospitalization may be indicated. When the lethal potential is high, the physician may need to sign necessary papers for commitment for psychiatric treatment "due to being a danger to self (or others)." Depending on local mental health laws, the patient may be held for observation from two to five days. At a hearing before a judge, the patient (with or without private legal counsel) may petition for release. Involuntary commitment is a legal decision. Therefore, the patient's and family's capacity to persuade the judge that the patient is safe for discharge may effect such release even if the doctor has strong reservations. Tragedy has followed some of these releases, leading to the comment that persons may indeed die with their (civil) rights on. On the other hand, a family's collaboration to achieve legal release of one member may herald the beginning of awareness of the seriousness of their problems. Changes may then follow with outpatient treatment or counseling and continued surveillance by probation officers and the child service agency.

FATHER-DAUGHTER DYADIC COUNSELING. Father-daughter dyadic counseling has been suggested as a form of incest therapy. If the two constitute the entire residual family, this modality may have value. If not, the therapist must be aware of potential tensions that the exclusive dyadic treatment may create within the rest of the family. Other family members may be resentful or rivalrous. They may worry about more secrets. Such a special therapeutic relationship may be more harmful than helpful to the integration of the family needed to eliminate the incest. In a sophisticated way, father-daughter counseling resembles marital therapy and may similarly enhance the father-daughter dyad. Traveling to and from therapy may also provide further intimacy, enjoyable or feared depending on the equality and reciprocity of the relationship.

Psychiatric disorders with incest

When present in any incest family member, psychiatric disorders will require appropriate and specific treatment at the same time as (and not instead of) family and marital therapy. Psychiatric problems may or may not be contributing factors in the incest behavior, but they must nonetheless be medically and psychiatrically understood and treated.

Either incest partner or another relative may reveal evidence of mental illness. Some of these conditions have today yielded to biological research and respond in some degree to medications that offer much relief, although no cures. Motivation for change and cooperation with treatment are essential. Health care professionals must recognize the important role played by educating the patient about the psychiatric condition for which the medications or treatment is prescribed. In a number of remediable disorders, it is not an "either-or" situation of medication or psychotherapy. Both psychotherapy and specific medications in adequate doses for a sustained period of time are required [180].

If the mental illness enters into the incest behavior, this must clearly be explained to the family, with the patient's consent and preferably in the patient's presence: "Mother has a problem where she hears voices from outside telling her things like God wanted her to take Billy to bed with her (or to have Jenny go to bed with father; or to stop having sex with father; or to hurt herself; or that she wants to have sex too much when she gets hyper, and then she slows down again). This kind of problem does happen to some people. There are special ways to help mother, like for her to take medications every day (or one injection every two weeks)."

Correct diagnosis is as important in this as in every other branch of medicine. A concerted effort must be made to match the patient's condition with specific medications, which differ in manic depression, anxiety, or schizophrenia. To some extent they may overlap, since some psychotropic medications are effective in more than one diagnostic category. The response to specific medication may also be useful as a diagnostic test, e.g., lithium carbonate or lithium citrate for manic-depressive disorder.

Diagnostic tools in psychiatry depend heavily on (1) a careful history from the patient and family, (2) observation of behavior, (3) the patient's subjective responses in a psychiatric evaluation, and (4) psychologic tests and rating scales. All of these have limitations. Careful and skillful combinations of diagnostic aids may improve accuracy. No diagnostic blood or urine tests yet exist to confirm schizophrenia or manic depression as elevated blood sugar or uric acid do for diabetes or gout.

SCHIZOPHRENIA. Schizophrenia is a major mental illness that occurs in 1 : 100 persons worldwide. Milder forms of the disorder that produce personal adjustment problems also exist. There are a variety of ways a schizophrenic may think and behave. Distortions of perception occur, and reality may be misperceived. Rarely, incest might be due to such an illness in a mother, father, grandparent, child, or other family member.

MANIC-DEPRESSIVE ILLNESS. Manic-depressive illness occurs in about 5 : 100 persons. Biological factors are emerging in research into this bipolar emotional disorder, which shows a strong familial incidence. Cycles of overactivity and underactivity, with dramatic changes in mood from elated to depressed and weepy, are noted in this condition. During either cycle, behavior problems may occur. In the "high" phase, excess activity, (over) jovial mood, and hypersexuality are known components of the illness.

An intense, insatiable sexual urgency or drive to find sexual release may propel the patient to show inappropriate sexual behavior (e.g., masturbate publicly); demand intercourse repeatedly in a short space of time (often without satisfaction); or turn to a child, to more than one relative, or even to strangers. Therefore, incest may occur in what is called the manic phase of the illness. The hypersexuality may spontaneously subside in the other phases of the disorder. Self-help educational books may be of great value to the whole family [38, 86].

ALCOHOL OR DRUG ABUSE. Alcohol or drug excess may at times play a role in incest behavior. A chemical psychosis may be induced. Then violent and sexual impulses may combine, as in the case of the girl whose stepfather, an alcohol and drug abuser, raped her at age 4 (Case 5-1, page 77). There was no record available about what became of him. Occasionally such a man is jailed without realization by the authorities that he is alcohol- and drug-intoxicated. Uncontrolled and lethal withdrawal from drugs—barbiturates, heroin— and alcohol may occur within 24 to 48 hours of his arrest. Moral outrage at the affinity adult-child heterosexual rape incest is expectable, but his death by professional neglect does not serve the greater good of the community in an age of available medical attention.

For years it has been stated that alcohol lowers sexual controls and fosters incest [20, 66, 165, 172]. However, alcohol may also be used to rationalize or excuse the incest behavior [107].

If alcohol is a life-adjustment problem for a parent or other family member, Alcoholics Anonymous (AA), Alateen, and Alanon are excellent and widely available support groups and social resources for the incestuous family as for nonincestuous families. Substance abuse, from smoking cigarettes to taking street drugs, is not a simple medical or social problem. Habit change is difficult. Recurrence of alcohol abuse increases the risk of repeating incest patterns; therefore, extra precautions are needed for protection of a minor in the home. Drug programs vary in quality, availability, and safety because of the criminal association with illicit street drugs.

PEDOPHILIA. Pedophilia is a sexual problem in which an adult is recurrently driven to seek a child of either sex for sexual arousal or release of sexual tension or both. It may be limited to fondling or exposure; however, oral, anal, or vaginal penetration may also occur. Theories of causation abound: fear of adult coitus; strong religious repression; early positive sexual experiences with child peers producing "sexual arrest" at that psychosexual developmental stage; cultural emphasis on youth and beauty in advertising causing adult males to turn to nymphets; need for a nonchallenging, compliant sexual companion; actual seduction of the adult by a pseudomature child turned prostitute [1, 56].

Incarceration of pedophilics protects society, but a jailed pedophilic suffers severe degradation in the prison system as "the worst" inmate. Prison is not treatment. Since all convicted pedophilics are men, an antimale hormone (cyproterone acetate) has been experimentally used to lower the sex drive by its antiandrogen effect [115]. Its side effects include breast enlargement and loss of hair. Compliance among outpatients in taking this medication or tranquilizing drugs to lower drives is low, whereas recidivism to pedophilia is high.

In addition to the treatment described for adult-child incest, for a pedophilic *constant surveillance* is an essential aspect of outpatient treatment. This sets up a "prison mentality" in a family unfortunate enough to have a pedophilic member; however, health care professionals must engage all family members, the pedophilic, and the probation system if outpatient family therapy is to be tested as an alternative to prison.

Clinically, control of human behavior is frustratingly far from the science-fiction level. What a legal or health professional considers inappropriate or unacceptable may be ardently pursued by a pedophilic patient who is a "childaholic" similar to an alcoholic. An AA approach with reformed pedophilics as helpers forming a support group may have something to recommend it, if and when successful therapy evolves.

OTHER PSYCHIATRIC DISORDERS. Other psychiatric disorders may afflict a child or adult incest partner. Severe depression, acute anxiety, a conversion disorder, a withdrawal reaction, psychosis, or a suicide attempt may be a form of crisis presentation of an incest partner. Guilt (internal) or shame (concern about external exposure) or fear of real harm may all be symptoms. There may be blocking of painful, pleasurable, or conflicting memories of incest experiences. Aggressive reactions may also occur in self-protection or even in jealous rage. Treatment may take the form of hospitalization (if indicated) or outpatient psychotherapy with or without medications or all of these at various stages.

The clinical course of incest treatment may be stormy and emotionally depleting. Certainly it is not a financially rewarding endeavour. Dedication—to child protection, to health care, or to the law—is required. Disillusionment may occur rapidly. It is *rare* that the patients involved are entirely cooperative or enthusiastic. Much is demanded of the maturity and integrity of the helping person, whose "giving power" is limited. Demands from schools, courts, and family may be unbounded. Knowing one's own limits—of time and responsibility—is important.

Consultation is always valuable when an additional opinion is needed. Sometimes a therapist may become so immersed in incest that it becomes easier not to see incest as a problem anymore. This is a danger signal that objectivity is lost. Adult-child incest is against the law. Knowing and ignoring the fact that incest is continuing has invited disaster in the form of a suicide attempt or hysterical seizure by a child who now feels totally helpless, when even a helping professional is not able to stop coercive sexual approaches from the family member. Then the psychiatric consultation unfortunately may have to be an emergency room visit after a stomach washout for a suicidal overdose. This has occurred. Far better for ethical practitioners to request a consultation during the treatment course. Sharing the responsibility not only halves it, but can also be a growth process for both professionals.

9

SOME CONCLUSIONS

INCEST is a forbidden sexualized love relationship in a family. Western culture speaks its name in shame, guilt, fear of destructive consequences, social isolation, pain, or bold headlines.

I have approached incest as a fact for noncondemnatory understanding so that optimum clinical treatment may reach those who seek help with incest experiences. Throughout this text, I have avoided legal *victim* and *perpetrator* terminology as being too narrow, since, in an incest-avoiding community, the entire family is usually damned.

In 20 years of medical practice, I have found members of incestuous families to be about as psychologically healthy or unhealthy as members of comparable nonincestuous families. The majority of those who have experienced incest do not stand out from their community in any special way. Many are average, responsible, churchgoing citizens. Some are not. They are, however, "invisible" until incest is voluntarily admitted or somehow discovered.

I have been privileged to perceive a very wide spectrum of incest behaviors. It is for this reason that I have made such an effort to delineate a definitional system that could become legally, clinically, and academically useful. I hope a more scientific data base on the incests may slowly be gathered. Research is long overdue but essential. Eventually, with greater specificity and clearer definition, the existing tendency to extrapolate from noncomparable, incomplete incest reports will lessen.

Not every woman who experiences some kind of sexual contact with a family member becomes a prostitute, although some prostitutes report this in their history. So do average, well-adjusted nonprostitutes. Well-meaning ovservations may become damaging pseudo-scientific predictions. The men, women, and children who experience any variant of the incests daily live out in the family the riddle of one or more of the complex causative factors.

The family itself has undergone very rapid change in the last 50 years as a result of urbanization, economic changes, and the rising divorce rate. How the family nurtures, teaches, and desexualizes affection has been carefully explored at length, with special emphasis on reconstituted families. Contrary to beliefs held in the past, there is no instinctive aversion to incest, nor is there always a catastrophic outcome to inbreeding. Sexual feelings and fantasies are a normal part of everyday life, and sexual attraction may quite naturally arise between affinity or consanguineous family members. One theory proposes that adolescent turmoil and negativism are defenses against parent-child incest as rivalry is against sibling incest. However, there are cases in which negativism, rivalry, turmoil, and incest coexist.

There are no easy explanations for why incest, rather than, say, adultery or divorce, occurs within a family. Glib generalizations do not help. Each family needs an in-depth evaluation, which should include all members both to understand the incest as well as to raise enough awareness to prevent recurrence.

Incest-preventing factors are still as dimly understood as are incest-fostering ones. The basic silence and uncomfortable avoidance of discussing sexuality in the home, especially with growing children, is several centuries old and has yielded little to better and more available sexual knowledge. When a couple cannot talk explicitly and comfortably about sex, affection, and love to each other, how will they do so with their children?

I therefore prefer to regard the incests as sexual learning disorders. Some family members have not learned to desexualize affectionate touch or have not learned or accepted that incest is socially inappropriate and morally wrong. These values may not have been taught. On the other hand, some incest participants do know that they violate the law yet are driven by strong attraction to continue their incestuous relationship. Each family must be objectively evaluated. How did each individual learn about sex, affection, and forbidden partners?

In our incest-avoiding culture, it is the task of parents and family members to provide persistent messages, from infancy onward, that desexualized affection, love, and loyalty are for closest relatives. Sexual and marital partners are to be chosen outside the family. Thus, conscious as well as unconscious controls may be developed and perpetuated in each new generation. Legal and religious reasons may be given to the growing child to reinforce incest as unacceptable behavior that must be controlled, repressed, or denied.

Childhood sex exploration and play quite normally occur between peers and siblings. When is sibling contact considered incest? This is one more unclear area. The recurrence and the *exclusivity* of the sexual partnering, as well as progression to intercourse, must be evaluated to answer this question when cases of sibling incest present.

Incest may present in widely differing circumstances. Crisis presentations of incest may be few, yet they are usually the most urgent and dramatic. They also most frequently involve adult-child coital incest, with pregnancy or physical harm (rape or abuse) an immediate concern. Sometimes the crisis is not in the incest participants but in a third person who discovers it. Direction may be needed from hospital hot lines; distress, damage, and discomfort may require emergency room attention. When incidentally emerging as part of a thorough, detailed life history, the report of incest experiences may be given matter-of-factly, without conflict or distress. Sometimes there may be unresolved feelings of shame and guilt in telling the story, even though it was volunteered to someone who is doing research on the incests.

In professionals working with the incests, emotional reactions to incest behaviors may at times unexpectedly arise and impede optimum conduct of a case. Feelings of aversion, anger, arousal, anxiety, or avoidance of involvement may be unhelpful to persons in need of assistance. By being aware of the possible reactions of professionals, relatives, and others to the very mention of the word *incest* or to dealing with incest participants, one can go a long way toward coping with an admittedly difficult task.

Over several centuries of criminalization of incest in Western culture, an adversary approach has evolved between helping professionals and patients, which makes forming a therapeutic alliance difficult. Where child protection (in coercive adult-child incest, coital or noncoital) is an evident need, a law enforcement approach has immediate validity. However, adequate data collection becomes questionable when the result of telling the truth means jail. On the other hand, presumptive or incomplete evidence may still condemn a man. A child's agony that his or her testimony has sent father to jail may be severe. To tell a child that father deserved jail when he was otherwise a loving and stable parent may relieve the distress of nonfamily adults only. The child must later return to the family, perhaps after years in a foster home. Treatment follow-up may be nil owing to poor professional resources. Some court experts comment that the real trauma of incest begins when it is discovered, referring to the insensitive way a child is handled by the social, health, and justice systems. Reform is long overdue.

The range of incest behaviors and of sequelae is wide. Blanket statements that all incest experiences are destructive and emotionally crippling err in the same way as does the sweeping fervor of the pro-incest lobbyists, namely, overgeneralization and unfounded extrapolations [67]. Without field study, the community proportions and patterns of incest cannot be reliably established. No matter how erudite the authority may be, assumptions are no more reliable than guesswork. Special clinics and advertising for incest participants collect a special sample, important but not necessarily representative of the population or community at large.

In the most favorable circumstances, research on human behavior is difficult to design scientifically. This is especially true in the study of incest. There may be clear objectives, satisfactory rationale, and plausible hypotheses, but data analysis and interpretation are open to valid criticism because of the numerous variables and interactional factors involved in family dynamics, because of the criminal status of incest, and because of the subjective nature of the sexual elements. However, study must begin at some baseline, whether or not it is of questionable significance. Generations of scholars have climbed to greater knowledge upon the shoulders of those who went before and shared their findings and theories.

Complexities are many and guidelines are few for the professionals who must deal with incestuous families. I have attempted to share some actual treatment techniques. Since explicit details must be obtained for a proper incest evaluation and for treatment, a special incest questionnaire tested at Loyola is included here for clinicians and researchers to begin with and perhaps improve.

A prime goal in writing this book was to help clinicians, teachers, pastors, and other helping persons to gain sensitivity toward each family member as well as to attain personal comfort, confidence, and professional skill. It has also been my goal to emphasize the importance of the family's integrity. Wholesome parenting with a satisfying sexual relationship plus affectionate bonds between parents and desexualized affectionate bonds with each child may turn out to be a buffer against forbidden sex in the family.

I hope that persons in the justice system—police, probation officers, lawyers, law students, judges, and law makers—will take a few hours to review this material. A deeper understanding of incest behaviors may prevent the miscarriage of justice. Under the framework of child abuse laws, family destruction may be perpetuated as the only legal response to adult-child incest allegations.

Both health care and law professionals must understand that it is virtually impossible for a legal investigator or psychiatric evaluator to ascertain the accuracy of a verbal report obtained from an incest partner or witnesses inside or outside the family. The clinical or legal case will have to be built on substantial amounts of additional evidence of sexual involvement, unless there is open admission of the illegal incest activity. Even when incest is admitted, can jail, child placement, and family disruption be considered treatment? Newly evolving treatment options favor judicial supervision with professional outpatient care as an alternative.

There are severe psychosocial limitations to the current penal treatment of incest as a felony in the United States. One blatant example is that although "carnal knowledge" is the legal definition of incest in Illinois, many men are behind bars for years for noncoital noncoercive incest. Jailing a few hundred fathers does not address or even touch incest as a family and social issue. There have always been questions about the effective control of intimate sexual conduct through law. My critique is not new or original. Social, moral, and religious pressures must all combine to maintain civilized or acceptable behaviors. For the sake of individual safety, child or adult protection by law is certainly in order when physical or emotional harm is inflicted by a powerful family member. When, however, there is no force or fear in an incest relationship, is justice served by condemning an otherwise law-abiding man to years in jail at public expense; by placing his family on public welfare and his child (also at enormous public expense) in custodial care; by the loss of his potential productivity during the prison years and on release; by the child's great loss of being in and belonging to his or her family; by the prisoner's loss of precious years with what may be his well-loved and loving family?

The recent Canadian Law Reform Commission Report on Sexual Offenses addressed a special segment, given here in Chapter 2, to incest. This report makes the cogent point that, in the absence of exploitation, incestuous behavior ought not to be treated and punished as a criminal act, since criminal laws provide no solutions for the family disturbances within which the incest occurs. The final phase is worth considering: ". . . In the final analysis it will be up to Parliament to assess public opinion and decide whether decriminalizing incest between adults would be impolitic at present." That was written in 1978. It still remains impolitic to consider because of other political priorities.

What about the United States? Decriminalization could be considered at least in selected situations in which confidential clinical treatment (family, marital, individual, or group therapy) could be of greater benefit than court pressure, publicity, family rupture, and great public cost. Reconstruction of state and federal laws on marriage, divorce, illegitimacy, and sex offenses are long overdue. Unfortunately, special interest groups influence legislators more than those who seek to attain justice in the everyday work of the courts, because seeking justice brings no personal glory or political recognition [121]. It is a fact that it is good party politics for a prosecutor to catch the public eye by "achieving" drastic penalties for an emotionally highly charged misdeed such as incest. For legislators, taxation, appropriations, patronage, and political fund raising will all take precedence over considering reform of incest laws. Political avoidance will continue until some mature and courageous legislator or a judiciary committee in the House of Representatives or the Senate initiates action toward change.

Law reform in any country is extremely slow and incredibly cumbersome. The lack of adequate machinery for reform of outdated and ineffective laws greatly reduces both individual and public respect for law. An excellent recommendation for achieving essential progressive, updated, lawmaking was made three decades ago, namely, appointment of a permanent body equivalent to a ministry of justice, with "security of tenure, adequate facilities, competent investigators, opportunity of dealing with questions as a whole rather than in detached local fragments, and scientific spirit and method" [121]. Only in this truly responsible way can we achieve successful preparation for reform of sex and relationship laws. Although the task may be politically feared as a lightening rod attracting a vocal antisex minority, it nonetheless must be done to prevent the miscarriage of justice through its own misguided, outdated tenets.

To incest participants who may read this book and who may identify with or relate to segments on any page, I would like to say, You are not alone. You have experienced another kind of love, which has been condemned in our society. It may have puzzled and distressed you, yet you have had strength and courage to live with quiet dignity. You have learned as you grew that life presents ambiguities and differences. You have gradually formed your own value system regarding sexual rights and wrongs. How have you adapted to the incest experience, and what will you teach your own children about affection, about sex, and about their right to the privacy of their bodies? Will you help them by telling them that secrets, although exciting, can also bring anxiety and often relate to forbidden acts? Will you tell them that they may always, with anything, bring their secrets, even sex secrets, to you?

You may read this book and be surprised that others were upset by incest experiences since you were not or that you were upset and some were not. You may, on your very own, have sorted out what was going on in your family, why affection and sex were mixed up, and why sex was sought from you or by you. You may not have condemned but forgiven or understood or even responded sexually, all of which were possible and natural responses. You cannot undo the past. Present and future sexual behavior remains your choice and your responsibility. This book reflects the fact that, for almost all of the United States today, choosing sexual partners in the close family remains forbidden morally and legally. If you wish to find help to talk about your incest experiences, call any hospital hot line, remain anonymous, and ask what resources there are in your own community.

I would like to end by saying once more that it is time to reassess some of our conventional notions about incest, both personally and professionally. Rhetoric, perpetuated preconceptions, partial evaluations, and vague definitions of incest are no longer defensible. Confusion has in part been due to the different ways in which incest emerges for scrutiny within each community: in a crisis, incidentally as part of a life history, or when a study of incest is in process.

A great range of incest practices has been documented in cross-cultural anthropological studies. Incest preferences, prohibitions, and penalties have differed through the centuries and among different groups of people. Personal and family attitudes may concur with or diverge from social, religious, or legal standards within the same community as a result of complex factors, one of which may be migration into a new area, as for example when persons from rural, island, or mountain communities seek employment in cities or move from family to college. What is condoned in an individual's birth community may be condemned in the new setting. Thus the cultural context in each family situation is a most important aspect of a professional's, and a patient's, understanding of the meaning of the incestuous behavior.

Since this book was conceived because of many of my own un-answered questions, I will conclude with these important clinical questions that should be considered in every case: Does incest maintain the cohesion of this family? Is this otherwise an endangered family structure? Is the incest a cultural mandate? Is the physical closeness considered to be important emotional nurturance? Is any member exploited or harmed? Is there public indecency or scandal? Why and how does the incest now come to professional or legal attention? How will legal intervention help or harm this family and the incest partners? How can I best be of help to this family? *What purpose did or does incest serve in this family?*

Scholarship and service must continue to go hand in hand in this special clinical frontier of understanding and treating the many presentations of incest: misdirected sexualized family love.

REFERENCES

1. Abel, G. G., Blanchard, E. B., and Barlow, D. H. Measurement of sexual arousal in several paraphilias: The effects of stimulus modality, instructional set and stimulus content on the objective. *Behav. Res. Ther.* 19(1):25, 1981.
2. Ackerman, N. W. *The Psychodynamics of Family Life* (1st ed.). New York: Basic Books, 1958. Pp. 223–225.
3. Adams, M. S., and Neel, J. F. Children of incest. *Pediatrics* 40:55, 1967.
4. Alstrom, C. H. A study of incest with special regards to the Swedish penal code. *Acta Psychiatr. Scand.* 56:357, 1977.
5. Andrews, V. *Flowers in the Attic.* New York: Pocket Books, 1980.
6. Andrews, V. *Petals in the Wind.* New York: Pocket Books, 1981(a).
7. Andrews, V. *If There Be Thorns.* New York: Pocket Books, 1981(b).
8. Armstrong, L. *Kiss Daddy Goodnight: A Speakout on Incest.* New York: Hawthorne, 1978.
9. Awad, G. A. Father-son incest: A case report. *J. Nerv. Ment. Dis.* 162:135, 1976.
10. Bagley, C. Incest behavior and incest taboo. *Social Problems* 16:505, 1969.
11. Barlow, D. H., and Wineze, J. P. Treatment of Sexual Deviations. In S. R. Leiblum and L. A. Pervin (Eds.), *Principles and Practice of Sex Therapy.* New York: Guilford Press, 1980.
12. Barzun, J. *Teacher in America.* Boston: Little, Brown, 1944.
13. Bender, L., and Blau, A. The reaction of children to sexual relations with adults. *Am. J. Orthopsychiatry* 7:500, 1937.
14. Bender, L., and Grugette, A. E. A follow-up report on children who had atypical sexual experience. *Am. J. Orthopsychiatry* 22:825, 1952.
15. Berman, C. *Making it as a Stepparent.* New York: Doubleday, 1980.
16. Berry, G. W. Incest: Some clinical variations on a classical theme. *J. Am. Acad. Psychoanal.* 3:151, 1975.
17. Bowlby, J. *Maternal Care and Mental Health.* Geneva: World Health Organization Monograph, 1951.
18. Bowlby, J. Attachment Theory, Separation Anxiety and Mourning. In D. H. Hamburg and H. K. Brodie (Eds.), *The American Handbook of Psychiatry.* New York: Basic Books, 1975.

19. Broderick, C. Children's romances. *Sexual behavior*, May, 1972. Pp. 16–21.
20. Browning, D. H., and Boatman, B. Incest: Children at risk. *Am. J. Psychiatry* 134:69, 1977.
21. Carter, C. O. Risk of offspring of incest. *Lancet* 1:436, 1967.
22. Cavallin, H. Incestuous fathers: A clinical report. *Am. J. Psychiatry* 122:1132, 1966.
23. Cavenar, J. O., Jr., Sullivan, J. L., and Maltbie, A. A. A clinical note on hysterical psychosis. *Am. J. Psychiatry* 136:830, 1979.
24. *Child Abuse Prevention and Treatment Act* (PL. 93–347), Washington, D.C.: National Center on Child Abuse and Neglect, 1974. P. 9.
25. Cohen, Y. The disappearance of the incest taboo. *Human Nature* July, 1978. Pp. 72–78.
26. Connell, H. M. The wider spectrum of child abuse. *Med. J. Aust.* 2: 391, 1978.
27. Cormier, B. M., Kennedy, M., and Sangowicz, J. Psychodynamics of father-daughter incest. *Can. Psychiatr. Assoc. J.* 7:203, 1962.
28. DeMott, B. The pro-incest lobby. *Psychology Today* 13:10, March, 1980. Pp. 11–16.
29. DeRachewiltz, B. *Black Eros*. London: George Allen & Unwin, 1964.
30. *Diagnostic and Statistical Manual of Mental Disorders, I*. Washington, D.C.: American Psychiatric Association, 1952.
31. *Diagnostic and Statistical Manual of Mental Disorders, II*. Washington, D.C.: American Psychiatric Association, 1968.
32. *Diagnostic and Statistical Manual of Mental Disorders, III*. Washington, D.C.: American Psychiatric Association, 1980.
33. Dixon, K. N., Arnold, L. E., and Calestro, K. Father-son incest: Under-reported psychiatric problem. *Am. J. Psychiatry* 135:835, 1978.
34. Eist, H. I., and Mandel, A. Family treatment of ongoing incest behavior. *Fam. Process* 7:216, 1968.
35. Erikson, E. *Identity, Youth and Crisis*. New York: Norton, 1968.
36. Fairbairn, W. R. *An Object-Relations Theory of Personality*. New York: Basic Books, 1974.
37. Ferenzi, S. Male and female. *Psychoanal. Q.* 5:249, 1936.
38. Fieve, R. *Moodswing*. New York: Bantam Books, 1975.
39. Finch, S. The effects of adult sexual seduction on children. *Medical Aspects of Human Sexuality* 7:3, 1973.
40. Finkelhor, D. *Sexually Victimized Children*. New York: Free Press, 1979.
41. Fleck, S. Family welfare, mental health and birth control. *J. Fam. Law* 3:241, 1964.
42. Fleck, S. Some Basic Aspects of Family Pathology. In B. J. Wolman (Ed.), *Manual of Child Psychopathology*. New York: McGraw-Hill, 1972.
43. Ford, C. S., and Beech, F. A. *Patterns of Sexual Behavior*. New York: Harper & Row, 1970.
44. Forward, S., and Buck, C. *Betrayal of Innocence*. Los Angeles: J. P. Tarcher, 1978.
45. Fox, J. R. Sibling incest. *Br. J. Sociol.* 13:128, 1962.
46. Fox, R. *Kinship and Marriage*. New York: Penguin Books, 1968.
47. Fox, R. *The Red Lamp of Incest*. New York: E. P. Dutton, 1980.
48. Franklin, D. Incest in middle class differs from that processed by police. *Clin. Psychiatr. News* 2:3, 1974.
49. Freedman, A. M., Kaplan, H. I., and Sadock, B. J. *Modern Synopsis of Comprehensive Textbook of Psychiatry II*. Baltimore: William & Wilkins, 1976. P. 769.

50. Freud, S. *Three Essays on the Theory of Sexuality.* New York: Basic Books, 1962.
51. Freud, S. Totem and Taboo (1913). In *The Standard Edition of the Complete Psychological Works of Sigmund Freud,* transl. and ed. by J. Strachey with others. London: Hogarth and Institute of Psycho-Analysis, 1968. Vol. 20, p. 34.
52. Freudenberger, H., and Richelson, G. *Preventing Burnout.* New York: Doubleday, 1980.
53. Fromm, E. *The Art of Loving.* New York: Harper & Row, 1956.
54. Gagnon, J. Female child victims of sex offenders. *Social Problems* 13: 176, 1965.
55. Garma, A. Oedipus was not the son of Laius and Jocasta. *Int. J. Psychoanal. Psychother.* 7:316, 1978–1979.
56. Gebhard, P. H., et al. *Sex Offenders: An Analysis of Types.* New York: Harper & Row, 1965.
57. Geiser, R. L. *Hidden Victims.* Boston: Beacon Press, 1979. Pp. 43–72.
58. Giarretto, H. The treatment of father-daughter incest: A psychosocial approach. *Child. Today* 5:2, 1976.
59. Giarretto, H., Giarretto, A., and Sgroi, S. Coordinated Community Treatment of Incest. In A. W. Burgess, A. N. Groth, L. L. Holmstrom, (Eds.), *Sexual Assault of Children and Adolescents.* Lexington, Mass.: Lexington Books, 1978.
60. Gil, E. M. Abuse of children in institutions. Presented at the Second International Congress on Child Abuse and Neglect, London, Sept. 12–15, 1978.
61. Gil, E. M. Personal communication, 1980.
62. Gligor, A. M. Incest and sexual delinquency: A comparative analysis of two forms of sexual behavior in minor females. Case Western Reserve University Ph.D. Thesis, 1966.
63. Goodall, J. *The Behavior of Freeliving Chimpanzees in the Gombe Stream Reserve,* Vol. 1. London: Balliere, Tindall & Cassell Animal Monographs, 1968.
64. Goodwin, J., Sahd, D., and Rada, R. T. Incest hoax: False accusations, false denials. *Bull. Am. Acad. Psychiatry Law* 6:269, 1978.
65. Groth, N. Guidelines for Assessment and Management of the Offender. In A. W. Burgess, A. N. Groth, L. L. Holmstrom (Eds.), *Sexual Assault of Children and Adolescents.* Lexington, Mass.: Lexington Books, 1978.
66. Groth, A. N. *Men Who Rape.* New York: Plenum Press, 1979.
67. Guyon, R. *The Ethics of Sexual Acts.* New York: Octagon Books, 1974. Pp. 321–330.
68. Hall, C. S., and Lindzey, G. *Theories of Personality.* New York: Wiley, 1970.
69. Halleck, S. L. Victims of sex offenders. *J.A.M.A.* 180:273, 1962.
70. Halleck, S. L. *Psychiatry and the Dilemmas of Crime.* Berkeley: University of California Press, 1971.
71. Hammer, E. F., and Gluck, B. C. Psychodynamic patterns in sex offence: A four factor theory. *Psychiatr. Q.* 3:325, 1957.
72. Harlow, H., and Harlow, M. Social deprivation in monkeys. *Sci. Am.* 207:136, 1962.
73. Harris, M. *Culture, Man and Nature.* New York: Crowell, 1971. P. 289.
74. Hartl, D. L. *Our Uncertain Heritage—Genetics and Human Diversity.* Philadelphia: Lippincott, 1977. P. 377.
75. Heard, D. H. From object relations to attachment theory: A basis for family therapy. *Br. J. Med. Psychol.* 51:67, 1978.
76. Henderson, D. J. Incest: A synthesis of data. *Can. Psychiatr. Assoc. J.* 17:299, 1972.

77. Holmes, T. H., and Rahe, R. H.   The social readjustment rating scale. *J. Psychosom. Res.* 2:213, 1967.
78. Howard, J.   *Families.* New York: Simon & Schuster, 1978.
79. James, J., and Meyerding, J.   Early sexual experience and prostitution. *Am. J. Psychiatry* 134:1381, 1977.
80. Jung, C. G.   *Modern Man in Search of a Soul.* New York: Harcourt Brace & World, 1933.
81. Justice, B., and Justice, R.   *The Broken Taboo.* New York: Human Sciences Press, 1979, Pp. 15, 245.
82. Katchadourian, H. A., and Lunde, D. T.   *Fundamentals of Human Sexuality.* New York: Holt, Rinehart and Winston, 1972.
83. Kaufman, I., Peck, A., and Taguiri, C. K.   The family constellation and overt incestuous relations between father and daughter. *Am. J. Orthopsychiatry* 24:266, 1954.
84. Kinsey, A. C., Pomeroy, W. B., and Martin, C. E.   *Sexual Behavior in the Human Male.* Philadelphia: Saunders, 1948.
85. Kinsey, A. C., Pomeroy, W. B., Martin, C. E., and Gebhard, P. H.   *Sexual Behavior in the Human Female.* Philadelphia: Saunders, 1953.
86. Kline, N.   *From Sad to Glad.* New York: Ballantine, 1974.
87. Kohut, H.   *The Analysis of the Self.* New York: International Press, 1971.
88. Kubo, S.   Researches and studies on incest in Japan, *Hiroshima J. Med. Sci.* 8:99, 1959.
89. Langsley, D. J., Schwartz, M. N., and Fairbairn, R. H.   Father-son incest. *Compr. Psychiatry* 9:218, 1968.
90. Law Reform Commission of Canada on Sexual Offenses, Minister of Supply and Services, J31-28/1978, Ottawa, Canada.
91. Layman, W. A.   Pseudo incest. *Compr. Psychiatry* 13:385, 1972.
92. Lee, J. A.   *The Colors of Love.* New York: Prentice-Hall, 1976.
93. Lewis, J. M., et al.   *No Single Thread: Psychological Health in Family Systems.* New York: Bruner-Mazel, 1976.
94. Li, C. C.   *Population Genetics.* Chicago: University of Chicago Press, 1955.
95. Li, C. C.   *Human Genetics.* New York: McGraw-Hill, 1961. P. 171.
96. Lidz, T.   *The Family and Human Adaptation.* New York: International Universities Press, 1963.
97. Lidz, T.   *The Person.* New York: Basic Books, 1970. P. 240.
98. Lindzey, G.   Some remarks concerning incest, the incest taboo and psychoanalytic theory. *Am. Psychol.* 22:1051, 1967.
99. Lukianowicz, N. Incest. *Br. J. Psychiatry* 120:301, 1972.
100. Lustig, N., Dresser, J. W., and Spellman, S.   Incest: A family group survival pattern. *Arch. Gen. Psychiatry* 14:31–40, 1966.
101. Mahler, M. S.   Separation-Individuation. In J. B. McDevitt and C. F. Settlage (Eds.), *Essays in Honor of Margaret S. Mahler.* New York: International Universities Press, 1971.
102. Mahler, M., Pine, F., and Berman, A.   *The Psychological Birth of the Human Infant.* New York: Basic Books, 1975.
103. Maisch, H.   *Incest.* New York: Stein & Day, 1973.
104. Marcuse, M.   Incest. *Am. J. Urol. Sexology* 16:273, 1923.
105. Martin, P. A.   Dynamics of family interactions. *Journal of Continuing Education in Psychiatry,* 40(1):23–35, Jan. 1979.
106. Masters, W., and Johnson, V.   *Human Sexual Inadequacy.* Boston: Little, Brown, 1970.
107. McCaghy, C.   Drinking and deviance disavowal: The case of child molesters. *J. Social Problems* 16:43, 1968.

108. McFarlane, K.   Sexual Abuse of Children. In J. R. Chapman and M. Gates (Eds.), *Victimization of Women*. Beverly Hills, Calif.: Sage Publications, 1978.

109. McKusick, V. A.   *Human Genetics*. Baltimore: Johns Hopkins University Press, 1964.

110. Meiselman, K. C.   *Incest*. San Francisco: Jessey-Bass, 1979. Pp. 62–68.

111. Miles, H.   *The Forbidden Fruit: The Incest Theme in Erotic Literature*. London: Luxor Press, 1973.

112. Minuchin, S.   *Families of the Slums*. New York: Basic Books, 1967.

113. Minuchin, S.   *Families and Family Therapy*. Cambridge, Mass.: Harvard University Press, 1974.

114. Money, J.   The Therapeutic Use of Androgen-Depleting Hormone. In H. L. P. Resnick and E. W. Marvin (Eds.), *Sexual Behaviors: Social, Clinical and Legal Aspects*. Boston: Little, Brown, 1972.

115. Money, J., and Ehrhardt, A.   *Man and Woman, Boy and Girl*. Baltimore: Johns Hopkins University Press, 1972.

116. Montagu, A.   *Touching*. New York: Harper & Row, 1971.

117. Nin, A.   *Winter of Artifice* (1945) and *House of Incest* (1958). London: Quartet Books, 1979.

118. Nobile, P.   Incest: The last taboo. *Penthouse*, Dec. 1977. Pp. 117–158.

119. Parsons, T.   The incest taboo in relation to social structure and the socialization of the child. *Br. J. Sociol.* 5:101, 1954.

120. Pomeroy, W.   Attacking the last taboo. *Time*, April 1980. P. 72.

121. Pound, R.   Introduction. In M. Ploscowe (Ed.), *Sex and the Law*. New York: Prentice-Hall, 1951. Pp. 8–10.

122. Quinsey, V. L.   Assessment and treatment of child molesters: A review. *Can. Psychol. Rev.* 18:104, 1977.

123. Rahe, R. H.   A start at quantifying stress in life. *J.A.M.A.* 232:699, 1975.

124. Raphling, D. L., Carpenter, B. L., and Davis, A.   Incest: A genealogical study. *Arch. Gen. Psychiatry* 16:505, 1967.

125. Rassmussen, A.   The importance of sexual attacks on children less than fourteen years of age for the development of mental diseases and character anomalies. *Acta Psychiatr. Neurol.* 9:351, 1934.

126. Raybin, J. B.   Homosexual incest. *J. Nerv. Ment. Dis.* 148:105, 1969.

127. Renshaw, D. C.   Sexuality in children. *Medical Aspects of Human Sexuality* 10:62, 1971.

128. Renshaw, D. C.   Sex education for educators. *J. Sch. Health* 43:645, 1973.

129. Renshaw, D. C.   Understanding masturbation. *J. Sch. Health* 46:2, 1976.

130. Renshaw, D. C.   Stresses in family life. *Chicago Medicine* 80(1):11, 1977(a).

131. Renshaw, D. C., and Renshaw, R. H.   Incest. *J. Sex Education Therapy* 3(2):3, 1977(b).

132. Renshaw, D. C.   Healing the incest wound. *Sexual Medicine Today* 1(1):27, 1977(c).

133. Renshaw, D. C.   Rape. *J. Sex Education Therapy* 4(2):11, 1978(a).

134. Renshaw, D. C.   I'm just not interested in sex, doctor. *Medical Aspects of Human Sexuality* 12(5):32, 1978(b).

135. Riemer, S. A.   A research note on incest. *Am. J. Sociol.* 45:554, 1940.

136. Roberts, J. A. F.   *An Introduction to Medical Genetics*. New York; London: Oxford University Press, 1959. Pp. 232–250.

137. Rosenfeld, A. A., Nadelson, C. C., and Krieger, M.   Fantasy and reality in patients' reports of incest. *J. Clin. Psychiatry* 40:159, 1979.

138. Rosenfeld, A. Sexuality in a normal parent-child relationship. *Sexual Medicine Today* 4(9):40, 1980.

139. Rossman, P. *Sexual Experiences Between Men and Boys.* New York: New York Association Press, 1976. P. 12.

140. Sagarin E. Incest: Problems of definition and frequency. *J. of Sex Research* 13(2): 126, 1977.

141. Sarles, R. Incest. *Pediatr. Clin. North Am.* 22:3, 1975.

142. Schlachter, M., and Cotte, S. A. A medical, physiological and social study of incest from a pedopsychiatric point of view. *Acta Paedopsychiatr. (Basel)* 27:139, 1960.

143. Schull, W. J., and Neel, J. V. *The Effects of Inbreeding on Japanese Children.* New York: Harper & Row, 1965.

144. Seemanova, E. A study of children of incestuous matings. *Hum. Hered.* 21:108, 1971.

145. Shelton, W. A study of incest. *Int. J. Offender Therapy Comp. Criminology* 19:139, 1975.

146. Shepher, J. Mate selection among second generation kibbutz adolescents and adults: Incest avoidance and negative imprinting. *Arch. Sex. Behav.* 1:293, 1971.

147. Sklar, R. B. The criminal law and the incest offender: A case for decriminalization? *Bull. Am. Assn. Psychiat. Law* 7(1):69, 1979.

148. Slotkin, J. S. On a Possible Lack of Incest Regulations in Old Iran. In R. E. L. Masters, *Patterns of Incest,* New York: Julian Press, 1963.

149. Smith, G. F. Genetic implications of incest. Presented at the Illinois Masonic Medical Center Intrafamilial Childhood Sexual Abuse (Incest) Conference at the Bismark Hotel. Chicago, October 24–27, 1978.

150. Smith, J. A., Renshaw, D. C., and Renshaw, R. H. Twins who want to be identified as twins. *Dis. Nerv. Sys.* 29:615, 1968.

151. *Special Report on Rape and Other Sexual Offenses.* VII:5. Australian Royal Commission on Human Relationships, 1977. P. 222.

152. Spiegel, J. The resolution of role conflict within the family. *Psychiatry* 20:1, 1957.

153. Spitz, R. A. Hospitalism: An inquiry into the genesis of psychiatric conditions in early childhood. *Psychoanal. Study Child* 1:53, 1945.

154. Spitz, R. A. The role of early sexual behavior patterns in personality formation. *Psychoanal. Study Child* 17:283, 1962.

155. Stein, R. *Incest and Human Love.* New York: Third Press, 1973.

156. Sullivan, H. S. *The Interpersonal Theory of Psychiatry.* New York: Norton, 1953.

157. Sutter, J. Recherches sur les effects de la consanguinité chez l'homme. *Biol. Med. (Paris)* 47:563, 1958.

158. Swanson, D. W. Adult sexual abuse of children. *Dis. Nerv. Sys.* 29: 677, 1968.

159. Swift, C. Sexual victimization of children: An urban M.H.C. Survey. *Victimology* 2:322, 1977.

160. Tennov, D. *Love and Limerance.* New York: Stein & Day, 1980.

161. Thayer, N. *Stepping.* New York: Doubleday, 1980.

162. Topiár, A., and Satková, V. Behavior of delinquents, victims of incest and their fathers. *Cesk. Psychiatr.* 70(1):55, 1974. (Cze.)

163. Touch of incest. *Time,* July 2, 1979. P. 76.

164. Trankell, A. Was Lars sexually assaulted? A study of the reliability of witnesses and experts. *J. Abnorm. Soc. Psychol.* 56:385, 1958.

165. Virkkunen, M. Incest offenses and alcoholism. *Med. Sci. Law* 14:124, 1974.

166. Visher, E. R., and Visher, J. S. *Stepfamilies: A Guide to Working with*

Stepparents and Stepchildren. New York: Atcom, Atlantic Institute, 1979.

167. Wahl, C. W. The psychodynamics of consummated maternal incest. *Arch. Gen. Psychiatry* 3:188, 1960.

168. Walters, D. R. *Physical and Sexual Abuse of Children: Causes and Treatment.* Bloomington: Indiana University Press, 1975.

169. *Webster's Third New International Dictionary of the English Language Unabridged.* Springfield, Mass.: Merriam, 1966.

170. Weeks, R. B. The sexually exploited child. *South Med. J.* 69:848, 1976.

171. Weich, M. J. The terms "Mother" and "Father" as a defense against incest *J. Am. Psychoanal. Assoc.* 16:4, 1958.

172. Weinberg, S. K. *Incest.* New York: Citadel, 1955.

173. Weiner, I. B. Incest: A survey. *Excerpta Criminologica* 4:137, 1964.

174. Weiner, I. B. A clinical perspective on incest. *Am. J. Dis. Child.* 132:123, 1978.

175. Weitzel, N. D., Powell, B. J., and Penick, E. C. Clinical management of father-daughter incest: A critical re-examination. *Am. J. Dis. Child.* 132:127, 1978.

176. Wells, H. M. *Your Child's Right to Sex.* New York: Scarborough Books, 1976.

177. Werman, D. S. On the occurrence of incest fantasies. *Psychoanal. Q.* 46:245, 1977.

178. Westermarck, E. *The History of Human Marriage.* London: Macmillan, 1894.

179. Westermeyer, J. Incest in psychiatric practice: A description of patients and incestuous relationships. *J. Clin. Psychiatry* 6:644, 1978.

180. Wender, P. H., and Klein, D. The promise of biological psychiatry. *Psychology Today* 15(2):25, 1981.

181. Winnicott, D. W. *The Family and Individual Development.* London: Tavistock, 1965.

182. Winnicott, D. W. *The Child, the Family and the Outside World.* New York: Penguin Books, 1975.

183. Wolberg, L. R. *Techniques of Psychotherapy,* Vols. 1, 2. New York: Grune & Stratton, 1977.

184. Yates, A. *Sex Without Shame.* New York: William Morrow, 1978.

185. Yorukoglu, A., and Kemph, J. Children not severely damaged by incest with a parent. *J. Am. Acad. Child Psychiatry* 5:111 124, 1966.

INDEX